Within You Without You

Within You Without You

Listening to George Harrison

Seth Rogovoy

OXFORD
UNIVERSITY PRESS

Oxford University Press is a department of the University of Oxford. It furthers
the University's objective of excellence in research, scholarship, and education
by publishing worldwide. Oxford is a registered trade mark of Oxford University
Press in the UK and certain other countries.

Published in the United States of America by Oxford University Press
198 Madison Avenue, New York, NY 10016, United States of America.

© Oxford University Press 2024

Library of Congress Cataloging-in-Publication Data
Names: Rogovoy, Seth, 1960– author.
Title: Within you without you : listening to George Harrison / Seth Rogovoy.
Description: New York : Oxford University Press, 2024. |
Includes bibliographical references and index.
Identifiers: LCCN 2024000740 (print) | LCCN 2024000741 (ebook) |
ISBN 9780197627822 (hardback) | ISBN 9780197627846 (epub)
Subjects: LCSH: Harrison, George, 1943–2001—Criticism and interpretation. |
Rock music—History and criticism. | Rock music—Religious aspects.
Classification: LCC ML420.H167 R65 2024 (print) | LCC ML420.H167 (ebook) |
DDC 782.42166092—dc23/eng/20240109
LC record available at https://lccn.loc.gov/2024000740
LC ebook record available at https://lccn.loc.gov/2024000741

DOI: 10.1093/oso/9780197627822.001.0001

Printed by Sheridan Books, Inc., United States of America

For Linda

Contents

Preface

What We Talk About When We Talk About George Harrison

This is not a biography of George Harrison, although readers will presumably learn a lot about Harrison's life and career, in and out of the Beatles, while reading these pages. In writing this book, however, I do not set out to retell all the details of Harrison's life, or even most of them. Rather, the focus of this book is George Harrison, the musician, and beyond that, the cultural figure. Reference to Harrison's biography and the story of the Beatles will and must be made in such an endeavor, especially as it relates to the topic at hand, whether that be a Beatles song or a Harrisong or a guitar lick or a concert appearance. But primarily this book is driven by Harrison's music, and, as the subtitle indicates, is meant to enhance the experience of listening to George Harrison, to illuminate Harrison's place in and outside of the Beatles, to strengthen one's appreciation for Harrison's genius: for his skills and innovations as a guitarist, a songwriter, an arranger, and a producer, and for the model he set for how to survive the insanity of global fame—in his case, in the form of Beatlemania— and for how to live a rich and meaningful life in the wake of that insanity.

George Harrison was an enigma, which was always part of his appeal. While Harrison was bitten by the rock 'n' roll bug at an early age, his musical influences, like those of his bandmates, went far beyond the sounds that exploded out of the blend of American rhythm and blues and country music in the form of rockabilly and early rock 'n' roll in the mid- to late 1950s. Being born in the early 1940s meant George and his fellow Beatles and their contemporaries were at the perfect age, their mid-teens, to inherit the mantle of the pioneers of the music—including Chuck Berry, Little Richard, Elvis Presley, and Buddy Holly. But like the others, especially Paul McCartney and Ringo Starr, growing up in a family that loved music and dancing meant Harrison was exposed from birth to the manifold sounds of the previous half-century, which meant the entirety of recorded music: vaudeville, early jazz, pop standards, swing, novelty recordings, blues, folk, ethnic music, even Indian music, that last of which his mother particularly enjoyed listening to on the BBC while George was in utero. The radio was always on in the Harrison household, and he soaked it all in—how else to account for Harrison recording songs by the likes of Hoagy Carmichael, Harold Arlen, and Cole Porter over the course of his solo career?

George was "the quiet one," yet he was no shrinking violet. Though not shy, he had introvert tendencies—his first proper song, after all, was called "Don't Bother Me"—but they never stood in the way of his speaking up for himself and his bandmates. He was one of four, and if sometimes it was hard to get a word in edgewise when your bandmates were the wickedly outrageous John Lennon, the voluble Paul McCartney, and the affable Ringo Starr, Harrison made every word count. His wit was as quick and biting as Lennon's. He did not suffer fools gladly—by the evidence of his songs, he despised them.

George was "the spiritual one" who found great solace in lessons learned from Eastern religion, which provided the very tools he needed—meditation, chanting, yoga, the basket of practices we now call "mindfulness"—to deal with his bandmates when they were at odds and the pressures that fell upon him from a world that was all too much. But as deeply spiritual as he was, he was never immune to earthly temptation, whether it be illicit substances or fast cars or the comfort of women to whom he was not married—even when he was indeed married. Blame it on being a Pisces, whose symbol is two fish going in opposite directions. He certainly did. It meant enough to him that he wrote about it in song ("Pisces Fish," on 2002's posthumous album, *Brainwashed*). And now is a good time to declare outright: I have little to no interest in writing about sex and drugs and the rock 'n' roll lifestyle as these pertain to Harrison, and only when and if it is needed to contextualize something musical or otherwise. This is not out of any prudery; rather, I just find reading and writing about that kind of thing superficial, sensationalist, and boring. Besides, others have already gone over that territory, so if that is what you are looking for, go find it elsewhere.

When George Harrison joined the Quarry Men, he was a junior partner. He was nearly two years younger than John Lennon, and the difference between being fifteen and seventeen is the equivalent of a decade in adult years. Although he was friends with Paul McCartney before the latter met John Lennon, by the time they signed him up as lead guitarist of the Quarry Men, Lennon and McCartney were already a tight unit, nascent songwriting partners with strong ideas about music and what direction their band should take. What George brought to the table—what made Paul repeatedly insist that John give him a listen—was that he was a much better guitarist than the other two. The proof of it, as far as Lennon and McCartney were concerned, was that he could play a perfect rendition of "Raunchy," a twangy guitar instrumental by Bill Justis (from a 1960 album called *Cloud 9*). Once Lennon heard Harrison play, he could no longer resist the idea of George joining the group. But to be fair, from day one, the idea was simply that George would play lead guitar. He did not come with any other skills—he was not a songwriter or composer (yet)—and any other contributions, perhaps excepting a few backing vocals, were not part of the original plan or vision for him.

Lennon and McCartney soon learned, however, that Harrison had much more to offer the group than the facility to play "Raunchy" and the ability to tune a guitar (a task that long evaded John Lennon's grasp). As the Quarry Men morphed from a skiffle group into a rock band requiring a new name, Harrison revealed himself to be a musician of many talents. While guitar was his instrument, and his vision of the role of the guitar in a rock band was like no other, his contributions often rose to the level of co-composition. In providing clever intros and codas and hooks and solos, Harrison colored the sound of the Beatles. His guitar often was the glue holding a song together. No single Beatle was more important than any other, and there probably has never been a greater example of the whole being more than the sum of its parts in music than the Fab Four. But Harrison's contributions have not always been given their due. To this day, he is sometimes viewed as a lesser guitarist, not one to be included in the pantheon of rock guitarists. Complaints about him include that he could not improvise, that he could not play fast, that he took too long to get his parts right, and that when push came to shove, Paul McCartney had to shoulder the most difficult guitar passages in the Beatles oeuvre. Just the fact that Harrison invited Eric Clapton to play the solo on his own song, "While My Guitar Gently Weeps," is used against Harrison, as proof that he knew that he was not up to playing the part himself.

None of this could be further from the truth. Music is not a contest, and lists of the "best guitarists" of all time defy logic. There are so many different styles and approaches to guitar that comparing Jimi Hendrix to Robbie Robertson, or Eric Clapton to Eddie Van Halen, belie a wholesale misunderstanding of what these unique artists brought to their music and their instrument. To denigrate Harrison for his professionalism and perfectionism, his insistence on taking a song home so he could work out his parts overnight, makes no sense. Perhaps without even realizing it, Harrison was a composer as much as he was a guitar player, and he wanted to (and did) come up with the best possible contributions he could make to a song. Harrison also had the mind of an arranger and producer, both of which he would become later on, so if he thought that Paul's style of playing could serve a song better than his own—even on one of his own songs, as was the case with the guitar solo in "Taxman"—he set his ego aside (whatever he had of one) and made the best choice to serve the song. The same goes for Eric Clapton's playing on "While My Guitar Gently Weeps." In his mind, Harrison heard Clapton's guitar sound on the number, so he asked his friend to come into the studio to contribute a solo. And in case anyone thinks that Clapton wound up playing something that George could not, just take a look at Harrison's rendition of the song in the *Concert for Bangladesh* film, where Clapton, standing right next to Harrison and for whatever reason, failed to recreate the magic of the original, leaving George to pick up where Clapton stumbled and rescue the tune with a pitch-perfect solo that indeed wrung the obligatory tears out of his guitar.

While it is moments and misconceptions like these that this book is meant in part to correct, what I really hope to show are Harrison's positive achievements, how the "quiet," "serious," and "spiritual" Beatle—perhaps even the "moody" Beatle—made some of the most compelling music of the rock era, both within and without the Beatles. If this book makes you hear a familiar song slightly differently, if it moves you to listen again to an old favorite or to a song that until now had escaped you, and makes you hear them with new ears, then I will consider what I have set out to accomplish here to be a success. Happy reading, and happy listening.

—*Seth Rogovoy, September 15, 2024, Hudson, New York*

Note to Readers

All references to Beatles albums are to the original versions of their albums as released in the United Kingdom by EMI. These often differed from the versions distributed in the United States by Capitol Records, which put out entire albums of Beatles songs as they saw fit, even when they did not correspond to the albums as the Beatles themselves imagined and configured them. Much to the consternation of some fans and listeners, songs originally issued as singles often did not appear on official Beatles albums until various compilations and greatest-hits packages were released in the 1970s and later. On the other hand, all references to chart positions refer to *Billboard*'s tallies of sales and radio play in the United States. Specific references to UK chart positions are those determined by the Official Charts Company unless otherwise denoted.

All quotations appearing in the text by Michael Lindsay-Hogg, Wesley Stace (a.k.a. John Wesley Harding), Robyn Hitchcock, Lauren Passarelli, Allan Kozinn, Sarah Beth Driver, Candy Leonard, and Gary Lucas are from interviews conducted by the author, unless otherwise indicated.

Why George Harrison?

George himself is no mystery. But the mystery inside of George is immense.

—John Lennon[1]

From an early age, John Lennon and Paul McCartney had dreams of stardom. They were bitten by the bug of Elvis Presley, and Lennon, for one, dreamed of nothing less than supplanting Presley himself. Of course, he knew he could not do this on his own. While he may have had the attitude and ambition, he lacked Presley's otherworldly voice, his raw and libidinal presence, and his innate ability to telegraph a forbidden sexuality with just the sneer of a lip and the twist of a hip. In Paul McCartney, however, John Lennon stumbled upon his near-perfect foil: a fellow Presley worshiper who was equally brash and extroverted with the bonus of a terrific voice made for rock 'n' roll hooting and hollering and an adorably pleasing visage. Plus, unlike Lennon, McCartney was a promising instrumentalist, one who when his full talent flowered could basically stand shoulder to shoulder with the best rock musicians on all the basic instruments in the rock 'n' roll arsenal, one who could seemingly write a huge pop hit over breakfast, and one who utterly thrived in the spotlight. The duo of Lennon and McCartney—who unlike Presley would soon generate their own material—came ready made for rock 'n' roll.

Later, they would draft a musician who was equally single-minded in his devotion to good old rock 'n' roll, to performing in front of an audience, and to enjoying the camaraderie of his bandmates and the fruits of rock 'n' roll success. Coming from a dirt-poor background, having spent much of his youth in and out of hospital because of various ailments, and consigning himself somewhat to the background by his choice of instrument, Ringo Starr simply loved playing the drums. By the time the Beatles drafted him, he had already tasted a hint of success with the prominent Liverpool group Rory Storm and the Hurricanes, such that he brought to the Beatles a modicum of professionalism and experience that the others lacked, a good balance when weighed against some of John Lennon's more anarchic instincts.

And then there was George.

Like his future bandmates John Lennon and Paul McCartney, George Harrison turned into a rock 'n' roll obsessive at an early age. For Harrison, though, it was less about rock 'n' roll fame and celebrity than it was about the essential sound that made the music—the sound of the rock 'n' roll guitar. Harrison went to great lengths to acquire his first guitar, an acoustic flat-top model, from a schoolmate for £3 and change, a gift from his parents. Once he had that guitar, he had discovered his best friend. His guitar served as his intermediary between his inner life and the world around him. It was the sight of George cradling his guitar on a bus to and from school that first caught the eye of the likeminded Paul McCartney. The two immediately bonded over their shared interest in rock 'n' roll, a bond that grew tighter with their shared interest in *playing* rock 'n' roll. And what McCartney—himself a guitarist at the time—discovered in Harrison was a student of the instrument who was, though younger by just short of a year, far more advanced in his skill on the instrument.

When the time came for John Lennon to add another guitarist to the ever-changing lineup of the Quarry Men, McCartney brought Harrison along to a few gigs, trying to get John to listen to George play. McCartney knew Harrison's talent would improve the band's sound exponentially, and when Lennon finally gave George a listen, he knew that more than anything else, his band needed this guy—who had the added advantage of knowing how to tune his instrument and play proper chords. Lennon, up until this time, had been transposing the banjo chords his mother had taught him onto four of his guitar's six strings, ignoring the other two. Harrison not only gave the group an adept guitar player; he also became a de facto guitar teacher to Lennon, although the latter is said to have been a terrible and unwilling student.

Recognizing how valuable a musical addition Harrison would be to his group was one thing. But Lennon (and McCartney) also probably sensed that the shy, retiring Harrison would not pose any threat as an aspiring frontman. Still a boyish teenager with stick-out ears and a goofy grin, Harrison had yet to develop the facial features that in just a few years would make him the handsomest of the foursome. Plus, he was, as the moniker would become, the "quiet one," although his shyness—his junior status no doubt contributing to this—could not hold back his rapier wit, and Lennon no doubt appreciated someone who could trade fours with him in that arena.

Again, another perfect foil for Lennon.

All the while, Harrison himself was the most unlikely of rock stars. After the first few years of the Beatles, he dreaded performing live and touring; he was unhappy about being seen as "a Beatle" rather than as himself; and, for the most part, he had little use for or interest in the accoutrements of fame, preferring to spend his time quietly in his garden at his beloved English country estate and with his few close friends and loved ones. In this manner, Harrison truly was "the dark one," and an introvert to boot. Imagine being a Beatle and an introvert. The mind boggles.

The very first song the Beatles recorded as the Beatles was a George Harrison instrumental called "Cry for a Shadow," a tribute—or a mockery?—of the sound of Cliff Richard's backup group, the Shadows. (Richard was England's homegrown, somewhat cut-rate answer to Elvis Presley.) The very last song the Beatles recorded as the Beatles was a George Harrison song called "I Me Mine." In between the two, the Beatles were primarily a band devoted to realizing the compositions of John Lennon and Paul McCartney, some of which they worked on together, many of which they wrote separately, but by early agreement, all of which were credited to the songwriting duo of John Lennon and Paul McCartney, regardless. Over the ten-year course of the Beatles' career, Lennon and McCartney would occasionally and often somewhat begrudgingly consent to recording a George Harrison composition. When Harrison was invited to join John Lennon's group the Quarry Men, it was on the basis of his facility on guitar and with the expectation that he would become the group's lead guitarist. There is no reason to believe that Harrison even entertained the idea that he would also contribute songs to the group upon gaining official membership, and it was apparently only because of Liverpool journalist Bill Harry's badgering that George finally put pen to paper and, while lying ill in bed in a hotel room in August 1963, came up with a song reflective of his feelings at that very moment: "Don't Bother Me."[2]

It would be several years before Harrison would come up with a follow-up to "Don't Bother Me," which was included on the 1963 album *With the Beatles*. But in the interim, he had a front-row seat to the creation of dozens of brilliant songs by Lennon and McCartney as well as a keen ear attuned to the astonishing new approaches to songwriting emanating from the American rock poet Bob Dylan. When, two years later, Harrison did finally come up with songs that were worthy of being included on a Beatles album next to those of Lennon and McCartney, on the summer 1965 album *Help!*, a listener could be excused for not realizing that "I Need You" and "You Like Me Too Much" were Harrison compositions. Just a few months later, the landmark album *Rubber Soul* would include two more Harrison compositions, "If I Needed Someone" and "Think for Yourself," that marked a huge leap in Harrison's standing as a songwriter. The album after that, 1966's *Revolver,* contained an unprecedented three songs by Harrison, including the lead-off track, "Taxman." Those who paid attention to such things soon realized that with his own songs ("I Want to Tell You" and "Love You To" were the other two) and with his significant musical and instrumental contributions to many of the other *Revolver* tracks, Harrison had become an equal creative force in the group, who no longer stood in the shadows of Lennon and McCartney.

It would be a while before Harrison would play such an essential role on a Beatles album to the extent he had on *Revolver*, but he would continue to give the group songs that would be considered among the best they ever produced, including "While My Guitar Gently Weeps," "Something," and "Here Comes the Sun." The last two would become the most popular Beatles songs in the streaming era of the early twenty-first century. Along with Ringo Starr, Harrison may have long been considered an "economy-class Beatle," a term he invented, but by end of the 1960s, his greatest achievements in the group had landed him an upgrade into first class. And early in his post-Beatles solo career, Harrison would record and produce albums that ranked with the best of his former bandmates. He would score several major solo hits throughout the 1970s as well as play a key role in aiding and abetting Ringo Starr's solo career: Harrison served as a producer, instrumentalist, and cowriter of Starr hits that included "It Don't Come Easy" (uncredited), "Photograph," and "Back Off Boogaloo."

The Beatles were unique, and they could have become the paradigm-shifting rock group they were only with the unique foursome of John Lennon, Paul McCartney, George Harrison, and Ringo Starr. The way their voices blended and veered off on their own, the manner in which their individual personalities balanced one another on and off record, and the musical and extra-musical talents they each brought to the whole enabled the group to become exponentially more than the sum of its parts, along the way birthing an entirely new form—the rock group—while transforming the rock 'n' roll music of the 1950s into the revolutionary, counterculture rock music of the 1960s. The bespoke recipe required these four individuals. In overseeing the Beatles, manager Brian Epstein was the essential catalyst, and producer George Martin was the genius behind the recording-studio curtain, the chef who knew just how to mix the various ingredients into a perfectly baked flaming pie.

There is no question that without Lennon and McCartney, there would be no Beatles and almost no Beatles songs. But a song is not a recording. Lennon and McCartney might have been the greatest songwriting partnership of the rock era—its answer to George and Ira Gershwin or Rodgers and

Hammerstein. And they may have been able to (and did) put together great demo recordings of their songs that would entice other singers and bands to record them. But without the essential contributions of George Harrison and Ringo Starr, there would have been no Beatles per se. Harrison and Starr were no mere backup musicians; they weren't there merely to add color or rhythm to the songs. Their contributions in the recording studio and onstage brought the Lennon and McCartney songs fully to life. George's guitar and Ringo's drums helped transform them from melodically inventive songs on the page into boundary-breaking hit records. And in this way, they were not secondary or "economy class"—they were utterly and totally coequals in the group. No one in the Beatles was more coequal than the others.

Especially George. "George Harrison was their secret weapon, bringing existential musings like 'But if I seem to act unkind, it's only me, it's not my mind that is confusing things' into the top twenty around the globe," English rock singer-songwriter Robyn Hitchcock told me. "He made them deep, just as John made them matter, and Paul made them fun."

Lennon and McCartney came to rely on George Harrison for creating so many of the memorable riffs and hooks that propelled their songs and gave the Beatles' their signature sounds. They brought in the lyrics, the melodies, and the chords, but then George created the latticework upon which to tie together and hang those elements. Later, the others deferred to George for his talent for arranging, for introducing unusual sonorities into the mixture, and for using experimental methods (e.g., found-sounds, back-masking) to add musical depth and sonic range to their recordings. Most notably, Harrison introduced Indian sounds and influences to the Beatles musical stew, beginning with his sitar playing on "Norwegian Wood" and running through (and beyond) the rest of the Beatles oeuvre. Even the use of a first-generation Moog synthesizer on *Abbey Road* was Harrison's innovation, another result of his restless musical curiosity.

While the electric guitar is the defining instrument of rock 'n' roll, and while George Harrison is known as one of the greatest rock guitarists of all time, George also found new ways to integrate the sound of acoustic guitars into rock music. The orchestral ring of Harrison's twelve-string acoustic guitar became a Beatles trademark and opened a whole new range of sounds and approaches in the rock 'n' roll band's toolkit. Inspired by Bob Dylan lyrically, musically, and personally, George was equally responsible with Dylan for the invention of what came to be known as "folk rock." Roger McGuinn bought a twelve-string Rickenbacker guitar after seeing George play one in the movie *A Hard Day's Night*, and subsequently made its jingle-jangle the defining sound of his group, the Byrds, who made a specialty of covering songs written by Bob

Dylan and who consciously modeled themselves after the Beatles, even down to naming themselves after an animal and purposely misspelling the name.

George Harrison was one of the most enigmatic figures in rock music history. A member of the most popular band of all time, he quickly came to dread fame and crave privacy—a veritable walking contradiction. He went to great lengths to pursue spiritual truths, frequently visiting India and studying with a panoply of Indian gurus, while at the same time amassing a collection of very expensive racing cars. (He reconciled these seemingly unrelated interests by finding in both a common pursuit of heightened states of consciousness.) While Harrison spurned the material world and was apparently quite humble and generous, neither was he a saint. He often attributed his contradictory nature to his being born under the sign of Pisces, whose symbol is two intertwined fish swimming in opposite directions. He was well aware of his puzzling nature, but with his disarming humility and sense of humor, he never came across as a phony or a hypocrite.

George Harrison faced down death several times in the late 1990s with varying and recurring bouts of cancer, but his deep study of Hinduism was in many ways a lifelong preparation for dying and the afterlife. (He even wrote a song called "Art of Dying" in the late 1960s, well before he turned thirty.) His fear of violence, dating back at least as far as several close calls with savage fans during the height of Beatlemania (including a particularly unpleasant trip to the Philippines, where Ferdinand and Imelda Marcos withdrew the government's security detail guarding the Beatles when they declined an invitation for a visit to the presidential palace[3]), was proven unfortunately prescient with the slaying of John Lennon in 1981, and then again when a crazed intruder broke into Harrison's country house in 1999 and stabbed him multiple times. Harrison survived the attack, but something broke inside him,[4] and he passed away from cancer within two years.

George Harrison left behind an incredible cultural legacy as well as a body of work as great as any other single recording artist and singer-songwriter of the rock era, perhaps with the exception of his good friend Bob Dylan. And from what we know of George's worship at the altar of Dylan—whose lyrics he could recite as chapter and verse—he would probably be totally OK with that.

1
I Saw Her Standing There

The song "I Saw Her Standing There" exemplifies so much of the best of the early Beatles sound: the urgent, dynamic vocals; the driving rhythms; the hint of danger and chaos, both in the form and content. The lyrics are full of insinuation and double entendre, while the music threatens to collapse in a heap but never does, given the tight group sound. One element, however, stands above all, and gives it that ineffable touch that makes it the Beatles instead of any other of many burgeoning Merseyside pop groups and other English, blues-based rock 'n' roll bands, and that is George Harrison's guitar. It provides the extra musical spark, the additional element that could almost be another vocal, adding color and dimension to what otherwise would be workmanlike revivalism. It captures the Beatles at a transitional moment—from being rock 'n' roll and rhythm-and-blues revivalists to creating something new, unprecedented, and outrageous. The early innovators and stars of rock 'n' roll were almost all solo artists—Fats Domino, Little Richard, Elvis Presley, and Jerry Lee Lewis. The Beatles were a whole other species: a rock 'n' roll group, and one in which each individual played a new and essential role. Certainly, Buddy Holly had his Crickets and Cliff Richard had his Shadows, but anyone other than the most ardent fan would be hard pressed to name a single member of either of those bands.

When he first formed the Quarry Men, John Lennon probably never had in mind the idea of a band of equals (and perhaps never fully came around to seeing the Beatles that way). But he knew talent when he saw it, which is why one by one he recognized that Paul McCartney and in turn George Harrison were essential to fulfilling his creative vision, and why he consented to have them join his group—even, as in the case of Harrison, when he did so only begrudgingly. As soon as the lineup got sorted, after his art-school friend Stuart Sutcliffe, who could never really play bass, left the band—freeing up Paul to shift from guitar to bass guitar—and the lumbering, odd man out, Pete Best, was replaced by Richard "Ringo Starr" Starkey, even when Lennon still clung to the idea that he was the ostensible leader of Johnny and the Moondogs, as he called his group for a split second, the band gelled in a way he never could have foreseen, because no one could have foreseen it.

It took two creative intimates standing just outside the group, manager Brian Epstein and producer George Martin, to gently nudge them and mold and shape the Liverpool quartet into a four-wheel-drive musical vehicle the likes of which had never been seen or heard (arguably before and since). Even they could not have predicted where the quartet would go—to the "toppermost of the poppermost," as John Lennon put it, to garnering recognition from the very British royalty they privately (or not so privately) scorned, to global fame, and to unimaginable fortune. If Lennon and McCartney sat in the front seats, sharing the driving and navigation, George and Ringo were right behind them in the back seat, filling in the gaps that made Lennon and McCartney not merely the second coming of the Everly Brothers, as they may well have been had they decided on remaining a duo, but the first coming of an entirely new approach to music—structurally, visually, sonically, and conceptually. The Beatles were the first true rock band. And as rock music was, at least for its first few decades, entirely guitar based, George Harrison's playing colored the Beatles' music as much as the wild, glorious vocals of John Lennon and Paul McCartney, along the way setting the parameters for the role of the lead guitarist in a rock band.

While the Beatles introduced themselves to the British Isles by way of several hit singles in the second half of 1962, including "Love Me Do" and "Please Please Me," the first track on their first studio album released in the United Kingdom—*Please Please Me*—was "I Saw Her Standing There." Written primarily by Paul McCartney with some input by John Lennon, it opened with a 1-2-3-4 count-in by McCartney before grabbing listeners by way of an update of 1950s rock 'n' roll. Indeed, McCartney later confessed to copping the bassline that propels the tune from Chuck Berry's 1961 hit, "I'm Talking About You," which the Beatles performed live on the BBC program "Saturday Club" six days before the release of *Please Please Me* on March 22, 1963. (They performed "I Saw Her Standing There" on that same program, alongside Berry's 1956 hit "Too Much Monkey Business.") Berry's 1958 hit "Sweet Little Sixteen" had been in the Beatles repertoire since their Hamburg residency in fall 1962; McCartney aged the subject of his very Berry-like number by one year (corresponding to a seventeen-year-old girl the twenty-year-old singer was dating at the time), but the Berry-Beatles connection was made abundantly clear.

There was nothing terribly unusual about the bassline of "I'm Talking About You." It was rather standard for rock 'n' roll of that vintage—derived from the boogie-woogie beat one might hear on a Fats Domino number—and it certainly worked well as the foundation for "I Saw Her Standing There." In McCartney's hands, the bass riff not only served as a rhythmic and harmonic device—it also offered a hint of McCartney's burgeoning style of playing bass, emphasizing melody as much as providing a rhythmic and harmonic foundation.

It also interlocked perfectly with Lennon's rhythm guitar and George Harrison's lead-guitar fills that pepper the song throughout. Once the song starts, it has a hang-on-for-dear-life feel, with its fast tempo and relentless pulse. While the debt to Chuck Berry's boogie-rock formula is clear, the Beatles utterly transform the overall sound and approach, most obviously in the vocals, featuring the harmonizing McCartney and Lennon. Even before the song gets going, Harrison's guitar offers a trebly, metallic counterpoint to what the other three are playing. When the song comes around to the middle eight—the part of the song where the chords and melody vary from the verse and refrain—Harrison's guitar tone changes, taking on a fat, reverb-drenched sound, more Carl Perkins than Chuck Berry.

"I Saw Her Standing There" is the first Beatles track to include a George Harrison guitar solo. It has all the basic elements of what will define Harrison's approach to solos: a mixture of single-note lines with double stops and chords; hammer-ons, bends, trills, and sliding notes and chords; and the liberal use of pauses and space—the *absence* of sound—as punctuation, as musical elements unto themselves, investing the solo with a sense of air and breath. "He was just expressing the right thing to play," says Lauren Passarelli, professor of guitar at Berklee College of Music in Boston, Massachusetts, and a specialist in playing the music of George Harrison and the Beatles. "He was responding to the song."

Talking about Harrison's "single, bent-note 'sighs'" on guitar, Beatles author Allan Kozinn said,

> For me, they basically underpin and further both the lyric and the subtext (i.e., that sort of longing—the overt lyric being kind of puppy-love, the subtext being sexual). Perhaps that "sigh" is a sort of innate human response, and something musicians have always captured and put into music that's about that sort of lovelorn/longing idea. But I think if you listen for it, you'll hear things like it all through the Beatles' catalogue, where the lead guitar offers a subdued but nevertheless running commentary that either captures something essential in the lyrics, or on a purely musical level, offering bits of counterpoint or just plain make-this-thing-sound-more-interesting texturing. . . . Another thing [Harrison] brought to the Beatles that people tend to overlook . . . is filigree, or detail, and not what one thinks of as a lead guitar line in the grand, showy solo sense.

Having workshopped "I Saw Her Standing There" in live performances for nearly half a year before recording it, the Beatles had the number down pat, and Harrison had his solo well-prepared and memorized. He simply played it live in the studio as the group tore through the number, with no need for overdubbing, as would soon become the practice for solos and other elements added beyond the basics of a song.

Harrison solos are never a sonic assault or an exercise in showmanship or in flaunting dexterity for its own sake, as would become de rigueur in rock music by the late 1960s. For Harrison, solos are carefully composed musical statements, worked out in advance as thoughtfully as any melody line, as we hear in "I Saw Her Standing There." The number comes to a halt with what would soon become another Beatles signature: one of Harrison's "naughty" unresolved chords—in this case, a ninth chord—that concludes the song on an ambiguous note that just hangs there, one that eschews closure and suggests that the song—and the "dancing," as the lyrics say—will continue through the night.

2

The Sheik of Araby's Three Cool Cats

American songwriter Ted Snyder, born in 1881, cowrote the 1921 Jazz Age hit "The Sheik of Araby" with lyricist Harry B. Smith, who was twenty years his elder. Their song was inspired by the 1921 silent film *The Sheik*, starring Rudolph Valentino, who up until that point was a contract player for Metro Pictures in Hollywood. The movie, based on a popular 1919 romance novel by Edith Maude Hull, made Valentino an international star and something of a sex symbol of the day. Forty-four years later, another international star and sex symbol named Elvis Presley would reprise Valentino's role in a musical comedy version of *The Sheik* called *Harum Scarum*, which is included on the list of the 100 Most Enjoyably Bad Movies Ever Made in *The Official Razzie Movie Guide*. But Snyder and Smith knew a good thing when they saw one, and their song, exploiting a nonexistent connection to the film, became a huge Tin Pan Alley hit. Within just a few years, the song was enough of a cultural touchstone that F. Scott Fitzgerald quoted a verse from it in his novel *The Great Gatsby*.

By the time George Harrison and the Beatles began performing "The Sheik of Araby" in their nightclub sets in 1961, the song had been steadily popular for four decades, performed or recorded by the likes of Fats Waller, Eddie Cantor, Louis Armstrong, Louis Prima, Duke Ellington, Nat "King" Cole, Oscar Peterson, Django Reinhardt, and Stephane Grappelli, Fats Domino, Art Tatum, and the Everly Brothers. Alice Faye and Betty Grable teamed up to sing and dance a somewhat risqué (for its time) version in the 1940 film musical *Tin Pan Alley*. The Beatles were no doubt familiar with Spike Jones's comic version of the tune, with one foot in Dixieland and the other in Jones's eccentric novelty style. But it was likely the swinging 1961 hit version made by their contemporary, Joe Brown—of whom they were big fans, especially Harrison—that caught their ears and made them want to add the tune to their ever-expanding repertoire. The Beatles' version did not merely copy Brown's arrangement; rather, they pulled the song kicking and screaming into full-fledged rock 'n' roll territory. That is to say, they made it into a Beatles song. Harrison leads off the recording with a guitar riff based on the nineteenth-century "Arabian riff," also known as "The Streets of Cairo" and "the snake charmer song." When I was a child, we sang a nursery-rhyme-like ditty to the same tune called "All the Girls in France," an apt variation, since the original melody may well date from an early-eighteenth-century French song called "*Colin prend sa hotte*," which may have been derived from a seventeenth-century Algerian folk song, perhaps accounting for its enduring "Arabian" mode. While Harrison could rightly be accused of Orientalism in his choice of intro, the song itself was already an "Oriental" pastiche as written in 1921, replete with stereotypes of harems and feudal rape, indicative of the Western view of the East at that time. Just a few years later, Harrison would go on to break down such stereotypes and, as much as any single individual, open the Western world's ears, hearts, and minds to the sounds and belief systems of the East.

After the intro, what follows is a rockabilly-based arrangement featuring stop-start rhythm guitar with Harrison's occasional chunky, surf-guitar-style lead riffs providing color and connective tissue. The song modulates its key several times in different ways—at the beginning, after the intro, and again toward the end. Harrison also displays a technique that will become one of his signatures: he moves to an unexpected chord at the end of a verse, momentarily shifting the song into a minor key before returning to the major tonic. In a nod to the song's novelty roots, John Lennon tosses in a couple of nonsense vocal interjections that mar an arrangement that otherwise plays it straight, guitars riffing down the highway, driven by Harrison's heavy use of vibrato courtesy of his whammy bar, while George claims his stake as a vocalist equal to the task of belting Presley- and Berry-inspired high-octane rock 'n' roll alongside Lennon and McCartney. Harrison also preternaturally phrases with extended melisma, stretching one syllable over several notes, a technique derived in large part from gospel music. At about forty seconds into the song, he divides the word "me" into five separate syllables dragged across three different notes. All that in just a minute and forty-three seconds.

Harrison's choice of "The Sheik of Araby" revealed more than just his appreciation for Joe Brown and Spike Jones. In choosing to cover a song with a forty-year pedigree, one that was firmly ensconced as a pre-rock pop standard—the kind of music his parents likely danced to when it came on the radio—Harrison showed his sympathy for a wide swath of musical history that extended far beyond the early days of rock 'n' roll and its R&B forebears. He may have rolled over Beethoven, but that did not mean he disliked or would ignore all music that preceded Elvis Presley.

John, Paul, and Ringo also counted music hall, vaudeville, operetta, jazz, swing, folk, country and western, Broadway, and pop standards as part of their musical backgrounds. This is in large part what set the Beatles apart from their contemporaries who, other than paying obeisance to acoustic and electric blues as avid fans and as early influences, were single minded in their devotion to "modern" music at the expense of all that came before. Not the Beatles, however. In his solo career, Ringo Starr would go on to record entire albums devoted to pre-rock pop, including his debut album, the aptly titled *Sentimental Journey*, which included songs by Cole Porter, Johnny Mercer, and Sammy Fain, best known from recordings by Bing Crosby, Doris Day, Frank Sinatra, and Fats Waller. The album also included Ringo's version of "Stardust" by Hoagy Carmichael, who was a favorite of Harrison's, too—George would likewise cover several Hoagy Carmichael songs in his solo career, alongside numbers by Cole Porter ("True Love") and Harold Arlen ("Between the Devil and the Deep Blue Sea"). The point is simply that with their incorporation of a panoply of pre-rock musical styles in their choice of cover tunes and in their own, pop-influenced melodies, the Beatles stood apart from their peers and also exhibited more musical sophistication in their melodies and chord choices than, for example, the Rolling Stones, the Yardbirds, the Bluesbreakers, and the seemingly endless parade of 1960s English blues-based rock bands, from Savoy Brown through Cream through Faces. (With Ray Davies's polyglot musical tastes and his persistent focus on British life and culture, the Kinks—beyond the proto-metal of "You Really Got Me" and "All Day and All of the Night"—shared more with the Beatles than with those other groups.)

This all plays out on a version of the song that was recorded as part of the infamous New Year's Day 1962 (ultimately unsuccessful) audition for Decca Records. The Beatles never included a version of "The Sheik of Araby" on an officially released single or album while they were together. Thanks to the *Anthology* project of the mid-1990s, several songs from the Decca audition finally saw the light of day on *Anthology 1* (there were three volumes in all), including "Hello Little Girl," "Searchin'," and "Like Dreamers Do."

The Decca audition included two covers of songs by Jerry Leiber and Mike Stoller, who had written hits for Elvis Presley, the Coasters, and the Drifters, including the aforementioned "Searchin'," sung by Paul McCartney with swoops into falsetto à la Little Richard and with answer vocals by Lennon and Harrison—a recording that serves as demonstrative evidence as to why the Beatles ultimately had to find a better drummer to replace a lagging, dragging Pete Best. Leiber and Stoller's "Three Cool Cats," like "Sheik of Araby," was another showcase for George Harrison. Originally recorded by the Coasters in 1958, featuring delicious three-part harmonies, sinuous rhythm guitar, and a haunting saxophone solo, the Beatles picked up the pace a couple of notches while making the most of it as a vocal-harmony number, albeit with

Harrison's vocals far out in front on the verses and his electric guitar taking the solo break instead of saxophone.

As with "The Sheik of Araby," Lennon and McCartney again interject comic nonsense vocals, audibly bringing George to the verge of laughter. But Harrison holds himself together enough to keep the tune going, and his surf-rock-inspired guitar lines are inventive, lending a Latin tinge to the rockabilly-based arrangement. (Incidentally, jazz musician Sidney Bechet broke new ground technically and creatively in 1941, when he used then-primitive over-dubbing technology to play every instrument on his version of "The Sheik of Araby," including soprano and tenor saxophones, clarinet, piano, bass, and drums.)

Both "The Sheik of Araby" and "Three Cool Cats" may have been unlikely source material for the Beatles, musical novelties that were already firmly established in listeners' minds. What makes them such fascinating listening to this day is how they manifest the emerging sound and vision of the Beatles. That George Harrison plays literal and figurative leading roles in both numbers is a tribute to his essential contribution toward shaping the group's aesthetic, even before Lennon and McCartney began writing and recording original compositions that would canonize that approach.

3

The Reluctant Beatle

From the very first song he wrote for the Beatles, "Don't Bother Me," through his feelings about the Beatles' famed final public performance on the roof of Apple—encapsulated in the single sentence, "I don't want to go on the roof," a statement that could well serve as his epitaph—George Harrison was the reluctant Beatle. Harrison could be said to have quit the Beatles a number of times, at least as early as August 1966, as the final world tour came to a crashing halt and he told his bandmates and his manager he was done with the Beatles. Harrison's extracurricular interests often took precedence over his day job, manifest in his relative indifference throughout the recording sessions of *Sgt. Pepper's Lonely Hearts Club Band*, during which he could hardly be bothered to pick up his guitar and play; during the recording of *The Beatles*, a.k.a. "The White Album," when *none* of the Beatles showed particular enthusiasm about recording as a group rather than as individual solo artists; and, most famously, in the January 1969 recording sessions captured on film, first in Michael Lindsay-Hogg's *Let It Be* and again in Peter Jackson's expanded remix of Lindsay-Hogg's film footage, 2022's *Get Back*. Harrison's ambivalence about the Beatles and fame could well be his defining characteristic, if it were not for the essential role he played in helping to create the Beatles sound and inspiring his bandmates to follow along on his musical and spiritual journeys.

Nevertheless, George Harrison was a charter member of the Beatles and remained with the group until it was dissolved by John Lennon in September 1969 or Paul McCartney in May 1970, depending on how you count or where you land. Harrison composed the very first track the Beatles recorded—"Cry for a Shadow"—*and* the final track they worked on in a recording studio as the Beatles—"I Me Mine." Decades after the group split up, in the music-streaming era, his songs "Here Comes the Sun" and "Something" were perennially the most streamed Beatles songs on the major streaming services. Even though millions of listeners did not realize it, George Harrison was, effectively, their favorite Beatle. And for long stretches—especially once the group had hung up their touring rock 'n' roll shoes and devoted themselves primarily to recording projects—Harrison was an eager participant, not only contributing songs, lead and harmony vocals, intricate guitar (and sitar) parts, and a host of musical ideas and technological innovations, but also continuing to shape the Beatles' sound and, to a significant extent, the group's meaning as a group. While the individual members of the Fab Four each had their own reactions to the Harrison-led excursions into Indian music, into Eastern spirituality, and to India itself, absorbing many of these influences into their subsequent songs and recordings, Harrison's passion for the East widened and changed the group's palette, musical and otherwise. That many of these changes happened in the wake of the musicians' experiments with mind-altering drugs, especially LSD, also heavily influenced what they sang about and how it sounded, further leading them down the path toward "psychedelia" as a style, a sound, and an overall worldview.

When at the ripe young age of fifteen Harrison was invited to join John Lennon's band the Quarry Men, it was based on his being a wizard on guitar. And being a guitarist in the group, much less the lead guitarist, was all to which Harrison aspired. There is no evidence that he ever held out early hopes of becoming a singer, a songwriter, or a frontman in a rock group. Even in his post-Beatles solo years, when he could have put together a new band on the model of Paul McCartney's Wings, he never came close to doing so (although he did repeatedly call on a close-knit group of musicians to record with him in the studio). He was always just George Harrison, being himself, bringing to the forefront whatever talents and ideas he had to bear (and they were often much more than he gave himself credit for), but never seeking the limelight in the manner that other singer-guitarists of his ilk did, people like Steve Winwood, Eric Clapton, and Neil Young. Nor was he inclined to hide himself within another band—although for two short weeks in late 1969 he seemed to enjoy precisely that when he toured as an unbilled musician with Delaney and Bonnie, and again when he found himself among a band of (mostly) equals with the Traveling Wilburys in 1988. Surely, he enjoyed the successful launch of his solo career with *All Things Must Pass* and the string of hit singles that followed over the course of the next few albums, and the unprecedented superstar benefit concert he largely produced himself to raise humanitarian aid for the people of Bangladesh. And in spite of contemporaneous reports of his late-1974 North American concert tour being a failure, that myth has been mostly put to bed by musical historians who have reviewed the mostly positive coverage the concerts received by local journalists who were not jumping on the bandwagon of negativity that seemed to come down from on high and infected the national rock press, unwilling or unable to accept George Harrison for who he was outside the Beatles, or as he chose to present himself, his music, and the collective of Indian musicians led by Ravi Shankar whom he brought along on the tour.

The point simply is that in getting in with the Beatles, Harrison did so with the understanding that he was being hired as a guitarist to play in a band that mostly played cover tunes mixed with an occasional original song by bandleader John Lennon and his writing partner and co-lead vocalist, Harrison's friend Paul McCartney. While one may argue that Lennon and McCartney should have recognized, at least by 1965 and *Rubber Soul*, the burgeoning talent of a third songwriter in the group—and especially, that they should not have cheated him and Ringo Starr out of their rightful share of their publishing royalties (a situation that decades later saw corrective efforts made in the negotiations that led to the three surviving Beatles and the Lennon estate collaborating on the mid-1990s *Anthology* project)—the fact is that the dynamic duo shared a tacit understanding of George's role in the group vis-à-vis their own. And it is not as if they had totally stifled Harrison's ideas, songs, and productivity. Several of Harrison's best songs *did* make it onto Beatles albums, after all, and Lennon and McCartney turned to Harrison to help them turn their basic song ideas into hit singles powered by his catchy and inventive hooks, riffs, and lead lines that never drew attention to themselves above or beyond their service to the song.

That, as much as anything else, is what made Harrison one of the greatest rock guitarists of all time, despite his lack of flash and his aversion to lengthy, self-indulgent solos. He was not and never wanted to be Eric Clapton or Jimi Hendrix. The one time he felt one of his songs needed a Clapton-style solo, he brought "Slowhand" into the studio to add one to his song "While My Guitar Gently Weeps." And when he could not quite nail the guitar solo needed for "Taxman," he turned to his own bandmate, Paul McCartney, and asked him to give it a try, *not* because McCartney was a better guitarist or because in time Harrison could not have come up with something on his own, but because he knew that sometimes another guitarist on his own song could provide something extra in the same way that dozens of Lennon and McCartney songs were fully and only brought to life once Harrison had added his musical commentary and punctuation to the tracks. That McCartney wound up playing a solo on "Taxman" that in significant ways referred to Harrison's own guitar style, even hinting at Indian sonorities, and that Clapton likewise came up with a tasteful, Harrison-like instrumental interlude for "While My Guitar Gently Weeps," speaks volumes, both to Harrison's brilliance in trusting his fellow musicians and to their honoring Harrison by not stepping all over his songs and attempting to turn them into something they were not.

Harrison, at least in his formative years and then in the early years of the Beatles, was all about his love of the instrument, the sounds it could make, the diversity of styles he could cop from his favorite players (Carl Perkins, Scotty

Moore, Chuck Berry, etc.) and make his own, and creating unique parts that would transform Lennon and McCartney's bare-bones songs into hit records, in defiance of the clueless English record-label honcho who, in turning down the Beatles, did so with the explanation that "groups of guitarists are on the way out."[1] Guitars, especially those employed as lead instruments and not just for rhythmic or chordal duties, were the very essence of rock 'n' roll music, soon to be just plain rock music. As the Byrds prescribed the formula in "So You Want to Be a Rock 'n' Roll Star," laying out the recipe for success (in one of the most cynical songs about the music scene at the time), "Just get an electric guitar, then take some time and learn how to play." Guitars largely usurped horns, especially saxophones, in the transition from rock's roots in rhythm and blues; lead-guitar solos—for better or worse—replaced sax solos.

Although in their later years the Beatles would occasionally add some horns to a few tracks (most memorably in McCartney's "Got to Get You into My Life"), what was most striking is how once George Harrison had become a solo artist, he incorporated the saxophone into many of his arrangements (along with contemporaries, including Lou Reed, David Bowie, Roxy Music, and Pink Floyd). First with Bobby Keys on *All Things Must Pass,* through Jim Horn at the Concert for Bangladesh and *Living in the Material World,* and then with Tom Scott on 1974's *Dark Horse* and the subsequent late-1974 American tour, Harrison's arrangements would be colored by the warm, soulful tones of the saxophone. Horn, Scott, and Willie Weeks would continue to record with Harrison into the late 1970s, with Scott adding a joyful solo to Harrison's Motown-influenced 1977 hit, "This Song." (After hearing him with Harrison, Lennon pinched Bobby Keys for his 1974 hit single "Whatever Gets You Through the Night." And McCartney borrowed Tom Scott to play on his 1975 hit single "Listen to What the Man Said.") Harrison continued featuring saxophone on his recordings through *Traveling Wilburys Vol. 1,* on which Jim Horn's sax sails above and through Harrison's song "Heading for the Light." Leave it to one of the most famous guitar players in the world to restore saxophone to its rightful place in the rock ensemble.

4

Leave Me Alone

A schoolteacher once described George Harrison as a "very quiet, introverted little boy, who would sit in the furthest corner and not even look up"[1]—not a far cry from how Harrison's dynamic role in the Beatles has been perceived and described for decades. George Harrison was the most unlikely of rock stars. After the first few years of the Beatles, he dreaded performing and touring; he was unhappy about being seen as "a Beatle" rather than as an individual; and, for the most part, he had little use for or interest in the accoutrements of fame, preferring to spend his time quietly in his garden at his beloved English country estate, hanging with a few close friends and loved ones. Harrison once told an interviewer, "The whole Beatles thing is like a horror story, a nightmare. I don't even like to talk about it. I just hate it."[2]

Therefore, one could not have asked for a more perfect song to announce George Harrison's debut as a songwriter for the Beatles than "Don't Bother Me." The very title of the song could well stand as a credo for Harrison, an early manifesto capturing his personality and entire mindset about fame, a topic to which he would frequently return in songs including "Only a Northern Song," "Dark Horse," "While My Guitar Gently Weeps," and "Cockamamie Business," that last a semiobscure 1989 song whose final line is "Didn't want to be a star, wanted just to play guitar."

Written in August 1963, even before full-fledged Beatlemania had taken hold, "Don't Bother Me" implored its interlocutor to "go away, leave me alone, don't bother me." Already Harrison was feeling put upon enough to make this the overall theme to his very first contribution to the group's repertoire. "Don't Bother Me" stood out especially in the context of the group's 1963 album, *With the Beatles*, alongside such sunny original numbers as "All My Loving," "I Wanna Be Your Man," and "Hold Me Tight," and next to covers of Smokey Robinson's "You Really Got a Hold on Me" (sung by George) and Meredith Willson's "Till There Was You" from the Broadway musical *The Music Man*. As Beatles author Rob Sheffield writes, "'Don't Bother Me,' his first real song, began the 'George is in a bad mood' phase of his songwriting, which never ended. . . . 'Don't Bother Me' is a sentiment he kept rewriting his entire life."[3]

For George, the very first message he chose to impart as a Beatles song-writer was that of a back turned: "Leave me alone, don't bother me." This, after all, came from the one member of the Fab Four whose first move upon arriving at the Plaza Hotel in New York City in February 1964 was to go to bed. The melody, chord structure, and guitar sound contributed to the song's overall negative vibe in keeping with its lyrics. The refrain employed a distinctive, descending melody sung over a complicated harmonic background that bounces from major to minor and back again. John Lennon's electric rhythm guitar is amped with a chunky tremolo, lending the effort an ominous, sickly feel, quite appropriate because Harrison was ill in bed when he wrote the tune. McCartney plays claves (hardwood sticks), adding a Latin feel to the rhythm, which occasionally stutter and trip, conjuring a sense of delirium. The fade-out features an odd, hammer-like sound, as if someone were knocking on the door, further enhancing the fever-dream nature of the number and providing final justification for his "don't bother me" plea. Little Richard's "You keep a-knockin' but you can't come in" might have been an inspiration. As Beatles historian Kenneth Womack writes, "'Don't Bother Me' would, at its core, prove a remarkably prescient sketch of the complicated relationship its composer would have with fame for the rest of his life."[4]

"Don't Bother Me" also hinted at a distinctive approach to songwriting for Harrison—that of the confessional singer-songwriter. Years before that term would come into common use as a reference to a more personal style of song-writing popularized in the early 1970s by the likes of James Taylor, Carole King, Leonard Cohen, and Joni Mitchell—inspired by the examples set by Bob Dylan and Paul Simon in the 1960s—Harrison's straightforward accounting of his emotional state in "Don't Bother Me" set him apart from what Lennon and McCartney were doing in song at that time. It would be a while before Harrison would produce another "confessional"-style song presumed to be a true accounting of his feelings, but with *Rubber Soul*–era songs, including "If I Needed Someone" and "Think for Yourself," Harrison cemented the approach, which he would carry on largely through his remaining work with the Beatles (in songs that included "I Want to Tell You," "It's All Too Much," and "Something") as well as in his post-Beatles solo career, which found him more aligned with the prominent singer-songwriters of the time than with his former bandmates, who largely continued to write and record as pop singers—perhaps with the exception of John Lennon. Thus, while it may have been a surprise to see Harrison performing in a duo with Paul Simon on the late-night TV program *Saturday Night Live* in November 1976, it seemed perfectly logical in retrospect. (The two duetted on Harrison's "Here Comes the Sun" and Simon's "Homeward Bound.")

Guitarist and composer Gary Lucas, perhaps best known for his work with Captain Beefheart and Jeff Buckley, finds the seeds of greatness in "Don't Bother Me." Lucas told me, "From his very first songwriting contribution of 'Don't Bother Me' on the second Beatles album, you knew you were in the presence of someone who was unafraid to break the mold of 'Beatles music,' as defined by Lennon and McCartney. Just to write a minor-key based song is astounding—very rarely done in those days and even now."

Lucas continues, "'Don't Bother Me' has a distinctively doom-laden quality to it and a very dark lyric of alienated rejection. . . . When you heard 'Don't Bother Me' you knew you were in the presence of greatness and that George Harrison was his own man with a distinctive voice, not only on guitar but in his songwriting. . . . From 'Don't Bother Me' you knew that anytime George was allowed a song it was going to be spectacular."

English rock singer-songwriter Robyn Hitchcock echoes Lucas's observations. "The moody, handsome, dark-eyed kid who wrote 'Don't Bother Me' was the chrysalis from which emerged rainbow Krishna George, a sensitive, quavering singer whose voice trembled at the onslaughts of the world," Hitchcock told me.

Harrison wrote "Don't Bother Me" in August 1963, while holed up in his room at the Palace Court Hotel in Bournemouth. The Beatles recorded it over the course of two days in the studio the next month. Harrison's vocals are double tracked, but not tightly, leaving space and occasionally time between the two vocal lines. This out-of-sync effect runs through the instrumentation, too—Lennon's heavily processed, woozy rhythm guitar adds to the sense of instability, as does the off-the-beat crack of the claves. On the verses, Harrison duets with his vocals on lead electric guitar, deftly blending individual notes with chordal figures. The music comes to a split-second halt before George sings the refrain, during which time he lays out on guitar, thereby forefronting his vocals atop John's tremolo-drenched rhythmic chords, Ringo's drums, and Paul's bass. The middle-eight section is a variant of the first two verses, with a different vocal melody line as well as an emotional shift in the lyrics, with the singer fearing he will "never be the same" unless the woman who walked out on him returns. The third verse returns to the main "don't bother me" theme, followed by an electric-guitar solo that adheres closely to the harmonic structure of the verse. Ringo Starr's drumming holds the song together when the other instruments threaten to go out of sync or just collapse into chaos—the perfect musical analog to the singer's emotional breakdown—and the song comes to an end with Harrison intoning "don't bother me" five times before all that remains is a knocking-on-the-door beat provided by the drummer.

"Don't Bother Me" was only the first not-love song that would come out of the pen of George Harrison. He would continue to explore the ambiguities of love and the difficulties of relationships in Beatles songs, including "You Like Me Too Much," "If I Needed Someone," "I Want to Tell You," "Long, Long, Long," and even "Something," that last often heralded as one of the greatest love songs of the rock era. Harrison would continue to write about love with a more sophisticated, mature understanding of its complexities than what was typical in pop music of the rock era in his solo career. "Don't Bother Me," which Harrison wrote at age twenty, was only the beginning.

5

Do You Promise Not to Tell?

One of the savvier policies that manager Brian Epstein instituted early on for the Beatles (along with wearing identical suits and not eating onstage) was that the four of them should keep their personal lives just that: personal. Brian Epstein himself was no stranger to this phenomenon—he was, as English law required him to be at the time, a closeted homosexual, whose anonymous trysts and hookups always came not only with the threat of danger and violence but also of public shaming and criminal prosecution. Epstein laid down a rule for the Fab Four: No member of the press or the public should know if they were in a steady relationship and certainly not with whom. The illusion that the members of the Beatles were free-floating individuals with no romantic ties was essential to fanning the flames of the Fab Four as potential love interests—fantastical or otherwise—to their female fans (and certainly to some of their male fans, perhaps none more so than Brian Epstein himself). Epstein saw the inherent power in presenting the fabulous foursome in a manner that the fantasies of the masses could be projected upon them by divorcing the image of the Beatles from their own humanity, reality, and life circumstances.

Therefore, when John Lennon wrote a song about his newlywed wife just a few months after secretly tying the knot with Cynthia Powell in Liverpool in late August 1962, he went to great lengths to keep the temporal meaning behind the song secret. Cheekily playing with fire, though, Lennon titled the song after its refrain: the very tantalizing, taunting, and teasing "Do You Want to Know a Secret." In the song itself, the secret the singer reveals to the object of his affection is that he is in love (although the genders of the subject and object of the song are nonspecific, further cloaking the song in a shroud of mystery and uncertainty). And to put further distance between the immediate impulse behind the song and Lennon's personal romantic situation, Lennon opted to have George Harrison sing the number. In a typically dismissive remark, Lennon later claimed he gave it to Harrison to sing because "it only had three notes and he wasn't the best singer in the world."[1] For the record, the song had more than three notes, and while George may not have been the world's best singer at that moment, he may well have been the third best. As for Lennon himself, while the musical form and structure of the song was somewhat inventive, the songwriter did not greatly exert himself with the lyrics: the song contains only one four-line verse that gets repeated three times, a three-line refrain that appears thrice, and a single, two-line bridge.

Nevertheless, Harrison laid his stamp on the tune with both his guitar and vocals. The song opens with a dramatic intro, as if Roy Orbison were singing a flamenco tune. George strums a few moody minor chords underneath his haunted, free-metered, exotica-tinged introductory vocals—"You'll never know how much I really love you; you'll never know how much I really care"— his voice drenched in so much echo it sounds as if it were emanating from the heavens above. Harrison resolves the introductory couplet with a leap to a major chord, as an ascending guitar arpeggio shifts the song proper into a major key for the duration of the tune. That minor-to-major transition[2] musically represents the emotional leap one takes from the feeling of vulnerability to the outward expression of love.

The arrangement of "Do You Want to Know a Secret" is deceptively minimalist. While George and John's guitars mostly provide rhythmic, chordal underpinning, and while Ringo keeps a simple, steady beat, the verses each build toward a climax with the aid of rhythmic variations introduced by guitar riffing and Paul McCartney's bundling of busy bass notes spilling forth at the end of each verse. Following the first verse, John and Paul chime in with "doo-dah-doo" vocals that echo George's vocals, almost as commentary—as id to George's ego, or as dreamy angels sprinkling their fairy dust of love on the unsuspecting young couple. After the recording's final crescendo, the song fades as George offers a vocal denouement of his own with a series of "ooh-ooh-ooh-ooh"s that echo Lennon and McCartney's doo-wop-derived interjections. The whole effort goes down easily—a sweet, catchy, somewhat mysterious love song, a simple profession of affection, all in the form of an economical, one-minute and fifty-seven-second pop tune.

The group continued to work on the song's arrangement even after the recording was in the can. A somewhat rare compilation called *Bootleg Recordings 1963*—in spite of its title, an official 2013 Beatles release—offers two live versions (in addition to an alternate studio take) recorded within days of each other, both taken at a faster pace—one fast, the other still faster—with McCartney driving the number along with a funkier bassline, along with a harder-rocking guitar accompaniment, much more lively and dynamic drumming by Ringo, and more assertive vocals by Harrison, here swinging harder to a more untethered beat. While the studio version merely sunsets on George's repeated "ooh-ooh"s, the live versions adopt that early Beatles trademark of concluding songs with one of those unexpected compound sixth or ninth chords that surprise the listener while bringing the proceedings to a close with a hint of ambiguity, perhaps leaving the sentiment of the number somewhat unresolved. (This had been tried on at least one take in the original recording session, but for some reason the Beatles or George Martin opted for the fade-out rather than the conclusive chord on the final track.) By the time the group performed the song live for the last time on the BBC's "Pop Goes the Beatles" program on July 30, 1963, the tune was so revved up it almost foreshadowed Ramones-style punk rock—only befitting, as the Ramones named themselves after one of Paul McCartney's early aliases, Paul Ramon. It is also the group's most soulful version of the song, and one could easily imagine it having been released by Motown Records under an assumed name ("the Ramones," say) and becoming a major hit on the R&B charts.

Lennon later attributed the creative inspiration behind the song to his mother; when he was a toddler she would sing "I'm Wishing" from the 1937 Walt Disney animated film *Snow White and the Seven Dwarfs*, which had a spoken-word intro that went, "Wanna know a secret? Promise not to tell?," which Lennon basically copped as the opening lines of his song proper, which follow his original spoken-word intro to the song. Years later, Harrison traced back the song's musical influence to the 1961 doo-wop hit "I Really Love You," by the Stereos—a song that the Beatles had likely played in their club days and that Harrison himself would revive in a relatively faithful cover version on his 1982 solo album, *Gone Troppo*.

Despite Lennon's patronizing comments about Harrison's abilities or lack of such as a singer, the recording was a great success. The song was included on the Beatles debut album, *Please Please Me*, released in the United Kingdom in March 1963. It would be a year almost to the day that "Do You Want to Know a Secret" was released as a single in the United States, where it shot up the charts to number two by early May 1964, prevented from hitting the top spot only by the Beatles' own "Can't Buy Me Love," which was firmly ensconced at number one for five weeks in all. (When "Can't Buy Me Love" first hit number one on April 4, Beatles songs occupied all top five positions in *Billboard*'s Hot 100 chart.) As number two, "Do You Want to Know a Secret" was the highest-charting Beatles song with a lead vocal by George Harrison until "Something" went to number one in late November 1969. Harrison's vocals were rhythmically inventive, and he made ample use of melisma (stretching a single syllable over a series of notes) and leaps into his falsetto range. Harrison also offered hints of John Lennon–like rock 'n' roll growls; listen to how he attacks the first word of the phrase "I'm in love with you," every time it comes around, adding a slight touch of menace to the proceedings. The overall effect was a blend of sweet, mid-tempo ballad singing with an undercurrent of raw lust.

The influence of both Lennon and McCartney on Harrison's vocals is clear, and one could not have asked for two finer role models.

Almost a year before "Do You Want to Know a Secret" became a huge hit in America, it had already enjoyed tremendous popular and commercial success in the United Kingdom—but not as a Beatles song. "Do You Want to Know a Secret" had also been recorded by Billy J. Kramer with the Dakotas, another Brian Epstein–managed pop group from northern England, in early 1963, and as a single it went to number two in May 1963, giving the songwriting team of Lennon and McCartney its first hit single performed by another artist. (Incidentally, Kramer's version, like the Beatles', was produced by George Martin.)

"Do You Want to Know a Secret" may well be the Rodney Dangerfield of early Beatles hits. Despite its key role as an exemplar of the Beatles sound during the Beatlemania year of 1964, it just seems to have been unable to garner much respect. This is not a question of lack of commercial success: one telling chart of Beatles recordings ranked by New York City radio station WABC[3] placed the song at number twelve, just below "Yesterday" and just above "Can't Buy Me Love." Perhaps "Do You Want to Know a Secret" has been overlooked because Harrison was the featured lead vocalist instead of John or Paul.

As Beatles songs went at the time, this was one of their tamer numbers, both lyrically and musically. One can easily imagine it being a track preferred by parents of teenaged Beatles fans, along with "A Taste of Honey"—the Broadway-like pop tune that followed it immediately on the *Please Please Me* album—and "Till There Was You," their cover of Meredith Willson's Broadway ballad that was used in *The Music Man* in the original 1957 Broadway musical and again in the film version in 1962. The Beatles released their version half a year later on their second album, *With the Beatles*. While primarily catering to their teen audience in their first few years, the Beatles, prodded by Brian Epstein, had grander ambitions to reach a broader, more diverse listenership with a broader, more diverse array of musical styles. Paul McCartney, after all, had already written a vaudeville-like jazzy tune called "When I'm Sixty-Four" at the ripe young age of fourteen in spring 1956.

But this still does not fully account for the lack of respect afforded "Do You Want to Know a Secret"—and the lack of respect given to George's performance. Perhaps just as it grew out of a secret about a secret and was shaped into the form of a secret, the song was destined to remain in the shadows, obscured by its origins and the deception at its heart. In that manner alone, the song must be measured a huge success.

As for Brian Epstein's role in all this, his marketing strategy of branding the Beatles' personal lives with the stamp of secrecy was largely a success by measure of his intentions: the Beatles became whatever their fans wanted and imagined them to be. For a while, this drove the fans—and the world around them—crazy, in a good way. What no one could have anticipated is how those fantasies would in just a few short years turn into something dangerous, ugly, and even violent, because such a phenomenon was unprecedented. And the psychic toll this dynamic wrought on Harrison and the Beatles, to say nothing of the mortal price Lennon and eventually Harrison would pay for it, would in the end prove to be the ultimate, defining tragedy of the Beatles.

Epstein would also fall victim to his own tragic secret-keeping. Although there is no evidence in or out of Lennon's song that he was channeling Epstein's emotional life as a closeted homosexual—which British law required at the time; sexual relations between men were outlawed in England until 1967—one could easily read it that way. Perhaps Epstein himself did. And perhaps it brought him little solace to know that his private life, like that of Lennon and the other Beatles, had to be kept a secret.

6
The Chord

"A Hard Day's Night" was one of the biggest hits in the initial wave of Beatlemania in the United States and around the globe in summer 1964. In addition to the song, *A Hard Day's Night* was the name of the first Beatles movie, as well as the name of the soundtrack album of the Richard Lester–directed film. The group's third studio album, it was the first one to contain only original compositions by the group, featuring a dozen new tunes by Lennon and McCartney, plus their previous hit single, "Can't Buy Me Love," which was given a home on the album. (Incidentally, this was the *only* Beatles album to exclusively contain songs by the main songwriting duo—all other Beatles albums included cover tunes or songs written by George Harrison.)

Thematically, "A Hard Day's Night" is a close relative of "Can't Buy Me Love," as both songs comment on the duality of work and love, or commerce and sex. The song was written and recorded in a single session, a final homework assignment given to Lennon and McCartney when the filmmakers decided they needed a song to match the film's title. Writing under deadline pressure proved to be a good impetus for John Lennon, who went home one night determined to beat Paul McCartney to the punch and returned to the studio the next day with the essentials of the tune worked out.

For producer George Martin, all that was needed was a proper intro to the song. As was increasingly the practice, Martin and band turned to George Harrison to see what he could come up with. Rather than a hook or a riff, Harrison devised a single chord, an unusual combination of notes that were not easily identifiable and that, as finally recorded by the group, was fleshed out by George Martin on piano and Paul McCartney on bass.[1]

And just what was that opening chord? This has been the stuff of great debate and analysis since 1964. Serious musicologists and even mathematicians have gone to great lengths to define the chord—to give a name to this atonal but not dissonant combination of notes that linger unresolved, that are neither "major" nor "minor" in any conventional use of the terms, that in spite of those efforts to deconstruct the chord defy analysis, and that Harrison cleverly dangles again at the end of the recording in the form of a single-note arpeggio played on his twelve-string electric guitar. Any attempt to define the chord by stripping it down into its constituent elements is destined to fail. If ever a chord—or a simultaneous assemblage of notes—was more than the sum of its parts, this was the one.

To no small extent, the opening chord of "A Hard Day's Night" remains the single most emblematic sound of the Beatles' entire recording catalog. The final chord to "A Day in the Life" on *Sgt. Pepper's Lonely Hearts Club Band* is a fascinating and dramatic musical choice that speaks to the Beatles' musical genius and avant-garde inclinations in 1967, "a forty-second meditation on finality that leaves each member of the audience listening with a new kind of attention and awareness to the sound of nothing at all."[2] But George Harrison's opening chord to "A Hard Day's Night" was equally avant-garde in its time, when such efforts were unknown and unprecedented.

Part of the magic of that opening *kerrang* is that, while built upon Harrison's "F with a G on top" chord, as he somewhat dismissively referred to it,[3] the chord was played by five musicians all told. In addition to Harrison's innovative guitar voicing, Paul McCartney gave it a "D" on bass; John Lennon played a variant of Harrison's chord on acoustic guitar; Ringo hit a rim shot; and George Martin played a triad of notes on piano. On record, everyone striking at once, it hits hard, like the crack of a snare drum, and then rings out and sustains for the longest three seconds in rock music, offering little to no hint of what is about to come. Before the chord has a chance to fully decay, the song proper begins with John Lennon's vocal joined by the full band, including Ringo's drums and overdubbed bongos. It is an attention-getting clarion call, the first sound the viewer of the *Hard Day's Night* film hears, and an announcement of a new dawn in music. It certainly represented a new beginning for the Beatles, introducing a new musical sophistication in their arrangements that would soon be followed by lyrical innovations worthy of the new music.

George Harrison's contributions to the song's success were not limited to that opening clang. He also provided a distinctive guitar solo halfway through, a quick melodic figure, a countermelody to the song's main tune, played twice in succession. Like the song's opening chord, the guitar solo bore a sound all its own, boasting a sharp, slicing tone full of fleet finger work. The unique tone was a result of George Martin running the tape at half-speed and having Harrison play the solo at half-speed, too. Then, when the resulting recording was brought up to full speed, it fit perfectly with the pitch of the track with a deep, rich tone. In addition, Martin himself doubled the solo on piano, playing the exact same notes as Harrison, thereby recapitulating to some extent the magical sound of the intro. And as previously noted, Harrison brought the curtain down on the number by playing the notes of the opening chord as a repetitive, linear ostinato. Even if listeners did not realize that the outro was just another form of the intro, their subconscious heard a song coming full circle back to its beginning, albeit with a different emotional effect, ending on something more akin to a question than the remarkable statement that kicked off the number.

It comes as little surprise that years later Paul McCartney would open a string of solo concerts with a song originally written and sung by John Lennon and heavily colored by the sounds of George Harrison's guitar. McCartney knew as well as anyone that "A Hard Day's Night" worked as a rip-roaring concert opener, one that with the mere sound of its opening chord would plunge his audiences into a frenzy of nostalgia, bringing them as close to the feeling of the original Beatlemania as they could ever get. Paul enlisted "A Hard Day's Night" as the kickoff tune on his "One on One" world tour that ran from April 2016 through December 2017, and again on his subsequent "Freshen Up" tour, which ran from September 2018 through July 2019.

7
Eight Arms to Hold You

The very first image a viewer sees in the 1965 Beatles movie *Help!* is a large statue of a Hindu-like god with multiple limbs. (Indeed, the working title of the film was *Eight Arms to Hold You*.) A young woman in a red dress is about to be sacrificed to the idol, until it is discovered that she is not wearing the required ring with a large red stone. Astute viewers get it immediately—if it is a ring that is missing, then Ringo must somehow be involved. And thus, for the next ninety minutes, the movie basically plays out in scenes in which this unnamed sacrificial cult tries to separate the ring from Ringo, who would happily turn over the ring, except that he cannot get it off his finger.

While in its own time the portrayal of the fictional Eastern cult may have seemed funny, it is impossible to watch it today without at best cringing or at worst being highly offended at the stereotypical portrayal of the violent and bloodthirsty group, its leaders, and its practices. What is doubly puzzling is how closely the sect seems to be identified with Indians and Hinduism. Indeed, it has been suggested that the cult was modeled after a medieval sword-carrying gang of highway robbers called *Thugs*, who blended Muslim and Hindu iconography and worshipped the goddess Kali. (In the film the cult members worship "Kaili.") And what is triply ironic is that in no small way, the making of the film *Help!* led directly to George Harrison's interest in Indian music, simply because a scene in a restaurant featured four musicians playing Indian instruments. George's curiosity about the Indian instruments on the set led him to pick up a sitar and try to play it. In the movie's final cut, the viewer hears Indian-style music even before the appearance of the restaurant scene; the musical score features sitar music that winds up being a version of the theme song to the Beatles' previous movie, *A Hard Day's Night*.

Other scenes and images from the film are eerily prescient of things to come in Harrison's and the other Beatles' lives and careers. Early on, the cult leader throws darts at images of the Beatles projected onto a home-movie screen, foreshadowing the real and threatened violence to which the Beatles would soon be subjected on their next worldwide tour, when they played concerts under a cloud of phoned-in bomb threats and death threats and all sorts of objects being thrown at them onstage. There is even a scene of a home invasion, in which each Beatle engages in hand-to-hand combat with murderous cult members intent on recovering their precious ring. Watching these scenes now, decades after John Lennon was assassinated in front of his New York City apartment and George Harrison was nearly stabbed to death by an intruder at his home in Friar Park in Henley-on-Thames, one cannot help shuddering at how these scenes anticipated real-life horrors to come in the lives of the Beatles.

This is not to say that the entire effort was without value and merit. Though not nearly as witty and engaging as *A Hard Day's Night*, and with a weaker selection of songs than those featured in their first film, *Help!* does offer occasional treasures. Many of the song set pieces are early versions of music videos, and self-referential Beatle-isms abound; e.g., at one point George comments, "I'm always getting winked at these days. It used to be you, didn't it, Paul?" The film is a veritable travelogue, with the Beatles on the run throughout London before escaping to the Austrian Alps, engaging the protective services of an inept Scotland Yard, and taking refuge in Buckingham Palace, before winding up in the Bahamas. Still, coming off the high of *A Hard Day's Night*, the movie was a letdown of sorts. And that is not even to mention the fact that the Fab Four were all high on marijuana throughout the filming of *Help!*, the results of which can often be seen right on the screen, with the individuals too stoned to speak their lines. John Lennon explained years later, "We were smoking marijuana for breakfast during that period. Nobody could communicate with us; it was all glazed eyes and giggling all the time."[1]

Part of the problem with *Help!* owed to its origins as a vehicle for comic actor Peter Sellers, whom the Beatles, incidentally, idolized from his early days as a cast member of the BBC radio comedy program *The Goon Show*. After Sellers opted instead to film *What's New Pussycat?* the script was hurriedly reworked for the Beatles. The effort was thus doomed from the start, an attempt at fitting a four-sided square peg into a round hole and taking next to no advantage of what the Beatles offered as individual characters beyond Ringo Starr's sad-sack, hangdog look and his penchant for bejeweled fingers.

Likewise, in the wake of the phenomenal success of the soundtrack to *A Hard Day's Night*, expectations were high for a repeat success with the *Help!* soundtrack. If *Help!* did not quite live up to *A Hard Day's Night* critically and commercially, it was not for lack of great songs and groundbreaking innovations—of those there were plenty. The album was rushed, however, and the Beatles had to scramble to write original material while bouncing from film sets to playing concerts with little to no down time. This undoubtedly accounted for the inclusion of an unprecedented two original George Harrison compositions—"I Need You" and "You Like Me Too Much"—on the album, as well as two cover tunes, marking the last time the Beatles would re-cord material written by outside songwriters until their raucous version of the traditional folk song "Maggie Mae" appeared on 1970's *Let It Be*. Still, *Help!* included such top-tier tunes as the title track, "You've Got to Hide Your Love Away," and "Ticket to Ride," all heard in the film, and a non-film song on the LP's obverse side called "Yesterday." The latter song, written and sung by Paul McCartney—the only member of the Beatles who appears on the track, with backing by a string quartet—would go on to become one of the most beloved of all Beatles tunes, a perennial top vote-getter in lists of the greatest songs of all time, and, with well over two thousand cover versions and counting, probably the single most-recorded song ever. As a Beatles song, however, "Yesterday" was and remains something of an outlier. It was a testament to the group's command of multiple musical idioms, to their ability and eagerness to defy constraints of genre, and to their willingness to indulge the occasional unconventional pursuits of the band's individual members. George Martin even suggested to Brian Epstein the possibility of releasing the track as a Paul McCartney solo record; fortunately, Epstein vetoed the idea, and "Yesterday" remained a Beatles song.

After "Don't Bother Me," which appeared on the Beatles' second album, 1963's *With the Beatles*, songwriter George Harrison would not be heard from again until the group's fifth album, which, despite its title, was not a soundtrack album to the movie per se. Only half of the album's fourteen songs were used in the film, and other than the title track, these were composed without refer-ence to the screenplay. All the songs used in the film were grouped on side one of the LP. Side two featured the non-movie songs, including Ringo Starr's ami-able rendition of Buck Owens's "Act Naturally," which became something of a signature song for the drummer—with its references to becoming a big star in the movies despite having no acting training nor ability—alongside a couple of McCartney highlights, including "I've Just Seen a Face" and "Yesterday."

Beginning with *Help!* George Harrison would place at least one but typi-cally two or more songs on every remaining Beatles album. Harrison's "I Need You" was the only non–Lennon and McCartney number to be used in the film; "You Like Me Too Much" was a side-two, non-film contribution. While the lyrics of "I Need You" did not break any new ground for Harrison or the Beatles—it was simply a love song sung from the point of view of a rejected lover, a last-ditch effort to win her back simply through pleading through the pain and the hurt—the composition and playing were intriguing. Most no-tably, "I Need You" is colored by some strange-sounding guitar notes played by Harrison. These were produced with the aid of a recent invention—a foot-controlled volume pedal. Plugged into his Rickenbacker twelve-string electric guitar, the effects pedal gave his guitar an inquisitive, elastic, organ-like tone. The resulting sound also offered an uncanny foreshadowing of the sound of a sitar, which Harrison would encounter on the set of *Help!* just a couple of months hence. One can also hear hints of the slide-guitar sound that would become Harrison's primary guitar language in his post-Beatles career.

Harrison's other *Help!* number, "You Like Me Too Much," is more in the vein of "Don't Bother Me" and telegraphs the shape of things to come from the songwriter. While in some ways it is closely related, lyrically, to "I Need You," this time out the singer is more confident, even full of braggadocio (and perhaps full of himself). "You'll never leave me and you know it's true, 'cause you like me too much and I like you," he sings, hinting at love with an edge, a competitive love with a hint of violence just shy of that found in contemporaneous Lennon songs, such as "Run for Your Life," in which Lennon threatens murder. Harrison's narrator betrays the mentality of a stalker in the line "I will follow you and bring you back where you belong," leaving it to our imagination what methods he will use, beyond the sort of persuasion employed in "I Need You." Looking ahead, Harrison fortunately drops this sort of macho posturing in his lyrics, while Lennon will continue to mine that emotional vein throughout the remainder of his work with the Beatles into his foreshortened solo career. Even while preaching "All you need is love" and "Imagine all the people living life in peace," Lennon returns to vengeful themes in "Jealous Guy" and "Steel and Glass."

Perhaps what is most interesting about Harrison's "You Like Me Too Much" is that it finds the group's lead guitarist writing a song that winds up being almost entirely a piano-driven number, with different piano parts played by Lennon, McCartney, and producer George Martin. Lennon plays a basic chordal pattern on acoustic guitar throughout the tune, but Harrison's electric lead is heard only during the song's instrumental break, when it does a pleasant call-and-response duet with the piano. What also can be heard, besides Ringo on drums and Paul on bass, is a steady tambourine beat throughout, not played by Ringo but rather by Harrison.

Beatles author Allan Kozinn finds distinctive characteristics in Harrison's two *Help!* songs that would come to characterize his songwriting approach. Kozinn writes, "[T]hey seem driven by their chord sequences rather than their melodies. Those sequences dart freely between major and minor keys, and yield melodies with the slightly exotic and sometimes mournful character typical of Harrison's work through the Beatles years and well into his solo work."[2]

The *Help!* song that fully represented the Beatles' changing sound the moment it was released, the song that pointed in the direction of what was yet to come, was "Ticket to Ride," released as a single in early April 1965, a full four months before the album *Help!* would hit record-store shelves. Mostly written and sung by John Lennon, the track combined commercial success—it shot to number one on the pop charts—with sophisticated and complex melody, harmonics, rhythms, and arrangements that, were it not for the song's popularity, might well have been perceived as a downright avant-garde experiment.

The song opens with a solo introduction by George Harrison, playing a jangly, ostinato riff on his Rickenbacker electric twelve-string guitar, a sound that was becoming one of the signature trademarks of the Beatles, soon to be copied by other groups on both sides of the Atlantic, most notably the Byrds. We have already seen how Byrds guitarist Jim McGuinn traded in his six-string for a Rickenbacker twelve-string after seeing *A Hard Day's Night*. McGuinn's Harrison-influenced guitar style would power the Byrds' folk-rock version of Bob Dylan's "Mr. Tambourine Man" to number one when it was released as a single in April 1965, just three days after the Beatles released "Ticket to Ride."

After Harrison's intro, the song proper begins, with Lennon on lead vocals and McCartney adding high harmonies. Ringo Starr patterned a distinctive, syncopated stop-start rhythm after Harrison's ostinato, which itself had an off-the-beat, syncopated swing to it, and which Harrison would continue to play in the background throughout the song. This highly effective use of pauses gave the illusion of stretching out the beats, a push-pull effect or stutter that implied a reluctance to move forward, the perfect musical representation of Lennon's lyrics, which find the singer confused about a girlfriend's departure, alternately feeling sad and vindictive—not an atypical pairing of emotions in a John Lennon song.

Beatles author Allan Kozinn told me,

The lead guitar was kind of a free agent, available for chording if it was needed—or for chording using different voicings than the rhythm guitarist was playing—but otherwise added texture, commentary . . . and a concise solo. Perhaps one thing he did was that where some lead guitarists basically repeated the vocal melody, perhaps with a few flourishes, George tended to prefer the solos to be their own thing, distinct from the melody, even though it's played against the same chord progression.

Somewhat mysteriously, the song opens with an extended passage based on a single chord. For the first twenty seconds, Lennon sings a raga-like melody over drone-like guitar figures and bass notes before the song modulates to a different chord.[3] In a short time, this sort of musical strategy would become de rigueur for the Beatles, but at this point it was utterly new and experimental. On their next album, *Rubber Soul*, and subsequent albums, the influence of Indian music would be fully present throughout many Beatles songs and in the resulting "raga-rock" craze they would spawn. But the sustained pedal point, similar to a Hindustani drone, beginning each verse of "Ticket to Ride" is nearly inexplicable, as the song was recorded on February 15, 1965, almost three months to the day before Harrison would famously hear Indian music for the first time on the film set of *Help!* in the restaurant scene featuring a trio of Indian musicians. We have noted that Harrison had neonatal exposure to the sounds of India when his mother would tune her radio to the regular BBC program devoted to Indian music. And it is not clear how much Harrison was responsible for the arrangement of Lennon's song. Whatever the case may be, all four Beatles were clearly and almost effortlessly predisposed toward the basic elements of raga; even Ringo's unusual drum pattern early in the tune approximates what a tabla—a pair of Indian hand drums—might play underneath such a drone.

Harrison's two songs on the Beatles' next album, 1965's *Rubber Soul*, are strong statements of his emerging role in the group as a songwriter and vocalist as well as an instrumentalist. Harrison's growing importance as lead guitarist—both in terms of his virtuosity and the intricacies of his contributions that nearly but unofficially made him a co-composer to several tunes—as well as his instrumental experiments would color the overall sound of *Rubber Soul*, contributing to the album's critical success, its increased musical sophistication compared to what had come before, and an overall shift in attitude that had begun with its predecessor, *Help!* This saw its full flowering on *Rubber Soul* and hinted at the full-fledged reinvention of the group's sound on *Revolver*, which would be recorded just a half year later. From his guitar line that snakes through the opening track, "Drive My Car," through his use of the sitar on "Norwegian Wood," to his deft fills and solos on "Nowhere Man," Harrison made manifest what had not been widely appreciated beforehand— that he was a coequal contributor to the Beatles' sound, and that he now squeezed into the driver's seat along with Lennon and McCartney on the way toward the musical revolution that would be 1966's *Revolver*.

8

On One Condition

By the time of *Rubber Soul*, the Beatles had ventured well beyond their original teenybopper approach embodied by songs like "She Loves You" and "I Want to Hold Your Hand." Fueled in part by Bob Dylan's influence as well as their own growth as individuals and songwriters, the Beatles left behind songs like "Love Me Do" and "Please Please Me" in favor of "Nowhere Man" and "I'm Looking Through You." Still, these were only half steps. *Rubber Soul* kicked off with McCartney's "Drive My Car," a number lighthearted enough to be covered eventually by former members of the Spice Girls. Lennon's "In My Life," while quite a leap forward from "Tell Me Why," was still basically a sentimental love song with a treacly melody. While McCartney's "You Won't See Me" added a little bite ("I've had enough so act your age") to what previously had been his specialty—silly teenage love songs—it was not so dark as to prevent it from becoming a Top 10 hit when covered by Canadian middle-of-the-road pop singer Anne Murray in 1974.

One of George Harrison's greatest early achievements as a songwriter was "If I Needed Someone," which was recorded in October 1965 and included on the British release of *Rubber Soul* in December and on the *Yesterday and Today* US release in June 1966. The song was an instant hit for the Hollies, whose version hit the top twenty in the United Kingdom, making it Harrison's first hit single as a songwriter. It must have rankled him that it took a group other than his own to drive one of his songs to the top of the pop charts. (Harrison, incidentally, hated the Hollies' version, telling an interviewer, "It's rubbish. . . . They've spoiled it," adding that they sounded like session musicians who had never before met or played together.[1] Graham Nash was not amused.)

Harrison acknowledged the influence that Roger (then Jim) McGuinn's opening hook on the Byrds' version of Pete Seeger's "The Bells of Rhymney" had on the intro to "If I Needed Someone," although this was no mere cut-and-paste job—more of a case of love rather than theft. The Byrds' sound itself, including the two- and three-part vocal harmonies and McGuinn's jangly, trebly guitar sound, was based upon the Beatles to begin with—Harrison referred to them as "the American Beatles."[2] It was all part of a give-and-take between mutually admiring musicians. The adoption of Indian modes, textures, and instrumentation was also a shared enthusiasm of both groups.

Harrison's "If I Needed Someone," however, broke new ground for a Beatles narrative; it was as complex as it was ambiguous. Ostensibly a love song, it is entirely delivered in the conditional mode (and a little subjunctive, too): *If* I needed someone; *had* you come some other day; it *might* not have been like this; *maybe* you will get a call. While it has often been seen as an ambivalent love song—perhaps meant for his soon-to-be wife Pattie Boyd—it is astonishingly jaded and cynical. There actually is no ambivalence at all in the lyrics. It is as much of a put-down song as that of his new pal Bob Dylan's "Positively 4th Street," which was released a few months earlier. In some ways it works as a love song—there is an implied lover other than the woman to whom the song is addressed, making it something of a not-so-subtle ode to infidelity.

Harrison's musical intuition and innate genius permeates the recording of "If I Needed Someone." We cannot know if he consciously said to himself, "If I sing on the offbeat, the disparity between the melody line and the song's rhythm will echo and imply the ambivalence of the lyrics," but that is exactly the effect this choice has. The melody line almost floats atop the downbeats, untethered by the song's rhythm, enhancing if not fully creating the dreamy, hesitant mood of the number. Just as the song's narrator is noncommittal—*if* this, *if* that, you *may*—so is the singer's delivery noncommittal, refusing to be pinned down by something as elementary as a downbeat. *It's all just too much exertion,* it seems to imply, which fits with the song's manifest and latent meaning, as well as with what we know of George's mindset at the time of the recording: that he feels imprisoned by his Beatle-hood, especially the obligation to tour relentlessly, to the point that he sometimes fantasizes about quitting the group.

Although the Beatles did not think highly enough of "If I Needed Someone" to release it as a single—not even a B-side—over time it has become one of the group's signature tunes. It certainly holds its own on the Beatles' first serious album qua album, *Rubber Soul,* and it was one of several tunes on that album to introduce Indian sounds and cadences into rock music. In essence, and in combination with "Norwegian Wood," written by John Lennon but with heavy-duty instrumental contributions from George, *Rubber Soul* simultaneously pioneered what would soon be called "raga rock" and, to a larger extent, ushered in the era of "world music." Lennon and McCartney did at least recognize that Harrison's greatest songwriting achievement up to that time was worth adding to the group's live set list in 1965, thus becoming the only Harrison-penned song the group ever played in concert once they had grown out of nightclubs and begun playing theaters, arenas, and stadiums (although it came at the expense of Harrison's only other lead vocal in the live repertoire, his cover version of Carl Perkins's "Everybody's Trying to Be My Baby").

At the same time of the recording of "If I Needed Someone," the Beatles also recorded what would become a Top 5 hit, "Day Tripper," one of the Beatles' iconic numbers, perhaps even overshadowing "We Can Work It Out," which was on the obverse side of the double-A-side single and which peaked at number one. While McCartney claims to have contributed significantly to the composition, Lennon claimed "Day Tripper" was all his, and that seems to be the consensus. Given the song's high pitch, McCartney wound up singing lead (as would occasionally happen when Lennon wrote himself out of a vocal in too high a key), with John's close harmonies, which might also have fed the idea that it was a cowrite rather than a complete Lennon composition top to bottom, as the latter claimed in his famous if occasionally disputed 1980 interview with *Playboy Magazine*.

The basic structure of "Day Tripper" is a twelve-bar blues—a rarity in Beatles compositions—but one that is almost fully disguised by the riff that drives the tune forward. All due credit must devolve to Ringo Starr, whose drumming on the track dances along with George's guitar and is some of the fiercest to be heard on any Beatles record. John's work on tambourine isn't half bad, either. In the end, the recording is a group effort. But what makes "Day Tripper" so memorable and so iconic is the guitar riff upon which the entire track is built. "I don't think there is any argument that this guitar riff is the most identifiable and loved riff within the entire Beatles catalog, arguably in all of rock/pop music," writes Dave Rybaczewski in his Beatles Music History website.[3] That riff, of course, is played by George Harrison, as is the mid-song guitar solo. Hum the song's melody—such as it is—to yourself, and you might discover that there hardly *is* a melody to the song. It is almost as if Paul and John are just declaiming the lyrics rather than singing them. All the heavy lifting, musically speaking, is done by George's riffing (and Paul's doubling of George's guitar riff in the bassline). Writing about "Day Tripper" in his Soundscapes blog, Alan W. Pollack echoes Rybaczewski, terming the ostinato riff "among the most memorable of the entire Beatles catalogue."[4] Pollack continues, "[B]y virtue of its handling of harmonic rhythm, ostinato guitar riff, and subtle textures in scoring, ['Day Tripper'] is remarkably instrumental, even orchestral in gesture for a 'pop song.'"

That orchestral quality is largely the work of George Harrison; indeed, what distinguishes George Harrison's guitar playing—or more precisely, his guitar *arranging*—is its "orchestral" quality. This is in total opposition to the prevailing approach to rock 'n' roll guitar up to that time and, in large part, throughout its history, whereby the lead guitarist essentially provides another vocal line to the tune, a direct extension of the blues guitar approach, epitomized by Chuck Berry and Elvis Presley guitarist Scotty Moore. This was also the underlying approach of Harrison's friend Eric Clapton. Despite their friendship and frequent collaborations, the two guitarists could not have been more different stylistically, and this is precisely why Harrison turned to Clapton on occasion to play on his own records and in his concerts. It is Clapton's guitar that "gently weeps" in Harrison's song of that name. George's guitar, on the other hand, is, well, *orchestral*. It is grand and fulfills multiple functions—rhythmic, harmonic, melodic—that make a song complete.

"George was very sure of what he wanted to play and when and what," says Lauren Passarelli. "And that's what I've always loved about his playing. He doesn't play the same old stuff on every song. You don't hear the same blues licks the way you do with all the other players. He didn't come from that blues vocabulary, and he didn't even come from the bebop vocabulary. He had his own melodic sense. Everything he comes up with had his own signature." While later, especially once he has made the move to slide guitar, Harrison's guitar does indeed weep on its own, for the most part it always is a central aspect of the musical material, with lines and licks and riffs and chords serving as the main musical element of his—and many of the Beatles'—songs, helping to provide their overall shape and structure. John Lennon and Paul McCartney, according to Rob Sheffield, "let the whole world listen in on their friendship, their memories of that friendship, and their mourning over the friendship's long and winding demise. George helped give that troubled, unmanageable, impossible friendship a sound, with a guitar that hiccupped like Buddy Holly and soared like the Chiffons."[5]

A close cousin to 1963's "Don't Bother Me," Harrison's *Rubber Soul* song "Think For Yourself" boosts the bile while reveling in wordplay obviously inspired by Bob Dylan. Harrison employs words like "opaque" and "rectify," the kind of words that had not appeared in earlier Beatles songs, if in any rock 'n' roll songs other than those by Dylan. Plus, Harrison makes use of the kind of internal rhyme that was a distinctive trait of Dylan's poetry; for example, in the line "And you've got time to rectify." He may be no Bob Dylan, but he aspires in the right direction, and those aspirations will eventually result in several collaborations over the ensuing decades between the Nobel Prize–winning rock poet and his number-one fan, culminating in their joining forces in the rock supergroup the Traveling Wilburys.

The song's title immediately clues in listeners that they are in for a scolding. The opening line, "I've got a word or two to say about the things that you do" lays out the purpose of the song, a rhetorical strategy to which Harrison would return repeatedly, putting as much care into his opening lines as he did into his introductory musical figures, most notably in "I Want to Tell You" (the opening phrase of which is the same as the title) and "Within You Without You" ("We were talking about the space between us all"). One cannot over-estimate the power of a great opening line, and it was certainly something Harrison saw was a favorite device used by Dylan, from "Come gather 'round people wherever you roam" to "You've got a lot of nerve to say you are my friend" to "You must leave now take what you need you think will last."

"Think for Yourself" is a song at the crossroads for Harrison. On one hand, its bitter tone, accentuated by McCartney's "fuzz bass," makes it something of a second cousin to "Don't Bother Me." The influence of Dylan's "Positively 4th Street"—one of the most visceral hate songs of all time—can be felt in every line. As in Dylan's number, Harrison's song is directed at an unknown "you." This is not to say "Think for Yourself" was inspired by a specific person, or that the song is in any way autobiographical. Rather, Harrison is presumably singing at—as opposed to "to"—a type of person. It is a kiss-off song that si-multaneously empowers the object—the "you"—to be independent while at the same time condescending to the "you"—"I left you far behind" and "Try thinking more if just for your own sake." Ouch! The attitude reflected here is "more schoolteacher than poet,"[6] and, assuming the "you" is a woman, and perhaps a former lover, it dabbles in that all too popular male-female dynamic of the time (and perhaps of all time), whereby the default assumption is that the woman should be subjugated to the man.

Harrison's impatience with hangers-on and disgust with celebrity "culture" has yet to be tempered by the empathy and compassion that will soon mani-fest in his songs once he has begun to absorb some of the lessons of humility and suppression of ego inherent in a Hindu worldview. Not that Harrison's personal character will undergo some sort of wholesale transformation, or that Eastern spirituality will imbue him with beatific love and understanding for everyone. As we will see, he will carry along some of these same attitudes into his life as an Eastern mystic. The biggest change will be that he will couch his impatience and disgust in different terms. He will also increasingly draw upon his innate sense of humor and absurdity once he has become more spiritually settled and philosophically reconciled to the bizarre outcome of picking up a guitar, learning to play, and joining in with a group of like-minded teenagers whose biggest dream was to play Buddy Holly songs at the Cavern Club.

The most distinctive musical elements of "Think for Yourself" are the bright, three-part vocal harmonies of George, Paul, and John, the somewhat unconventional chord progression, and the unprecedented, growly string sound that is not produced by Harrison's guitar but rather by McCartney playing an additional bassline through a "fuzzbox" device, lending it the distorted sound and essentially functioning as a lead-guitar line, albeit coloring the track with a bitter, acid tone reflective of the song's lyrics. Paul's fuzz bass also gives the number an urban quality—one hears car and bus horns blasting, the buzz of electric scooters, the rumbling of the underground. Contrast this with McCartney's idyllic "Michelle" and Lennon's pastoral "In My Life," both of which also appear on *Rubber Soul*.

Of all four Beatles, Harrison's Liverpool accent remained strongest when he sang. Paul McCartney made a concerted effort not only to lose his Scouse pronunciation but also to hide any hint of an English accent when he sang. The strength of John Lennon's accent in song remained somewhere in between Harrison's and McCartney's, and any hint of accent in Ringo's vocals was overwhelmed by the distinctive, sad-sack sound of his voice. "Think for Yourself" offers a perfect example of Harrison's clinging to his Liverpool origins: listen to how he pronounces the word "there" in the last phrase of the refrain, "'cause I won't be there with you." To American ears, the word in isolation would hardly be recognizable, sounding more like "thurr" than "there." Since these remnants of Harrison's accent are always heard in context of the overall song, they can and probably are mostly overlooked by English speakers of American origin. They are still *thurr*, though, and on some subliminal level they must have an effect on listeners, placing the singer in some kind of liminal space, geographically, emotionally, and otherwise. To a non-British English speaker, the way Harrison's "thurr" falls on their ears can sound lazy, mumbled, or very "English." This is not the result of any purposeful intent on Harrison's part, but just a happy accident that imputes a subtle meaning from his pronunciation alone.

Harrison's contributions to *Rubber Soul* go far beyond the two songs he wrote and sang on the album. The use of sitar on "Norwegian Wood," making his guitar sound like a Greek bouzouki on "Girl," and the Gallic-jazz tones of his guitar playing on "Michelle" lent an international flavor to the album. But it was the introduction of the sonorities of the sitar—even at this early stage when Harrison did not know how to play it properly, but approached it like a guitar—that would have the greatest lasting impact upon the music and the lives of the Beatles over the next few years, as it opened the doors to all things Eastern, including philosophy, religion, spirituality, meditation, yoga, and vegetarianism, not only for the Fab Four but for millions of enthusiastic adherents. As new-music composer Philip Glass wrote in an appreciation of Harrison for the *New York Times* just ten days after he passed away,

I see the great musical adventure of our time as the emergence of a world-music culture, which crosses lines of geography, race and gender. From this perspective, the impact of George Harrison's life and times has been enormous. He played a major role in bringing several generations of young musicians out of the parched and dying desert of Eurocentric music into a new world. I have no doubt that this part of his legacy will be his most enduring. And not only that. He opened the doors to this new world of music with deep conviction, great energy and his own remarkable clarity and simplicity.[7]

That it all happened almost accidentally on a John Lennon song takes nothing away from the impact of George's use of sitar on "Norwegian Wood." Lennon had difficulty with all aspects of the song—its story, the lyrics, the music, and the instrumentation. All kinds of myths have grown up around how true to life the song really was—that it was a not so subtle confession of his infidelities while he was still married to Cynthia Lennon, that there was a lover who, although German, insisted on calling herself Norwegian, that back in his student days in Liverpool Lennon would keep warm in winter by burning castoff furniture in a fireplace. In trying to brainstorm how to get the Dylanesque song across, Lennon saw Harrison's sitar lying around and asked him if he would try playing the song's melody on the nineteen-stringed "Indian guitar," which is exactly what Harrison did. While Harrison's entire approach to the instrument on this track was incorrect in terms of the proper way to address a sitar, it did not matter. Even Ravi Shankar, the world's most famous sitarist, soon to become Harrison's mentor, would admit this soon after the record's release. The prominence of the sitar's sonorities on the second song on the album—a song with an Indian accent titled after a Scandinavian country—was truly a musical and cultural blast from seemingly nowhere. And if no one, including Harrison, quite yet knew or understood the impact of that blast or its aftershocks, it did not matter. There was only one destination, and that was the land and culture of the instrument's birthplace.

9
The Black Album

George Harrison, spawn of the working class (his father was a ship steward and a bus driver), was not a very good Socialist. At least not by virtue of "Taxman," his hard-rocking song of protest against paying upward of ninety-five percent of his income to the Inland Revenue (now called the HMRC)—the United Kingdom's version of America's Internal Revenue Service. When in the song, which is sung from the taxman's point of view, Harrison sings "Here's one for you, nineteen for me," it was no exaggeration. Harrison did the math, which recurs toward the end of the song, when mean old taxman says, "If five percent appears too small, be thankful I don't take it all."

But even if Harrison's complaints about having to pay the millionaire's tax did not sit right with some of the Beatles' more astute, politically minded, leftward-leaning fans, there was no denying the allure of the song itself, a heavily R&B-influenced taste of metallic rock that Harrison's bandmates chose as the lead-off track for their 1966 album, *Revolver*. The song established the somewhat arrogant, bitter tone that ran through the album, albeit with a heavy dose of sarcasm that once again betrayed Harrison's literary sophistication in his reliance on unreliable narrators to get across his more pointed songs, whether they be indictments of fickle lovers, establishment figures, or the incurious, sheeplike masses.

"Taxman" was also that rare George Harrison composition that got full and complete buy-in from his bandmates, all of whom participated creatively in the construction and arrangement of the number that remains one of the group's most enduring hard-rock numbers. Lennon helped by suggesting the interpolation of the names of Britain's two leading politicians of the mid-1960s: "Mr. Wilson" and "Mr. Heath," the former being Harold Wilson, leader of the Labor Party and prime minister at the time of the song's writing and release, and the latter being the leader of the Conservative opposition and a future prime minister. Paul McCartney overdubbed a bubbling, stuttering bassline that, in its evocation of American soul music, nodded to the original idea of recording *Revolver* at Stax Studios in Memphis, Tennessee, where the likes of Otis Redding, Sam & Dave, Carla Thomas, and Booker T. & the M.G.s made some of their greatest recordings. Ringo Starr, like McCartney, patterned his drumming along the lines of American soul, swinging the whole number with a delayed backbeat and coloring it with more cowbell than usual. While Harrison scatters his sharp-edged, cutting lead-guitar fills throughout the song, it was McCartney who played the fiery, sitar-flavored electric guitar solo that appears halfway through the number—another case of Harrison demonstrating how much of a team player he was, willing to subsume whatever ego he had invested in "his" song to the greater good of the group's sound.

Says Lauren Passarelli, "The Beatles didn't get into music to be guitar gods. . . . And none of them had the ego that said, 'I have to do that, I'm the lead guitarist.' It was whoever had the best idea for the song, put it in, because they're having to do it so fast. And Paul says, 'Hey I've got a thing, it's kind of Indian-like,' and George says, 'That's great, put it in there.'"

While "Taxman" was written by Harrison, in its own time it was simply considered a Beatles song. Most listeners considered all Beatles songs the product of the collective, with very few paying attention to who wrote the songs (song credits, for one, made no distinction between songs written mostly or wholly by John Lennon or Paul McCartney), and only a few more even knowing who the lead singer was on any given song. As the first Beatles song that could be considered wholly topical in the sense of its being a political protest song, "Taxman" was received by the world not as a missive from George Harrison but rather as a group complaint. And almost everyone hates paying taxes, regardless of their income. Besides, the song makes its point with humor; it is a clever, funny song with a narrative strategy that Harrison would make use of frequently throughout his songwriting career, often casting himself as the butt of the joke.

George Harrison's songwriting contributions to *Revolver* hardly ended with the opening track—the album included three of his compositions. With "Love You To," George Harrison—along with the Beatles—took the full plunge into Hindustani classical music. The move was not unprecedented; as we have seen, going at least as far back as "If I Needed Someone," whose modal melody was possibly influenced by Harrison's exposure to raga, and in his sitar accompaniment to Lennon's "Norwegian Wood," Indian influences had already been creeping into Harrison's playing and his compositions (and Lennon's, to a lesser extent, often with the aid of Harrison). "Love You To" was the ultimate expression of these tendencies and perhaps the first and fullest example of "raga rock," a new subgenre of popular music that saw groups that included the Kinks, the Rolling Stones, and the Byrds, among others, variously combining basic Indian scales and sonorities with rock music.

This fusion of East and West made sense both musically and culturally—or more precisely, counterculturally—at a time when, in no small part because of Harrison and the Beatles, Anglo-American minds were opening to what the East had to offer, especially when Western values and mores were viewed as retrograde, shallow, violent, or worse. This dynamic was undoubtedly a gross simplification of both Eastern and Western cultures, but at least it posed questions about and challenged the dominance of the received materialism of postwar capitalism, as Harrison addressed in "Taxman" and in subsequent Beatles and post-Beatles songs, including "Piggies" and "Living in the Material World."

"Love You To" opens with a thirty-five-second, mostly free-metered instrumental introduction played by Harrison on sitar, fully establishing the Indian context while providing listeners with a basic vocabulary for what will follow. The song is the first in which Harrison employs melodic fragments from an actual Indian raga (*raag khamaj*), influencing the twisting and turning melodic lines. One can still hear the musical vision of the lead guitarist in a rock band behind the notes; Harrison finds the perfect fusion of Hindustani classical-based sitar and rock-based guitar music in these few bars. Harrison also employs subtle acoustic-guitar strumming and splashes of fuzz-toned electric guitar throughout the main part of the song, somehow never detracting from the impact of the Indian aesthetic.

According to musicologist David R. Reck, "Love You To" was "absolutely unprecedented . . . in the history both of popular music and of European orientalism. For the first time an Asian music was not parodied utilizing familiar Western stereotypes and misconceptions, but rather transferred almost in toto into its new environment, with sympathy and rare understanding."[1]

The song ingeniously employed authentic Indian percussion to lend a hint of rock rhythm, courtesy of tabla player Anil Bhagwat, kicking in around the half-minute mark and adapting to the familiar $\frac{4}{4}$ rock beat—no great stretch, given its close proximity to the eight-beat Hindustani rhythmic cycle called *teentaal*. Harrison references his opening improvisation on sitar later in the song, before it gallops to its conclusion with a very non-Indian fade-out—a technique frequently employed, however, in Western pop music. The whole thing wisely clocks in at three minutes, so as not to challenge listeners beyond their patience or breaking point and with consideration for how the song flowed on the album. Following Lennon's "I'm Only Sleeping" and preceding McCartney's "Here, There and Everywhere," the (then) exotic number sits comfortably between two of the album's most conventional songs.

Harrison had yet to meet Ravi Shankar when he recorded "Love You To" in two sessions on April 11 and April 13, 1966. He had already befriended musicians in the Asian Music Circle in London, where he had taken some rudimentary lessons on sitar. He also had immersed himself in North Indian music via recordings and attending recitals, and he saw Shankar in concert at the Royal Festival Hall that spring. The two finally met in June 1966, beginning a close friendship and a deep musical collaboration that would last until Harrison's death in 2001. (Shankar, who was Harrison's elder by twenty-three years, outlived the latter by eleven years, passing away in December 2012 at age ninety-two).

Harrison always struggled with titling his songs, and for a while the working title of "Love You To" was "Granny Smith," courtesy of engineer Geoff Emerick, who was not a huge fan of George or of his music and his recording practices. That same variety, however, would later become the symbol for the Beatles' star-crossed company, Apple Corps. The eventual song title, "Love You To," may have slightly hindered appreciation for the song: those three words do not appear in the lyrics in that order, it is not clear to what they refer (or how they relate to the song's lyrics), and the final "To" in the title was often misspelled, even in official products, as "Too." Harrison may have simply thought it was funny to scramble the last three words of the phrase "I'll make love to you" to create a title for the song. (The title may also have been a sly reference to the Beatles first hit single, "Love Me Do.")

"Love You To" stands as an essential transitional song, combining Harrison's cynical outlook up until then (as heard in songs that included "Don't Bother Me," "Think for Yourself," and "If I Needed Someone") with his burgeoning emphasis on spirituality (as reflected in soon-to-be-recorded songs that included "Within You Without You," "The Inner Light," and "My Sweet Lord"). "Love You To," for example, reverses the dynamic of "If I Needed Someone." In the latter song, the narrator puts off potential suitors with the conditional tense as implied in the song's title; he is saying, by implication, that he is unavailable (because he is now "too much in love"). "Love You To" represents a softening of that posture and offers a hint of Harrison's burgeoning philosophical beliefs, particularly the concept common to many mystical traditions that says sexual relations have the potential to bring about the ecstatic experience for which all mystics strive: the direct experience of the divinity. As Harrison put it just a few years later in his all-time greatest hit, "Really want to be with you, really want to see you, Lord." While in "Love You To," he has not quite gotten to that point yet, he does connect singing with lovemaking and concludes simply, "I'll make love to you, if you want me to" (once again hedging his bets through use of the conditional tense). That is a far cry and a long way from the sentiment expressed in 1963's "Don't Bother Me," with its clear and unambiguous directive: "Go away, leave me alone, don't bother me."

That Harrison accomplishes this in a piece of music that sounds nothing like anything that has ever come before only adds to the revolutionary effect of the song itself. It cannot be overstated how "Love You To" firmly established Indian sonorities—to say nothing of Indian instruments, raga scales, and drones—as an essential part of the Beatles musical vocabulary. This revolutionary aspect spills over to other songs on *Revolver*, which introduced stunning new sounds, effects, and approaches to songwriting from the group that until this point were the very avatars of 1960s Western pop-rock music. George's enthusiasm for Northern Indian classical techniques infected the other members of the Beatles. As English rock singer-songwriter Robyn Hitchcock told me, "George Harrison came into his own around 1966, when the Beatles had already been at the top for three years. He brought in the sitar and other Indian instruments—that sound spread throughout Christendom. He defined the psychedelic Beatles."

While Paul McCartney initially laid down backing vocals for "Love You To," these were dropped in the mix in favor of double-tracking Harrison's voice. And while a palimpsest of Ringo Starr's tambourine is buried in the final mix, this Beatles track basically includes only one member of the band on guitar and vocals, otherwise assisted exclusively by musicians from outside the group. This was not unprecedented; McCartney's "Yesterday" had previously dispensed with the services of John, George, and Ringo in favor of a string quartet a year earlier. Elsewhere on *Revolver*, McCartney repeated and expanded upon his solo approach to "Yesterday" by recording "Eleanor Rigby" with musical accompaniment provided solely by a doubled string quartet arranged by George Martin, in spite of the fact that the other three Beatles (and reportedly Beatles friends and associates Pete Shotton, Mal Evans, Neil Aspinall, and George Martin) variously contributed bits of lyrics, music, and arrangements—most prominently Harrison's idea to seed the song with the recurring antiphonal phrase "Ah, look at all the lonely people."

When *Revolver* was first released, it was greeted as something of a disappointment. Its dark, at times somber musical aesthetic was matched by the LP's sleeve, all black and white and gray, totally lacking color. The previous album, *Rubber Soul,* while certainly a huge leap forward in terms of musical and lyrical sophistication and an expanded scope beyond the teenage love songs that previously dominated their oeuvre, still sounded largely like the pop group the Beatles. And indeed, *Rubber Soul* may well have been the apotheosis of the Beatles-as-pop-band, loaded as it was with catchy melodies, inviting three-part harmonies, and a plethora of memorable guitar riffs and hooks—all the elements that made the Beatles the most popular group of all time.

Never mind that *Rubber Soul* was already chock full of hints of things to come—Lennon's Dylanesque turns on songs that included "Nowhere Man" and "In My Life," Harrison's burgeoning musical and philosophical turns toward India ("Think for Yourself" and his sitar-playing on "Norwegian Wood"), McCartney's growing musical experimentation on the Francophile "Michelle" and the Motown-flavored arrangements of "Drive My Car" and "You Won't See Me." For good measure, the group even touched down in Greek music on "Girl," with Harrison and Lennon's acoustic guitars voiced in such a way that they sounded like bouzoukis. Taken together, the Indian sitar, the Greek sonorities, and the French lyrics made the bright sound of *Rubber Soul* something of an early precursor to the "world music" genre yet to be coined as such.

Revolver, by contrast, was literally a dark album, from its black-and-white cover photo to its stories of bitter, lonely, and broken-hearted people who found it impossible to communicate effectively, sometimes preferring escape via mind-altering drugs or other means of bending consciousness. To be sure, the album was leavened with the comic relief of the children's sing-along "Yellow Submarine" (although the song was also something of a psychedelic manifesto, inspiring the full-length animated feature film of the same name) and "Good Day Sunshine," which opened side two with a typical McCartneyesque burst of optimism ("I'm in love and it's a sunny day") that either provided much-needed relief or was wholly out of place on *Revolver*, as if it had wandered over from another album.

Harrison's three songwriting contributions to *Revolver*—the first and only time he would place three songs on a single Beatles album—plus his considerable involvement in shaping the sound and arrangement of several other tracks, particularly Lennon's, were largely responsible for the somber cast of the overall project. As the fifth of seven songs on side two of *Revolver*, Harrison's "I Want to Tell You" was somewhat buried in the program, despite its ineffable guitar hook and its direct expression of the album's theme: the ultimate impossibility of effective communication. The hook, which eventually became one of the most recognizable ostinatos in all of rock music, fades in, played twice by Harrison alone before the drums and piano kick in the third time around, with the addition of a prominent tambourine courtesy of John Lennon and Paul McCartney's bass joining in on the fourth go-round before the song proper begins with Harrison's vocals, propelled largely by McCartney's insistent block chords on piano.

As startling as the jagged, dissonant piano chords that color the song's overall sound is how perfectly they replicate in music the lyrical meaning. While McCartney played piano on the basic track, there was also an overdub of the jagged chord in question—what Harrison called "an E and an F at the same time"[2]—and it's not clear if that was played by George or Paul. But even if it *was* played by Paul, George claimed credit for having "invented" the chord, whose atonal quality would give the song its unique character, echoing in music the narrator's stated inability to communicate clearly, while introducing a sound rather alien to pop music.

In contrast to a long-standing beef about Harrison requiring multiple takes and sessions on his own songs (fed largely by Geoff Emerick's memoir of his time as Beatles engineer), the five basic takes for "I Want to Tell You" were recorded in the course of a single day, Thursday, June 2 (coincidentally, the day after Harrison met Ravi Shankar for the first time), and required only one follow-up session the next day, during which McCartney overdubbed his electric bass for the first time ever. This was not standard practice for the Beatles or for any group at the time: typically, the rhythm track of bass and drums would be recorded first and other instruments and lead vocals layered on top of the rhythm track, with harmony vocals, handclaps, and other touches of percussion added at the end. This in and of itself was a somewhat revolutionary innovation that played to McCartney's strength as a melodic bassist, one whose unusual runs could re-harmonize a song as well as add rhythmic twists, and one that would become common practice in subsequent Beatles recording sessions.

In less than three years, the Beatles had gone from "I Want to Hold Your Hand" to "I Want to Tell You." That alone speaks volumes of the difference between Lennon and McCartney's songwriting and Harrison's—from puppy love to preaching, both in the form of two-and-a-half-minute pop songs. The former song was the group's first to hit number one in the United States; "I Want to Tell You" remained overlooked for quite a while, even by Harrison himself—it was not part of the set list at the Concert for Bangladesh nor did it show up in any of the concerts during his tour of North America in 1974. Not until Harrison's tour of Japan in 1991 did he trot out "I Want to Tell You" for live performance, when it held the lead-off spot during the twelve-concert tour, as heard on the *Live in Japan* album he released the following year. George also opened with the song at a benefit concert for the newly formed Natural Law Party, founded by the Transcendental Meditation movement, at London's Royal Albert Hall in April 1992, which, somewhat remarkably, turned out to be Harrison's only full-length concert as a solo artist in the United Kingdom. The song has otherwise proved enduring, with other artists performing it live (including Jeff Lynne and the Grateful Dead) and on recording (most famously by Ted Nugent, as well as the Smithereens, Thea Gilmore, and the Melvins).

In what may or may not be an apocryphal story, Paul McCartney played *Revolver* for Bob Dylan before its release. As the story goes, after listening to the whole thing, the future Nobel Prize winner and amateur rock critic said to Paul, "I get it—you don't want to be cute anymore."

10

I Know What It's Like to Be Dead

"She Said She Said," the final song recorded for *Revolver*, was credited to John Lennon and Paul McCartney, was written by John Lennon, and bears the fingerprints of George Harrison all over. The story behind the song's inspiration has been often told: at a party in California in a house the Beatles were renting in Beverly Hills in August 1965, actor Peter Fonda harangued John Lennon with the tale of how he knew what it was like to be dead, having survived a near-fatal accident as a boy. (He had accidentally shot himself on his eleventh birthday.) LSD was in the air, at the party in question and running through the veins of Lennon, Harrison, and Ringo Starr in varying amounts ever since their dentist spiked their after-dinner coffee with tabs of acid the previous March. The incident with Peter Fonda at that fateful party, at which Lennon supposedly ordered Fonda to leave the premises after making a nuisance of himself, stuck with Lennon, and in March 1966, when he sat down to write songs for what would become *Revolver*, Fonda's annoying mantra became the opening line to Lennon's trippy song, an acid-laced retelling of the event in the form of a debate or argument, in which time collapses between the present, childhood, and birth.

Lennon struggled with the song, as can be heard on an early demo in which he had only the first two verses (much in need of editing) and two lines of a refrain. Harrison visited Lennon at the latter's home to go over some of the songs the two were working on, and he wound up helping John expand the song by piecing together bits of other songs Lennon had in early stages of development. Harrison urged Lennon to incorporate the "when I was a boy" passage into the song, replete with a change in meter from $\frac{4}{4}$ to waltz time ($\frac{3}{4}$). The two also worked out harmony vocals and George's elaborate lead-guitar lines, which drove the song with a stinging, stuttering, sitar-like tone that at times functioned as an additional voice, echoing Lennon's vocal melody, further suggesting an elastic rather than linear sense of time in accordance with the song's lyrics and meaning. Likewise, Harrison's harmony vocals, double tracked like Lennon's lead vocals, stuck close to Lennon's, leaving just enough space between the two to provide a dreamy, floating effect.

The success of Lennon and Harrison's partnership on "She Said She Said" may have unintentionally caused some friction within the band. Paul McCartney is said to have walked out of the recording session for the tune in a huff, leaving behind a number of questions that have never decisively been answered. Why did Paul leave the session? It is generally assumed that he felt dismissed when it came time to record a track whose arrangement had already been agreed upon. Supposedly there was a piano part for the number that has never surfaced; was this an attempt by Paul to add to the song's arrangement, one that John vetoed? Was Paul embarrassed to have been left out of the creative process entirely, and perhaps resentful of Harrison's significant role in the development of the song? And regarding the song's bass track, it has never been definitively established one way or the other if the final version of the song features a bassline overdubbed by George Harrison (which McCartney once claimed), or if it was indeed the work of McCartney, as many historians insist (and as the credits read on the *Revolver* boxed set of remixes released in 2022).

Adding to the uncertainty over just what went down at this session and the lingering bad feelings it established was a private conversation that Lennon and McCartney had several years later after Harrison walked out of the rehearsals at Twickenham Film Studios in January 1969. Unbeknown to Lennon and McCartney, film director Michael Lindsay-Hogg had placed a hidden microphone in a flowerpot in the lunch room at the studio. When Peter Jackson worked on the dozens of hours of film and audio footage recorded by Lindsay-Hogg for his eight-hour documentary, *Get Back*, he was able to recover most of the conversation, long thought to be beyond retrieval. Lennon and McCartney's heart-to-heart about Harrison's role in the Beatles and his frustrations, about which both seemed quite empathetic, included discussion of their own issues. Lennon confessed to McCartney that there were times when he allowed McCartney to take his songs to "somewhere I didn't want" rather than to confront McCartney over it. The latter seemed to understand Lennon's complaint, and in the *Get Back* film, there are other times when he clearly is uncomfortable pushing the individual Beatles to do things that they did not want to do, but unwillingly and uneasily found himself in the awkward role of band director. Lennon confesses that there were moments in the past where he would turn to George in a strategic maneuver to bypass Paul, knowing that Harrison was likely to be more amenable to Lennon's ideas. McCartney's reply to that observation was simply, "'She Said She Said,'" to which Lennon replied affirmatively, "'She Said She Said.'" With Harrison and Lennon no longer around to offer their versions of what happened, the complete story of what went down in the "She Said She Said" sessions will probably never be known. Is this a tragedy? No. A mystery? Perhaps. An enigma? Yes, and one that can be addressed only by close listening to what exists on the recordings that came out of the session.

It is often suggested that "She Said She Said" was a harbinger of psychedelic rock, and perhaps it strongly influenced the "acid-rock" sounds to come out of the San Francisco Bay Area scene over the next two years or so. It certainly pointed toward a future trend in Beatles music, as heard on *Sgt. Pepper's Lonely Hearts Club Band* and concurrent singles, including "Strawberry Fields Forever." But in this case, the attempt to situate a particular Beatles song in the prevailing musical zeitgeist is less than illuminating, especially when the Beatles are driving that zeitgeist. What is most fascinating about this track is how it melds the voices (in the generic sense) of Lennon and Harrison, with all its suggestions of what might have happened had the two spent more time in working with each other. They would of course continue to play together on many subsequent Beatles tracks, and Lennon would call on Harrison to lend his instrumental support on a few of his earliest solo albums. But rarely if ever would the two collaborate on the creation of a song at the level of "She Said She Said," seeing it through to its logical conclusion, producing one of the standout tracks on *Revolver* and, arguably, one of the most memorable tracks in the Beatles' body of work.

11

The Space Between Us All

Had producer George Martin (and, presumably, Paul McCartney and John Lennon) felt kindlier toward "Only a Northern Song," George Harrison's initial contribution intended for the album that would become *Sgt. Pepper's Lonely Hearts Club Band*, Harrison might never have written "Within You Without You," the song considered by some to be the "philosophical centrepiece"[1] or "conscience"[2] of the landmark 1967 concept album. Fortunately for the Beatles and for us, after recording George's "Only a Northern Song," Martin suggested that Harrison come up with something more suitable for *Sgt. Pepper's*.

The previous year saw Harrison's emergence as a songwriter of considerable talent and heft with his unprecedented three songs on *Revolver*. Additionally, Harrison's experiments with guitar loops and other studio trickery colored *Revolver* even beyond his own songs, such that some view it as Harrison's album as much as McCartney's, with the latter's estimable contributions that included "Eleanor Rigby," "For No One," "Here, There and Everywhere," and "Got to Get You into My Life."

But 1966 also marked the nadir of Harrison's experience as a member of the Beatles, with that summer's world tour—the group's last—convincing Harrison (as well as Lennon) that performing before live audiences had become untenable, marked by real and threatened violence, risky air travel, and an utter lack of musical value. Given that technology had yet to catch up with the needs of rock bands for proper amplification, monitoring, and public-address systems capable of overcoming the screaming of thirty-, forty-, or fifty-thousand fans at a time, the music the Beatles played onstage was something of a joke—they could not hear one another over the din created by the overenthusiastic vocal contributions of concertgoers. When the summer tour concluded, Harrison made clear to manager Brian Epstein and his bandmates that he would remain in the group only if membership was limited to working in the studio as a recording group. With John Lennon sharing most of Harrison's concerns, the four continued working together for several years with this new understanding of their job descriptions.

When the band came off the road after four years of near-incessant touring (and several years of marathon club residencies before that), the Fab Four each took time to themselves to rest, relax, and pursue interests outside of the group. For Harrison, this meant a dedicated plunge into studying sitar under the guidance of Ravi Shankar, both in India—where he spent a month and a half in September and October 1966—and back home in England. Along the way, Harrison continued absorbing tenets of Hinduism, immersing himself fully in Indian culture, including cuisine (he became a vegetarian), spirituality, and fashion. Eventually, Harrison's enthusiasm for all things Indian would rub off on his bandmates, and after they all met Maharishi Mahesh Yogi in London the following summer—in the wake of the May 1967 release of *Sgt. Pepper's Lonely Hearts Club Band*—they joined Harrison at the Maharishi's ashram in Rishikesh, India, in February 1968, where they studied the Maharishi's brand of Transcendental Meditation.

By the time the Beatles began the recording sessions for *Sgt. Pepper's* in December 1966, sessions that would continue through the following April, Harrison's mind, spirit, and muse were already heavily influenced by his Indian experiences. Harrison had hardly picked up his guitar since he had put it down at the end of the Beatles' final concert at Candlestick Park in San Francisco, California, on August 29, 1966, favoring instead the sitar. If Harrison was not entirely enthusiastic about interrupting his studies to return to the recording studio, especially without having written any new songs of his own and being somewhat skeptical of McCartney's vague concept for the new album, on which the Beatles would profess to cloak their identity as, well, not the Beatles but as the fictional Sgt. Pepper's Lonely Hearts Club Band, he rallied, collected his guitars, and showed up at Abbey Road Studios ready to play.

As it turned out, there would not be a lot of playing for Harrison to do. The sessions firmly marked the ascension of Paul McCartney as the group's driving force, if something short of the nominal bandleader, although by all accounts his heavy hand made him the de facto leader of the group. Looking back on the sessions, even Ringo Starr said he was mostly bored as he sat around and waited for his turn to come to get behind his drum kit, as McCartney assembled many of the parts piece by piece, rather than the group working its way through the numbers in search of the right arrangement, as they had done in the past and would do so again, most notably in the sessions for *Get Back*. Ringo often says that his biggest memory of the *Sgt. Pepper's* sessions is the time he spent in the studio in learning to play chess.

Harrison was also somewhat sidelined, partly because of bringing very little original material to the sessions, and also because of McCartney's piecemeal approach to building the arrangements along with producer George Martin. McCartney played the guitar solo on the title track that led off the album, although Harrison took lead duty on the song's reprise version on side two. Harrison did contribute an evocative drone to "Getting Better" on tambura, which he also played on "Lucy in the Sky with Diamonds," and his lead-guitar licks and solo on "Fixing a Hole" color that track heavily, lending some much-needed, bluesy grit to what otherwise might have been a merely sappy novelty tune.

Having been given the assignment to come up with a song that was "better" than "Only a Northern Song" (or at least one that, however witty, did not complain about Harrison's relatively low status in the band as measured by his publishing royalties), Harrison returned with the makings of "Within You Without You," his most sophisticated Hindustani-pop fusion effort, all sketched out in his head. The structure of the song adhered mostly to the Northern Indian classical format, albeit with verses and refrain in a recognizable Western pop style. The vocal and instrumental melodies followed the *raag khamaj* mode (familiar from "Love You To"), and the instruments, including the sitar and tambura played by Harrison, were almost entirely unique to Indian music, including dilruba, swaramandala, and tabla, all played by members of the Asian Music Circle in London.

After the Indian foundation of the recording of "Within You Without You" was completed, under Harrison's guidance Martin wrote an accompanying arrangement for Western classical musicians, including eight violinists and three cellists, which was synced to the Indian tracks. Martin had previously worked with members of the Asian Music Circle when he was producing a Hindustani-flavored remake of "Wouldn't It Be Loverly" from *My Fair Lady* for Peter Sellers, so he had some basic familiarity with how the music worked. Also, the fusion of Indian and Western classical music had just reached its apex on the January 1967 album, *West Meets East*, a collaboration between American violin virtuoso Yehudi Menuhin and Ravi Shankar.

"Within You Without You" may have been a case of careful what you wish for, but Martin, Lennon, and McCartney all seemed pleased with the finished product, even though Harrison was the only member of the Beatles to appear on the track. In that vein, and most appropriately, Harrison owned and was fully responsible for "Within You Without You." There was nothing else remotely like it on *Sgt. Pepper's*, other than those few Indian accents that Harrison lent to a couple of other songs on the album. Yet "Within You Without You" sat comfortably alongside numbers such as "When I'm Sixty-Four" and "Lucy in the Sky with Diamonds" in its highly personal approach. Besides, McCartney's original concept for the album was to break all expectations that it would sound like what one would expect from the Beatles. "Within You Without You" certainly met that rubric, enough to have the song sequenced as the opening track of side two. It grounded the weaker side of the album—the song was followed by "When I'm Sixty-Four," "Lovely Rita," "Good Morning Good Morning," and "Sgt. Pepper's Lonely Hearts Club Band (Reprise)—providing a weighty bookend to the album's concluding track, the equally experimental and profound "A Day in the Life."

"Within You Without You" opens in typical George Harrison style, with an introduction setting the musical context for what follows, in this case establishing the mode of the tune via a drone on tambura over which the stringed dilruba plays the notes contained in the melody. In Northern Indian classical music this section is called the *alap*. Harrison employed a similar strategy in Beatles songs such as "If I Needed Someone," "And I Love Her," and "I'll Be Back," as well as in solo songs that included "Wah-Wah," "Beware of Darkness," and "So Sad." About twenty-three seconds into the number (a very brief *alap* by Indian standards), tabla kicks the song's rhythm into gear, before Harrison's vocal enters. The first three words he sings are "We were talking," before he relates the philosophical thoughts from a real-life conversation that took place between Harrison and longtime Beatles friend and associate Klaus Voormann, at whose house the song began to take shape one night after dinner. Once again, Harrison's narrative strategy was to address the listener directly about addressing the listener, as he previously did in "I Want to Tell You," whose first five words gave the song its title, and in "Taxman," in which he grabs attention with the direct approach, embodied in the phrase "Let me tell you how it will be." Harrison would continue to use this meta-narrative strategy, in which the singer begins a song with an acknowledgment that he is about to sing a song or deliver a message, often betraying a sense of unease or difficulty in communication, as heard in "Only a Northern Song" ("If you're listening to this song"), "What Is Life" ("What I feel I can't say"), "This Song" ("This song has nothing tricky about it"), and in the extended recitative that sets the scene for the plea for help in "Bangla Desh."

Harrison's vocal melody was doubled by bowed dilrubas; his natural tendency toward melismatic singing—stretching syllables across multiple notes—combined with the plaintive quality of his voice served him well on this number. By this time in his study of Indian music, he had gained a natural feel for what to Western ears sounds like irregular rhythms, such that his phrasing, which could have presented difficulties to a novice, was fluid and organic. The Western classical chamber ensemble comes in at the very end of the first verse and remains throughout the rest of the song. George Martin did a terrific job of coaxing the classical musicians to slide and bend the notes on their cellos and violins in the style of the Indian dilrubas, making for a fully realized, successful fusion of Indian and Western classical music contained in the form of a Western pop song.

After the opening verse and first chorus, an all-instrumental section follows—the equivalent of the typical "middle eight" of a Beatles song. Loosely based harmonically on the pattern of the verses, the instrumental section features improvisations and call and response between the Eastern and Western ensembles. Harrison plays sitar during this section, in what would be analogous to a guitar solo in a conventional rock song. The section ends with the harp-like swoop of a swarmandal, answered by strings playing a descending passage, leading to a near-pause in the track, almost a false ending, before Harrison can be heard counting down the beats toward another iteration of the fixed melody (or, in Hindi, *gat*). Harrison's verse implicates those who have fallen prey to materialism—a theme to which he will return in subsequent songs, most notably the title track to *Living in the Material World*—succumbing to something of an uncharitable them-versus-us outlook, betraying a tendency toward self-righteousness that will repeatedly surface in song in coming years. In the return to the final chorus, which has different lyrics from those of the first, save for the final line, arguably the most important line in the song, Harrison backs off a bit from his indictment of those who have yet to see or understand "the truth" as he names it, suggesting that eventually everyone will come around to appreciate the unity of humanity and the cosmos.

Harrison insisted on ending the track with a bit of canned laughter found in the sound effects archive. Many have pointed to this as a self-subverting gesture wholly inappropriate to the serious nature of the song, or as a self-conscious admission of Harrison's holier-than-thou attitude as expressed in the song. Harrison defended the choice as an intentional effort to lighten the mood, in keeping with his sense of humility and his sense of humor, and, most aptly, as a gesture in keeping with the overall concept of *Sgt. Pepper's* as a concert being played out before a live audience, making for a smoother transition into the following number, Paul McCartney's jaunty, music-hall-influenced "When I'm Sixty-Four."

The "Within You Without You" track as originally played wound up being six minutes and twenty-five seconds long. George Martin shaved off one minute and twenty seconds merely by speeding up the tape just enough so that the final track is a half-step higher than what was initially recorded. One can hear how this played out by listening to the instrumental version of "Within You Without You" on the Beatles' compilation *Anthology 2*, which captures the original key played by the musicians, followed by the completed version as it appeared on *Sgt. Pepper's Lonely Hearts Club Band*, raising the key from C to C sharp.

"Within You Without You" is often grouped with other songs from *Sgt. Pepper's* and Beatles songs of that era under the umbrella of "psychedelia," a term sometimes used as a euphemism for music influenced by hallucinogenic drugs, in particular LSD. Other so-called psychedelic songs by the Beatles included "Strawberry Fields Forever," originally intended for *Sgt. Pepper's* but instead released as a single, eventually finding a home with "Penny Lane" on the soundtrack to *Magical Mystery Tour*, and "Lucy in the Sky with Diamonds," a stand-out track on *Sgt. Pepper's* which, no matter how much protesting to the contrary claiming it was inspired by the title of a drawing his young son brought home from school, saw John Lennon embed the letters "LSD" in the title of a song that clearly described an acid trip.

Psychedelia in 1967 was certainly in the air and found its way into rock music—including *Their Satanic Majesties Request* by the Rolling Stones, Moby Grape's eponymous debut album, *Surrealistic Pillow* by the Jefferson Airplane, Cream's *Disraeli Gears*, and *Smiley Smile* by the Beach Boys—but the categorization of some music as "psychedelic" or "psychedelia," and attributing its influence or subject matter to drug trips, is ultimately limiting, if not demeaning. Harrison and Martin went to great lengths to create a new fusion of styles, motivated by the sheer creative, musical challenge it presented, in a way that the resulting music would echo the song's message. While Harrison had taken LSD in the past, and while he spoke about its mind-expanding qualities, that was just one minor element that went into the creative composition of the song.

Nevertheless, George Harrison's adoption of Indian sounds and instruments and his lyrical focus on transcendental consciousness as heard in songs that included "Love You To" and "The Inner Light" saw them being grouped in with the overall psychedelic craze, even after Harrison had renounced the use of hallucinogenic drugs in favor of meditation and other Eastern forms of mind expansion, as expressed in "Within You Without You," which could be heard as a manifesto for the *post*-psychedelic era. Harrison sings of a universal life force that flows through human beings, a force related to or synonymous with love. He calls on his listeners to realize the power of harnessing this life force, this love and mindfulness, as a means to bring about a state of equanimity, to conclude the endless recycling of one's soul through multiple reincarnations, and along the way to do nothing less than save the world. Embedded inside "Within You Without You" is the seed of

Indian philosophy that will reach its full flowering on Harrison's first two proper solo albums.

As for the rejected "Only a Northern Song," Harrison's witty dig at the Beatles' publishing company would go on to find a comfortable home on the soundtrack album for the animated film, *Yellow Submarine*, released in mid-January 1969.

12

Gone for Baroque

John Lennon has the reputation of being the most politically minded of the four Beatles and given his forays into activism—especially his post-Beatles efforts with Yoko Ono that fused political protest and conceptual art, his various be-ins and bed-ins—perhaps deservedly so. While solidly antiwar, however, Lennon was no knee-jerk leftist. In fact, in probably his most famous "political" song, the aptly titled "Revolution"—released as the B-side of the single "Hey Jude" in August 1968, before finding a home on *The Beatles* the following November—Lennon distanced himself from the culture of the New Left when he sang, "But if you go carrying pictures of Chairman Mao, you ain't gonna make it with anyone anyhow." Taken as a whole, the song can be read as a repudiation of the tactics, if not the ideology, behind the protest movements of the late 1960s—especially regarding the use of violence. "Count me out," Lennon sang.

In response, Lennon was excoriated by the leftist press as well as the mainstream press. Rock critic Ellen Willis wrote in the *New Yorker*, "Deep within John Lennon there's a fusty old Tory struggling to get out."[1] The song made Lennon enemies of everyone from French filmmaker Jean-Luc Godard to African-American singer Nina Simone while gaining him the most unlikeliest of supporters in right-wing columnist William F. Buckley, Jr. In 1971, Lennon backed away from the sentiments expressed in "Revolution" in a Maoist gesture of self-criticism, calling it "a mistake" and recording the single "Power to the People" as a gesture of apology and recompense. By the late 1970s, Lennon reversed himself once again, decrying his own "Power to the People" and defending the pacifism espoused in "Revolution." The song "Power to the People" nevertheless lived on, used notably as a theme song for Democratic Socialist Bernie Sanders's failed US presidential campaigns in 2016 and 2020. Lennon's song also inspired Patti Smith's 1988 populist anthem, "People Have the Power," which went on to become an all-purpose rallying cry of the American left.

George Harrison—whose "Taxman," with its complaint about wealthy people being taxed at an exorbitantly high rate in the United Kingdom, could be interpreted as a conservative or anti-Socialist critique—turned the tables with the song "Piggies" (which he began writing about the same time as "Taxman"), an indictment of the establishment, adopting language and imagery borrowed from George Orwell's *Animal Farm* and from Lewis Carroll. The song portrays an alternative world where "piggies" are the dominant species, divided into "little piggies"—think the common man—and "bigger piggies," roughly analogous to the hereditary rich, capitalists, and power brokers.

At the time that Harrison wrote the song, the descriptor "pig" was already used in common parlance as a derogatory reference to a police officer, dating back at least as far as nineteenth-century England, where it appeared in the Oxford English Dictionary in 1811, thereby suggesting it was in use even earlier. The term appears again in *The Slang Dictionary: Etymological, Historical, and Anecdotal*, written by John Camden Hotten and published in London in 1859. Fast-forward nearly one hundred years, when the term was adopted by American antiwar protesters in the mid-1960s, culminating in its widespread use by the so-called Youth International Party, or Yippies, at the 1968 National Democratic Convention in Chicago, where it was employed as a verbal weapon in face-to-face showdowns between protesters and law-enforcement officers ordered to disband political protest rallies. The term soon spread beyond Chicago—where some activists were seen in possession of actual live pigs—gaining more widespread usage in the late 1960s and early 1970s.

George Harrison began writing his song "Piggies" in early 1966, promptly set it aside and forgot about it, and then rediscovered it when the Beatles began work on what would become *The Beatles*, or "The White Album," in 1968. Although it has sometimes been dismissed as a period piece that has not aged well, over time it has grown in status as a timeless indictment of the gulf between the haves and the have-nots. Harrison's "piggies," after all, were not police officers—he wrote that the song had "absolutely nothing to do with American policemen"[2]—but rather representatives of all humanity. His song was really a musical version of Orwell's *Animal Farm*. As the song's barbs are aimed at the "bigger piggies," the "piggies" of the song's title are generally thought of as synonymous with the "bigger piggies" who bear the brunt of the song's ridicule, and exclusive of the "little piggies," who are repressed, economically and otherwise, by the wealthy ruling class. In this way, the evolution of Harrison's "piggies" both tracked and spurred on the more widespread use of the term as a sociopolitical critique of those few who benefit the most from modern capitalism at the expense of the mass of humanity, who never enjoy the full fruits of their labor.

"Piggies" is an exhibit in how far Harrison's songwriting had come from "Don't Bother Me" and "I Need You." He employs just a few colorful details to paint the entire character of the upper and lower classes. The former—the "bigger piggies"—wear starched white shirts, while the latter—the "little piggies"—are consigned to playing around in dirt, their lives offering no hope for upward mobility. It is all the more delicious that one of the song's most violent images, one that actually still had the power to shock in its day (only half a century later, with the normalization of political violence and terrorism, it began to seem downright quaint), originates not with George Harrison but with, of all people, his gentle, fun-loving mother, Louise. One can just imagine the scene: George, back in Liverpool sitting in his mother's kitchen, paper and pen in hand, laboring over his lyrics, trying to nail the song down before returning to London and presenting it to the group, asking his mother, "What rhymes with 'something lacking'?" Imagine his shock and delight when Louise replied, "A damn good whacking!" Never underestimate the power of a mother to contribute, however slightly, to the work of some of the greatest geniuses of our time—they did, after all, raise their sons and daughters and presumably deserve some credit for having helped shape their world outlook, if not their slide-guitar technique.

The roots of the Baroque stylings that wound up being played on harpsichord on the final recording can be heard on the acoustic demos recorded at Harrison's home in Esher, where Harrison plays some very classical-sounding guitar. The demo version captures the infant "Piggies" in the style of a folk song. The more Harrison worked on the music, the more he veered toward the faux-Baroque touches. This was as much a case of serendipity as it was an intentional effort to color the tune with the hues of a classical salon. Chris Thomas, who was assisting George Martin as producer for the extensive sessions for *The Beatles* that were spread out over five months, happened to see that a harpsichord was set up in the studio adjacent to the one where the Beatles were working. Thomas suggested to Harrison that harpsichord might lend just the right note to "Piggies," and Harrison, McCartney, and Starr, along with Thomas, set themselves up next door to take advantage of the Baroque keyboard. Thomas had classical-music training on keyboard instruments, so he handled harpsichord duties, and thus was the song given its mock-Baroque setting, which only enhanced the song's message of the starchy "bigger piggies," who would certainly prefer Baroque music to 1960s rock 'n' roll. Ample vocal overdubs further gave the number the flavor of a Baroque chorus, and when George Martin returned and heard what they had come up with, he wrote out an arrangement for a string octet. Thus had "Piggies" morphed from a deceptively simple, nursery-rhyme-like folk song into a fully produced, classically influenced opus in which, once again, the medium paralleled the message. "Piggies" was sequenced on side two of the double LP, sandwiched in between "Blackbird" and "Rocky Raccoon," making for an animal-themed suite.

While "Piggies" fit just fine on the eclectic, everything-but-the-kitchen-sink approach of the White Album, it may have been better served had it been included on *Sgt. Pepper's*, which in itself may have benefited from its inclusion. With its unusual orchestration and Baroque touches, it would have sat comfortably next to "Being for the Benefit of Mr. Kite" and "Fixing a Hole." The inclusion of actual pig noises on the track also lends it the feel of a *Sgt. Pepper's* number, given that album's sprinkling of barnyard noises across several tunes, a literal rejoinder to *Pet Sounds* by the Beach Boys.

Like several tracks on *The Beatles*, including "Revolution" and "Helter Skelter," "Piggies" was unfortunately co-opted by the maniacal cult leader Charles Manson, who believed that the Beatles were speaking directly to him through these songs, urging him through coded messages to provoke a violent race war. Manson and his cadre got as far as the gruesome, notorious Tate-LaBianca murders before being caught and jailed, putting a quick end to their vicious crime spree. The episode tainted "Piggies" and the other songs for several years. But with the passage of time, "Piggies" has grown in peoples' estimation as one of the best tracks on *The Beatles*. While Harrison steered clear of it on his 1974 North American concert tour, he performed a live version on his 1991 tour of Japan and again the following year at his Natural Law Party concert in England.

Given its quirky musical eccentricity, "Piggies"—unlike several other White Album tunes, most notably Harrison's "While My Guitar Gently Weeps"—never made it into the rock 'n' roll canon. Few other artists attempted their own versions of the tune. One of the few covers of "Piggies" does stick out, as much for how unusual it was and for the artist who performed it. Austrian-born American-Israeli folksinger and political activist Theodore Bikel included a version of "Piggies" on his 1970 album *A New Day*. Bikel, as it happens, had been a delegate to the 1968 Democratic convention in Chicago, and was therefore quite sympathetic to the song's sociopolitical critique of capitalism, as well as being familiar with the main image upon which the song was based. Bikel's arch, spoken-sung vocals are somewhat at odds with the original's childlike vibe—perhaps more "bigger piggies" than "little piggies"—but credit his attempt to decorate his standard folk approach with Beatlesesque touches, including an ad-libbed "All together now!," a reference to the Beatles song by that title included on the soundtrack album to *Yellow Submarine*.

13

The Waiting Is the Hardest Part

What do you get when you cross jet lag with a foggy view of Los Angeles?

On August 1, 1967, George Harrison and Pattie Boyd flew from England to California, where they planned over the course of a week to meet with former Beatles publicist Derek Taylor in Los Angeles, attend a Ravi Shankar concert at the Hollywood Bowl, and visit Pattie's sister Jenny in San Francisco. Taylor and his wife, Joan, were due to visit George and Pattie at their rental house in the Hollywood Hills on the night they arrived. As the hours ticked by and Harrison, waiting for his guests to show up, struggled with the familiar, contradictory effects of jet lag that render one tired but unable to fall asleep, he noticed a Hammond organ in the corner. He flipped it on and began messing around with it, playing with ideas for a song about waiting for Derek and Joan to appear. By the time the couple finally found their way through the fog to the house on Blue Jay Way, Harrison had all but completed the song.

The song lyrics begin with the basic who, what, and where of journalism: "There's a fog upon L.A., and my friends have lost their way." That was the situation, and it was basically all anyone needed to know. What follows are three-plus minutes of Harrison importuning his visitors not to take too long, lest their host fall asleep before their arrival. Most of this plays out over a single, unvarying droning note that George played on the Hammond, capturing the feeling and mood of timelessness that characterizes the wee hours when one is alone. (Mrs. Harrison presumably told her husband to wake her up when the Taylors got there, and in the meantime went to bed.) What was initially intended by George as an idle bit of fun to help pass the time wound up becoming the song "Blue Jay Way."

Within five weeks, the Beatles were back at EMI Studios in London to record songs for the soundtrack to their next project, a TV film called *Magical Mystery Tour*, but not before their manager, Brian Epstein, died from an accidental drug overdose on August 27, 1967. Amid all this, the Beatles had also for the first time met Maharishi Mahesh Yogi in London, before following him to Wales for a meditation retreat. The foursome had about a week to work in the studio on their songs before setting out to record the movie itself, a mostly improvisational, absurdist road film with avant-garde touches, largely concocted by Paul McCartney, who had taken up making short experimental movies of his own. The title track had already been recorded the previous spring, immediately on the heels of the final sessions for *Sgt. Pepper's Lonely Hearts Club Band*, and the music that wound up on *Magical Mystery Tour* was very much in the same vein as its predecessor. Beside the title track and "Blue Jay Way," songs included "I Am the Walrus," "The Fool on the Hill," and "Your Mother Should Know." The album was released as a six-song double EP in the United Kingdom, while Capitol Records released it as a full-length LP in the United States, pairing the songs from the UK EP with non-album singles from the previous year, including "Strawberry Fields Forever," "Penny Lane," "Hello, Goodbye," and "All You Need Is Love." Not too shabby a collection of tunes, even if it was not produced or sequenced as a regular Beatles album.

From its origins as an early-morning lark, "Blue Jay Way" was given the full psychedelic treatment in the studio on September 6. Backward voices, processed to the limit before they sound mechanical, pop in and out of the track, as if breaking through the time-space continuum; a cello dances above and below the drone note; Harrison's vocals are multitracked to the point of wooziness. Instruments and voices are treated to phasing and flanging, sent through the Hammond organ's Leslie speaker, whose rotating innards lend the sound a Doppler effect, used widely on the aptly titled *Revolver*. George sings in a laconic, understated voice, as if he did not want to wake those who had thrown in the towel and gone to sleep before the guests arrived. The sum effect is that of late-night delirium, the sound of a dream.

The length of verses is irregular, further lending an off-kilter, trippy sense to the number. There are no guitars on the track; George plays the drone on organ, just as he did when he wrote the song a month earlier. While no Indian instruments were used (or abused) in the making of "Blue Jay Way," the influence of Harrison's studies with Ravi Shankar are evident in the employment of the tambura-like drone and raga-like melody. Paul's bass, Ringo's drums, and John's backup vocals serve to propel the song along without drawing attention to themselves. A few weeks after the bulk of recording on the track had been completed, classical cellist Peter Willison arrived straight from a gig at the Royal Albert Hall shortly before midnight, still bedecked in his tuxedo, to record an unwritten, improvised part with coaching from George Martin. They worked on the part through the night into the morning, and the resulting overdub added just the right touch that had been missing. In a sense, the cello took on the lead instrumental role ordinarily provided by Harrison's guitar.

Recorded just days after John Lennon's "I Am the Walrus," the track is something of the latter's dark twin (in the similar manner that Lennon's "All You Need Is Love" is a brighter version of Harrison's equally brassy and anthemic but ultimately pessimistic "It's All Too Much"). As in other Harrison songs, the music of "Blue Jay Way" directly recapitulates the meaning of the lyrics. Through the gauzy, trippy haze, the incessant repetition of the line "Please don't be long" that constitutes the bulk of the song slowly imparts another aspect of meaning, as the emphasis of the phrase moves from the word "be" to the word "long," such that by the end one hears in it an entirely different request: "Please don't belong." This change in meaning from the very particular to a more universal, social appeal winds up recontextualizing the entire song, suggesting a new connotation of the opening phrase about George's friends having "lost their way" in the Los Angeles fog. What began in real life and in the beginning of the song as a simple observation about the Taylors trying to find Harrison's house is now heard as a critique of the California-inspired counterculture; Harrison now seems to be asking his listeners not to "belong" to the movement, or any movement. Perhaps the song took this turn after that first night; just days later, George, Pattie, and the Taylors would venture north to the Bay Area to visit Jenny Boyd and to get a firsthand look at the much-vaunted hippie scene in the Haight-Ashbury district, a visit that in itself would start from a sincere place motivated by idealism and a desire to see the revolution firsthand, only to stumble upon a horrific, nightmarish scene out of the Decameron, the Inferno, a Hieronymus Bosch painting, or *The Night of the Living Dead.* "Please don't belong," indeed. Harrison is said to have eschewed dropping acid from that day on.

14

The Love There That's Sleeping

While highly regarded as one of George Harrison's best Beatles songs, "While My Guitar Gently Weeps" is always identified as the one Beatles track featuring an outside guitarist, in the person of Eric Clapton. (The only other rock musician of significance to appear on Beatles recordings was Billy Preston, whose keyboards are heard on the *Get Back/Let It Be* sessions and on two *Abbey Road* tracks.) Far too often Clapton's appearance on the track is said to be the result of Harrison's inability to come up with his own solo for the song. One listen to the number disproves the theory. To Clapton's credit, he molds his guitar lines to fit within the parameters of the Beatles sound, eschewing his signature blues-based approach. He serves the song by not playing anything that George could not—or more importantly, would not—have played, such that when *The Beatles* was first released, it was not widely known that Clapton played on the number (his contribution was left uncredited), and there was little reason to suspect that he did. Partial credit goes to Clapton for requesting that his guitar sound be processed in such a way to make it sound less like Eric Clapton and more like something one would hear Harrison play on a Beatles track. Granted, if Harrison had assumed the lead-guitar role, he would likely have played something very different—probably something more melodic— and when listening to the track knowing that it is Clapton on guitar, one can indeed distinguish his touch and tone from Harrison's.

Frustrated by his bandmates' apparent lack of interest in helping to create and record the song's arrangement, Harrison invited Clapton to join him in a nighttime session in something of a last-minute whim; Clapton even had to borrow one of George's guitars, albeit one that Clapton had just recently given to Harrison as a gift—a red Gibson Les Paul model called Lucy, manufactured in 1957, and previously owned by John Sebastian and Rick Derringer, before Clapton purchased it from a New York City guitar shop.

In fact, the track had gone through several iterations, beginning with a solo acoustic version and a band rendition featuring a backward guitar solo, before Harrison brought Clapton in to overdub his guitar solo. At his most mischievous and frisky, George "stole" an eight-track recording console that EMI's Abbey Road studios had not yet seen fit to make available to the Beatles.

Harrison co-opted some of the studio engineers to help liberate the machine from an office where a technician was taking his sweet time slowly and studiously examining it, as was his general practice and EMI policy.

Impatient to make use of the machine at a time when eight-track recorders were popping up at independent studios around London, Harrison immediately set out to take advantage of the opportunities the multitrack machine had to offer, including multiple vocal overdubs and extra percussion. Still unhappy with the results, Harrison scrapped everything and had the group start from scratch, playing acoustic guitar with John assuming lead-guitar duties and Paul on keyboards. Finally pleased with the band's input, Harrison returned to the studio the next evening with a somewhat hesitant Clapton, who was self-conscious about being the first outsider to assist on a Beatles recording (aside from various orchestral players and Indian musicians whom the Beatles employed on several previous albums, including *Revolver* and *Sgt. Pepper's*). With Clapton in the studio, the group was able to put the finishing touches on the track, which also included McCartney's fuzz-toned bass guitar, Harrison on organ, additional percussion by Ringo, and, finally, George's lead vocals. A lot of work went into the making of the track, but it paid off—to this day "While My Guitar Gently Weeps" is considered one of the best songs on *The Beatles* and one of the greatest songs in the Beatles repertoire. Harrison was obviously proud of the song; he included it in all his post-Beatles live performances, including the Concert for Bangladesh, his 1974 Dark Horse tour, and his 1991 tour of Japan.

As Harrison so often did, he built "While My Guitar Gently Weeps" on a musical metaphor. From "Only a Northern Song," which poked fun at the Beatles publishing company and even delved into a bit of musical criticism of the group, through "Wah-Wah," a tribute to a guitar effects pedal, Harrison always found ways to create meaning from music itself.

One month after they recorded the song, Harrison repaid Clapton's favor when he helped Eric write "Badge," a song for Cream's farewell album, *Goodbye*, on which Harrison played rhythm guitar.

15
Take a Piece, But Not Too Much

Many interpret George Harrison's "It's All Too Much" as an expression of an acid trip, but to reduce it to drugs is to miss the greater point: it is a song about spiritual transcendence. Additionally, it is a love song (for his wife Pattie), a reflection on fame, a drug song, yes, but also an anti-drug song, one that puts forth meditation as the ultimate mind-altering practice. For Harrison, taking LSD was just one step along the way toward achieving cosmic consciousness, but immersing himself in Indian music, Vedic philosophy, meditation, and chanting played equal if not greater roles in leading him on his spiritual journey. The ending, with several minutes of the boys in the band relentlessly chanting "too much, too much," was in itself a kind of mantra. To reduce it all merely to drugs minimizes other aspects of the song that make it so compelling: the song's wit, its negativity, its hint of the preacherly scolding yet to come, and its kaleidoscopic musical vision that led one critic to rate it one of "the top five all-time psychedelic freakouts in rock history."[1]

The track, recorded May 25–26, 1967, shortly after the *Sgt. Pepper's* sessions, with the Beatles idling until its release on May 26, opens with sixteen seconds of guitar feedback, unprecedented for a Beatles song or any song by a major pop band at the time, and three times the length of the guitar feedback that kicked off "I Feel Fine." The feedback-drenched opening is often said to have been influenced by Jimi Hendrix, but that underestimates the Beatles' own experimentation and innovations with feedback and distortion, as well as the Beatles' own influence on Hendrix, who played versions of "Rain," "Day Tripper," and "Tomorrow Never Knows" in concert. Hendrix famously performed the title track to *Sgt. Pepper's Lonely Hearts Club Band* onstage just three days after the album was released, with several members of the Beatles in the audience. (Hendrix's supposed influence on the Beatles is also belied by simple chronology: Hendrix's solo career began only in late 1966 in London; his debut album, *Are You Experienced,* was released just a few weeks before the recording session for "It's All Too Much" in the United Kingdom, on May 12, 1967. Coincidentally, "It's All Too Much" was the rare Beatles track *not* recorded in EMI's studios at Abbey Road—it was recorded at De Lane

Lea Studios, where much of *Are You Experienced* was tracked. Also, like the Beatles before him, Hendrix was rejected by Decca Records.)

The basic Hammond organ figure that powers "It's All Too Much," played by Harrison, emerges from the din of the feedback. Guitars enter just shy of the half-minute mark, echoing the organ riff. (Who exactly played those guitars has never been conclusively determined; experts variously credit Lennon, McCartney, Harrison, or some combination of the three.) Harrison's first utterance of "It's all too much" comes in at about forty-five seconds on an off-beat—not where one would expect it, as does his vocal line in the verses (the first of which does not begin until just after the one-minute mark), a strategy Harrison had used at least as far back as "If I Needed Someone" in late 1965, and one that would become one of his compositional trademarks. Singing off the beat is a method that surprises listeners, or even unsettles them, adding a kind of ambivalence to the music that, in Harrison's hands, often underscores the ambivalence in his lyrics. Chances are most listeners are not even aware of this dynamic on a conscious level, but it cannot help engaging listeners on a subconscious level, setting up an underlying tension in the performance that is as meaningful musically as the manifest meaning of the lyrics.

"It's All Too Much" is full of oddball effects: machine-like noises, whirring sounds, vocals in reverse, instruments—particularly Ringo's drums—that phase in and out, suddenly get boosted in the mix, or experience a radical change of tone. A linear electric-guitar part politely winds in and around Harrison's vocals on the second verse before taking flight on an instrumental interlude, featuring a guitar solo followed by a brass passage, out of which emerges one piercing note on guitar that sustains and decays over the third verse for about twelve seconds. With about two minutes left in the song, the layers of sound begin to detach from one another: rhythms trip and stutter, the horns begin to lose their way, the other singers make their presence known, the music fades into a false ending before the group vocals repeating "too much, too much" slowly morph their verbal rhythm into a military-style "hup-two, hup-two, hup-two" count against the prevailing rhythmic pattern that has run throughout the entire song. In the last few seconds, one hears the ticking of a metronome or an egg timer, as if to say time marches on.

The brass interlude, apparently foisted on Harrison by George Martin, connects the song musically to *Sgt. Pepper's Lonely Hearts Club Band*. "It's All Too Much" could have easily found a comfortable home on that album, which otherwise included only one Harrison composition ("Within You Without You"). By the time the song was recorded, however, the *Sgt. Pepper's* album was already being manufactured. Harrison later expressed unhappiness with the horns on the track, but touches like that and the extended jamming—especially in the ad-lib vocals at the end—are what makes this very Harrisonian composition a Beatles song—indeed, what one critic termed "the great lost Beatle song."[2] Harrison, the third writer in the group, wound up creating the quintessential recording of the Beatles psychedelic phase, even as its lyrics argued largely against psychedelia.

The title alone is vintage Harrison, with its suggestion of a reaction against whatever it is that you've got. What exactly is too much? Too much Beatlehood, Beatlemania, acid, love shining all around here? The song is in some ways an update of his 1963 song "Don't Bother Me," writ for the psychedelic era. It partially extols the psychedelic mindset while cautioning against putting too much stock in it; no more than, say, a proper cup of tea. (Note how the handclaps throughout the song are treated in such a way as to make them sound like knocking on a door, also connecting the number to "Don't Bother Me," which ends with the ominous sound of someone knocking on a door despite the singer's pleas to be left alone.)

The dualities expressed in lines like "All the world is birthday cake, so take a piece but not too much" and "Show me that I'm everywhere and get me home for tea" express Harrison's ambivalence about fame, as well as his sense of humor that says that even among great abundance, even among the heights of the culture of the love-in, still, everything in moderation is recommended. And this tired, somewhat conservative or tradition-minded Englishman suggests that as much as we recognize and celebrate the awakening of universal consciousness, let's not throw the baby out with the bathwater: tripping to one's heart's content is OK, universal love is just dandy—just so long as we get a grip in late afternoon and stop all the nonsense and make time to enjoy the simple pleasure of a nice cuppa. All this works on two levels—the direct meaning of the words being stated, but also the level at which what is being stated is a false consciousness, a sendup, or, in other terms, meant ironically.

In its skepticism about the ultimate merits of acid-infused flower power, "It's All Too Much" foreshadows Harrison's final break with the hippie counterculture after his infamous visit to that subculture's ground zero in the Haight-Ashbury district of San Francisco just a couple of months after recording the song. What Harrison found after walking the streets was frightening and disheartening: rather than in a progressive model of social and spiritual activism among a community of enlightened beings, he found himself having wandered onto the set of a real-life zombie movie, where the crowds of unwashed, glassy-eyed dopeheads all too easily turned on a dime from initially hailing a real-life Beatle among them to attacking him and his small entourage, leaving them to flee to their automobile to escape the rampaging fanatics disappointed by Harrison's inability or unwillingness to . . . to what? To give them an impromptu concert? To turn water into wine? To feed them all with five loaves and a couple of fish?

Just a few weeks after the Beatles recorded "It's All Too Much," John Lennon, perhaps inspired by Harrison's complex commentary on love, consciousness, and excess, brought a similar but much simpler song to the group, one that would eventually wind up overshadowing Harrison's number. While John Lennon is often thought of as the most cynical member of the group—and in his personal bearing, his cynicism outshone that of Harrison's—his "All You Need Is Love" is almost childlike in its surface-level innocence and naiveté; as Brian Epstein told an interviewer, "The nice thing about it is that it cannot be misinterpreted. It is a clear message saying that love is everything."[3] There was nothing ambivalent about Lennon's tune, which would instantly become the anthem of the so-called Summer of Love after its world premiere on June 25, 1967, in the form of a live performance broadcast globally over a satellite TV link, reportedly watched by nearly a half-billion viewers.

Like Harrison's song, Lennon chose the key of G—the so-called people's key—for his universal message that opens with the phrase, "Love, love, love," repeated three times. Not to be outdone by Harrison—whose song quoted English Baroque composer Jeremiah Clarke's "Prince of Denmark's March," also called "Trumpet Voluntary"—Lennon, with the help of George Martin, expanded upon that strategy, opening "All You Need Is Love" with the clarion call from the French national anthem, "*La Marseillaise*," and interpolating snatches of Glenn Miller's big-band hit "In the Mood," an "invention" by J.S. Bach, and the traditional English folk song "Greensleeves," throughout the song. (Not realizing that Miller's "In the Mood" was not in the public domain, the Beatles wound up having to pay royalties to the song's publisher.) The final recording also cleverly quoted a bit of the Beatles' own "Yesterday" and, very aptly, given the subject matter, "She Loves You."

In addition to punctuating the song with well-placed guitar fills, Harrison also added some distinctive parts on violin—Lennon played harpsichord and banjo on the track and McCartney bowed a double bass. A who's who of English rock royalty added background vocals, including Mick Jagger, Keith Richards, Graham Nash, Eric Clapton, Marianne Faithfull, and Keith Moon.

Both "It's All Too Much" and "All You Need Is Love" were used in the animated film *Yellow Submarine* and included on the soundtrack album of the same name. "All You Need Is Love" also found a home on the Beatles' album *Magical Mystery Tour*. While the anthem was part and parcel of its time, encapsulating the utopian spirit of the counterculture—"It's easy / All you need is love / Love is all you need"—it could do so only by dumbing down the musical and lyrical innovations and complexity of its immediate predecessor in the recording studio, no doubt accounting for its huge popularity; released as a single, it topped charts in the United Kingdom, the United States, and around the world. But popularity is rarely a measure of creative achievement—more times than not, it suggests exactly the opposite. The banality of "All You Need Is Love" would be exceeded only by Lennon's 1971 piano ballad, "Imagine." Granted, that Lennon song has gained the status of a canonized hymn, trotted out for any and all occasions where a nod to idealism with a faux-hip quotient is required. In his 1991 song "The Other Side of Summer," Liverpool native and rock singer-songwriter Elvis Costello, an occasional collaborator with Paul McCartney, asks, "Was it a millionaire who said 'imagine no possessions?'" Costello expanded on the sentiment in a *New York Times* interview that same year, saying, "John Lennon wrote some wonderful songs, but 'Imagine,' which has been so sanctified, was one of his worst."[4]

In his 1981 postassassination tribute to Lennon, "All Those Years Ago," Harrison, on the other hand, namechecks two John Lennon songs: "All You Need Is Love" and "Imagine."

16

When George "Quit" the Beatles

For fifty years or so, it was accepted as fact that George Harrison quit the Beatles in January 1969, when he walked out of Twickenham Film Studios, where the band was rehearsing old and new songs for a projected album and concert. The event that supposedly precipitated George's walkout was a conversation during which a heavy-handed Paul McCartney tried to dictate to Harrison how to play his guitar part on the song "Two of Us." The evidence was right there in plain sight in Michael Lindsay-Hogg's eighty-minute 1970 documentary film, *Let It Be*, which showed McCartney lecturing a somewhat chastened Harrison, who responds, "I'll play whatever you want me to play, or I won't play at all if you don't want me to play. Whatever it is that'll please you, I'll do it."

But in November 2021, a nearly eight-hour documentary, *Get Back*—assembled by director Peter Jackson (best known for his *Lord of the Rings* film trilogy) from well over a hundred hours of unused audio and video film footage recorded by Lindsay-Hogg—fully recontextualized the McCartney-Harrison showdown. For one, it made clear that the discussion over the guitar part was just that: a discussion, not an argument. As Lindsay-Hogg told me,

> For them it wasn't a rift or a fight, it was two people talking about something to do with the music, as they had for the last fifteen years, and they always wanted it to be in the movie because it showed they weren't teenagers anymore. It showed that they were men—in Paul's case, approaching twenty-nine, and George probably twenty-six—it showed that they were able to have this discussion and it didn't blow them up or send them to the clinic. And this was part of working together. A lot of people say that this was the scene where Paul dumps on George. Not at all. They never wanted it out of the movie. Although a lot of people have looked at it as the electric light flashing "break up, break up." It wasn't like that at all.

Second, in the full version of the conversation, McCartney comes across less as a dictator and more as a reluctant, apologetic guide. And perhaps most importantly, the newly released footage made clear that far from provoking Harrison's departure, the tiff between the two, if it even was a tiff, happened a full five days before the day George packed up his guitar and told his bandmates he was leaving.

The entire received narrative, as it turned out, had to be rewritten. The new *Get Back* poked holes in much of the legend surrounding the *Let It Be* documentary, in large part a legend that grew with time, with only tangential reference to scenes in the actual movie, especially as the original film largely lived on in the fading memories of those who saw it when it was first released in 1970, or in the few years afterwards, before the movie was withdrawn from circulation.

Peter Jackson's *Get Back*, like Lindsay-Hogg's *Let It Be*, was still one director's edited view of what happened at Twickenham and Apple, where the filmed rehearsal sessions picked up after Harrison negotiated his return to the band just a few days after leaving. Without access to the complete footage, we can never really know the entire story. And even then, we cannot be sure that Lindsay-Hogg's recordings captured everything pertinent to Harrison's departure. They certainly did not capture what was happening in George's life and the others' lives outside the studio sessions. But Jackson's eight-hour version did open a remarkable window into the Beatles' relationships, working methods, and creative process at this pivotal period in their career, suggesting that all was not bitterness and rancor. And, in particular, it belied the notion that Harrison was pushed out of the band through a combination of neglect and disrespect.

Far from it. In *Get Back*, viewers see the Beatles going to great strides to get down on tape a usable version of Harrison's song "All Things Must Pass." The song was seriously being considered by Paul and John for inclusion in the set list for the live concert that would bring the January project to its culmination, until George withdrew the song from consideration. The group also listens attentively as George sings a beautiful, flawless, solo acoustic version of Bob Dylan's "Mama You Been on My Mind" (a difficult song to get right), and they all join in while George sings Dylan's "I Shall Be Released" (which at the time was best known for its version by the Band that appeared on their debut album, *Music from Big Pink*) and a shambolic, quickly aborted rendition of Dylan's "The Mighty Quinn." For "All Things Must Pass," John and Paul earnestly attempted to come up with vocal harmonies in the style of The Band, as per George's request to make the entire song sound "Band-y." If the group never quite nails it enough to have made it worthy of inclusion on *Let It Be*, the album resulting from these sessions, it was not for lack of trying. Indeed, what they did come up with sounds more "Band-y" than the version Harrison would rerecord the following year for his debut solo album of the same name. But all's well that ends well; *All Things Must Pass* would just not have been the same without "All Things Must Pass," which served as the landmark album's theme and mission statement.

The *Get Back* documentary also shows that George was not the only troubled member of the Fab Four in January 1969. At one point, upon his arrival to the studio in the morning, Ringo confesses that he's not feeling well, an obvious reference to being hung over. Throughout *Get Back*, Ringo can be seen yawning, rolling his head sideways as if he cannot hold it up straight, and even nodding off amid all the racket and chaos. Plus, the poor soul's eyes are perpetually red rimmed. Something's going on with him, but to his credit, it never seems to get in the way of his drumming.

John Lennon is a whole other case. A basket case. For the first few days of the sessions, he barely says a word. He has brought almost no new songs to the sessions, and the ones he does have are by no means up to par (although we do hear an early version of what will become his solo hit "Gimme Some Truth"). His pinpoint pupils are so constricted they are hardly there. A woman is glued to his side like an appendage almost the entire time, even while he is playing and singing. Lennon is no longer around to defend himself, but it has seemed clear to just about everyone who has ever watched *Let It Be* or *Get Back* that, at least for the first few days of the recording sessions, he was smacked out on heroin. It devolves to his credit, however, that like Ringo, he is still able to function—to play and sing—if not at his best, at least halfway decently, which is pretty much the arena where most people's best efforts live. And as the days tick by, Lennon seems to sober up and play a more active role in the sessions, contributing new songs and good ideas for improving the others' songs, as well as stepping back toward his role as co-bandleader.

The month of rehearsal and recording sessions worked to revive the long-dormant creative and emotional ties among the Fab Four as a group. Harrison himself notes toward the end of the month that the near-daily rehearsals have done wonders for getting his guitar-playing fingers back up to speed. And within just a couple of months after the rooftop concert at Apple that would conclude the project, the quartet would return to the recording studio for several months of sessions to create a new album, produced by George Martin, which would become *Abbey Road*, generally considered to be one of the Beatles' finest works.

Before the January 1969 sessions, playing live in the studio for hours on end had seemingly become a thing of the past for the foursome. More recent albums, especially *The Beatles*, had been largely pieced together in individual recording sessions with one or two members laying down tracks and overdubs at any given time. Part of the meaning of the title *Get Back* was that the Beatles were returning to the old way of doing things, playing and recording songs live as a band in the studio, albeit at this point without the oversight of their late manager, Brian Epstein (the loss of whom McCartney frequently laments in the film), and without the hands-on leadership of producer George Martin, who did attend some of the *Get Back* sessions and helped out whenever he could, but who was not called upon to produce the sessions in any meaningful sense of the term.

Neither was Glyn Johns by any stretch the producer of the sessions; his role was more that of chief engineer (and a fine one at that), which in this situation was no easy job, in part because the session lacked a producer—at the very least, someone to oversee the sessions and keep the musicians on track. A producer and engineer go together like toast and jam; you cannot have one without the other and expect the result to be any good. This left the Fab Four as their own producers, with the lion's share of those duties falling to the capable but reluctant hands of Paul McCartney, who as seen in *Get Back* is palpably uncomfortable playing that role, knowing that he comes across as "annoying" and bossy when all he is trying to do is make things happen (like getting the group to agree on what song to work on at any given moment). At one point, McCartney can be seen talking to himself (or to anyone within earshot who cares to listen) about the need for a precise schedule of song rehearsals and wishing there were someone besides himself who could keep the sessions moving and coach the band through the process. (This would have been part of George Martin's remit had he been enlisted officially as producer of the sessions.)

The "I'll play whatever you want me to play" back and forth between Harrison and McCartney took place on Monday, January 6, fully five days before Harrison took the opportunity of the lunch break on Friday, January 10, to pack up his gear, don his coat, and, without any drama, matter of factly remark to his fellow musicians, "I'm leaving the band now." (To which John replied, "When?" and to which George answered, "Now.") So, while Harrison may indeed have filed McCartney's attempt to "help" him with his guitar part on "Two of Us" with all his other gripes about working with Paul and his perceived lesser status in the Beatles, this conversation did not immediately result in George's departure. Footage from the following few days' rehearsals shows the players cooperating, helping one another, jamming together, and even having fun.

Running through the entire affair, however, is an undercurrent of tension based on several factors, including a lack of clarity about just what these sessions were for. Are the Beatles recording a new album? Rehearsing for a live concert before an audience . . . in *Libya*, as advocated by Lindsay-Hogg? Or are they first and foremost making another movie? Or is it some combination of the three? There was no clear consensus or agreement, and no sense of a path toward figuring out the answers to these questions. All they knew was that they were going to Twickenham every day and plugging in and playing together, while Lindsay-Hogg's camera crew and Glyn Johns's mobile unit recorded the mostly directionless proceedings—including aimless conversations about just what it was they were doing and why.

Thus, it is totally understandable that moments of discord kept bubbling to the surface, whether it be a tepid response to one of George's songs or an overeager McCartney trying to stage-manage a song's arrangement—or disagreement among the musicians over just how best to go about creating an arrangement (again, showing how much the lack of a producer was costing them merely on procedural grounds, and how invaluable George Martin had been in the past in these situations). McCartney himself was the most vocal in his frustrations with how things were proceeding, bemoaning how the role of rehearsal leader, and possibly even bandleader, had fallen to him merely by default. McCartney's ill-begotten reputation as a control freak is belied by *Get Back*, in which he comes across as a sympathetic figure, albeit one caught between a rock and a hard place. If he had not stepped up to lead the band, nothing would have been delivered.

One watches *Get Back* and *Let It Be* closely for clues to see what drove George Harrison to decide at the lunch break on that fateful Friday to quit the Beatles, but neither of the films provides a clear-cut answer. This is not necessarily because something did not happen. It is simply because we are not *shown* what might have happened, what might have been a precipitating event or a straw that broke the camel's back. And that very well could be because the filmmakers may not have included footage that may have explained what happened that morning. Perhaps Lindsay-Hogg's cameras were not rolling at a certain moment when the camel's back was broken. Perhaps one or more of the Beatles insisted that footage of an argument not be included in the final cut. The London tabloids, for example, had a field day in reporting an alleged row between Harrison and Lennon, claiming that they even came to blows. We see nothing of the sort in the films; rather, we see Harrison and Lennon shadowboxing while making fun of those news reports. But was there indeed an argument of some sort between Harrison and Lennon that Friday morning? Did Yoko Ono say or do something that put George over the edge? Perhaps she did—Paul is captured later on as saying, "It's gonna be such an incredible sort of comical thing like in fifty years' time, you know . . . 'they broke up 'cause Yoko sat on an amp.'" McCartney could have been speaking figuratively, or perhaps his tossed-off comment offers a clue to the final skirmish, which, if it was about Yoko's presence in the studio, would certainly have earned George the wrath of John. Could George just take no more of McCartney's imperious direction or Lennon's disparagement of his songs? If footage of any of this exists, the filmmakers have withheld it from us, either on the basis of their own editorial judgment or on orders from on high, i.e., the Beatles. Or was it all just a slow burn, one small microaggression after another, until George could no longer tolerate being in the same room with Paul and John?

For the most part, on the basis of the documentary footage, Harrison seemed to be having a fine time working with his bandmates. There are moments of boredom, moments of joy, moments of frustration, and moments of conviviality. In sum, the atmosphere is typical of group recording sessions—as typical as anything regarding the Beatles can be. There are musical false starts balanced with inspired music-making. We see all of this, but we see nothing that hints at an unavoidable break.

That is, we see nothing out of the ordinary until the morning of Friday, January 10. Because the truth is, from the moment Harrison appears at Twickenham that morning, George *does* seem different. He is quiet, sullen, and humorless. Whatever *is* bothering him that day he seems to have brought with him from home to the studio.

When an already troubled George arrives, McCartney, Starr, and a few others are seated in a circle with the Beatles' longtime music publisher Dick James. James had dropped by Twickenham to deliver in person the news that Northern Songs had acquired the Lawrence Wright Music catalog, a huge backlist of songs featuring popular material that the Beatles and their parents had grown up listening to on radio, including "Stardust," "Home on the Range," "Ain't Misbehavin'," "Basin Street Blues," "On the Sunny Side of the Street," and "My Yiddishe Momme." McCartney perused the catalog with great glee, spotting favorite songs that he now owned (in partnership with James, Lennon, and Brian Epstein's heirs). James bragged to McCartney about the staggering revenue that would begin to flow from the publishing royalties for these songs, doing so right in front of Ringo Starr, who, like Harrison, owned a ridiculously small share of the publishing company, something to the tune of a half percent (as opposed to Lennon and McCartney's twenty percent apiece). Starr was a good sport about it, but his face betrays a confusion of emotions and embarrassment.

Overhearing the news about the purchase of the Lawrence Wright catalog, Michael Lindsay-Hogg says to James, "You bought it. Oh, great." James corrects Lindsay-Hogg, specifying that the purchaser was not himself but Northern Songs, "which includes Paul and John and . . ." Before James has a chance to stick his foot in his mouth by mentioning George and Ringo's minuscule shares in the company, McCartney takes exception to James, replying, "Just about," in reference to his and John's share of ownership. James, somewhat miffed and unable to suppress his annoyance at the resurfacing of a long-standing rift between him and the group, who resented James's fifty-percent share of their publishing royalties, says to Paul, "What are you talking about, 'Just about'?" To which Paul replies, "Nothing. Uh, no comment." But James refuses to let it go, saying, "Very substantially, sir," referring again to Paul's and John's ownership share. No doubt from James's point of view, Lennon and McCartney's share *was* substantial, as measured by music industry standards at the time he signed the publishing deal with the Beatles in February 1963. If there was any argument at Twickenham that morning, it was this testy exchange between McCartney and James. And indeed, just a little over two months after this conversation, James will secretly sell his fifty-percent share in Northern Songs to Associated Television, or ATV, without even giving Lennon and McCartney the chance to purchase his shares. Harrison has arrived at the tail end of this conversation, and when Starr asks him if he wants to look at the catalog of which he owns a half percent, Harrison offers an abrupt "no" and walks away. Clearly the last thing Harrison needed right then was to have it rubbed in his face how low he ranked in the Beatles inner circle in terms of his financial earnings.

If he was already harboring resentment over not getting the group to take his songs seriously enough to record and release, which in and of itself limited his income, this unfortunate encounter illustrating Harrison's "economy class" status in the Beatles on this fateful morning merely fanned those flames, coming on top of whatever was bothering him before he even arrived at the studio, which may have had nothing to do with Beatles. Harrison's emotional state could have been the result of problems back home. Eric Clapton had recently split with his French girlfriend, Charlotte Martin, after which George's wife Pattie invited her to stay with the Harrisons at Kinfauns. Martin turned Pattie's hospitable offer of lodging into an opportunity to move in on more than just her home. When Pattie caught onto the subterfuge, she left Kinfauns to stay with friends in London, where she remained for six days. George finally called her on Thursday, January 9, to tell her that Martin was gone and to plead with her to return home. If this drama had played itself out overnight while January 9 turned into January 10, it is no wonder that Harrison was not in the best of spirits when he arrived at Twickenham that morning. Perhaps his leaving the session early was in part owing to his eagerness to get back home to begin the reconciliation process with his wife.

All the attention over the years has been focused on the events of Monday, January 6—the dressing down of George by Paul over a guitar part—and

Friday, January 10, when George says, "I'm leaving the band now." Less attention is paid to an exchange that takes place on Tuesday, January 7. It is important to keep in mind that this comes a day after the tense conversation between Paul and George, although as we have noted, in the fuller context that was revealed in *Get Back*, McCartney seems more frustrated with the situation and his own role than with Harrison himself. The next day, however, talk among the musicians reveals the depths of the black cloud hovering over the group. George muses, "Ever since Mr. Epstein passed away . . . ," to which John snaps back, "Who passed away?" before allowing George to complete his thought, "it's never been the same." In one of several bantering sessions exploring just what is happening in Twickenham and why the four musicians are finding it difficult to work together in a focused manner, George says, "The Beatles have been in doldrums for at least a year," presumably a reference to the difficulty the band had in getting together and working cooperatively on the recording sessions for *The Beatles,* which by all accounts were even more acrimonious and divided than what went down at Twickenham in January 1969. Then, ominously, George says, "I think we should have a divorce." To which Paul immediately replies, "Well, I said that at the last meeting. But it's getting near it." John tries to lighten the mood by asking, "Who'd have the children?" to which Paul replies "Dick James," a quick-witted reference to the publisher's majority ownership of the Beatles songs, three days before James would drop by for his ill-fated visit.

Filmmaker Michael Lindsay-Hogg was one of the few people always in the room that fateful week and for the duration of the remaining month of filming. Lindsay-Hogg told me there was no fight or crisis that took place on Friday, January 10, that might explain Harrison's impulsive decision to leave. "It was cumulative," says Lindsay-Hogg. "I think George was frustrated and felt undervalued by Paul and John. And why it was that morning . . . ? Maybe he hadn't slept well, that this was chewing at him."

Having worked with the Beatles since 1966, directing music videos (what were then called "promo films") for songs including "Paperback Writer," "Rain," "Hey Jude," and "Revolution," Lindsay-Hogg gained a sense of where Harrison fit in the group in the minds of Lennon and McCartney and the humiliation he suffered over having his songs dismissed or treated as a second-tier material.

Says Lindsay-Hogg,

George, I think, knew that he was a songwriter. And that what was in him were songs as they turned out to be, as wonderful as they were. But he couldn't get much traction with Lennon and McCartney. Because if there was going to be an album, if there were twelve tracks, there'd be ten Lennon/McCartney tracks, one Harrisong, and one for Ringo. And when George would offer songs, it was kind of like, "Yeah they're nice, they're good, they're fine." And then they'd go back to what they were doing. And there's the thing which opens in *Let It Be* part two, where George is playing "Something," and he's kind of auditioning for them. You see a look in his eyes that says, "I hope you like it." And they do, but they don't give him the . . . we used to call it in the mafia world, "the respect that he deserved."

I genuinely saw what I think was his frustration. It would be artistic frustration, it would be frustration to do with his friends, and it also probably to a degree would be financial frustration. Not that they all weren't rich, except that they were going through money like a knife through butter. But if there are twelve tracks on an album and ten of them go to Lennon and McCartney and there's only one to George, then he only gets one-twelfth of the album.

As we have seen, the deal for George was even worse than that while his compositions were being published by Northern Songs, given Lennon and McCartney's significant ownership stake in the company. John and Paul would wind up earning more income on a Harrison song than Harrison himself. The situation was finally amended in 1968, beginning with his contributions to *The Beatles*, when Harrison escaped the clutches of Northern Songs and began publishing his songs with his own company, Harrisongs. The switch came just in the nick of time for George, as 1969's *Abbey Road* contained his two greatest Beatles hits, "Something" and "Here Comes the Sun," which were published by Harrisongs, thereby insuring him a steady flow of royalty income from the Beatles versions as well as the cover versions of the songs, which numbered well over one hundred.

George Harrison was not the first member of the Beatles to leave a recording studio in the middle of a session. As we have already seen, in June 1966, a frustrated Paul McCartney walked out during the recording of "She Said She Said" in a huff over the song's arrangement, which had been worked out beforehand by Lennon and Harrison. A demoralized Ringo Starr "quit" the Beatles in August 1968 for nearly two weeks during the sessions for the White Album, taking his family on holiday in the Mediterranean. Before recording began for *Let It Be*, John Lennon had already begun working on non-Beatles projects with Yoko Ono; their debut recording was released in November 1968—the same month as *The Beatles*. And, as captured in *Get Back*, Paul acknowledged that he himself thinks breaking up the band may be the best thing to do. By the time George walked out of Twickenham declaring that he was leaving the group, quitting the Beatles was practically just another day in the life of the Fab Four.

But George Harrison did not quit the Beatles. He just *said* he did. After a few days off to cool his jets, reconnect with his wife, and visit his parents in Liverpool, a stretch of time during which the foursome met at least twice at John Lennon's house to discuss the situation, George and his bandmates came to a new agreement about how to proceed. Mostly, his bandmates conceded to George's wishes: that they leave the cavernous Twickenham film soundstage in favor of the more amenable environs of the recording studio at Apple headquarters, that they cease talk of staging a concert at ancient ruins in Libya, and that they consider dropping the idea of a live concert altogether. George had called their bluff, and for the most part he got his way, proving, at least existentially, that he did not really want to quit the band after all. Much to his own dismay and after insistent protesting—"I don't want to go on the roof, you know"—he finally went along with the group's plan to stage a surprise concert on the rooftop of Apple headquarters.

"In those days, going up to the roof was mainly workmen going up to the roof to repair the boarding or whatever it was," says Lindsay-Hogg.

> But it was the six of us, me, the four of them, and Yoko, and I realized that things were not secure. Ringo said it's cold out there, which it was. He was thinking of the guitar players, I think, because of their fingers. And George said what's the point? Why do we want to go up there? Why do we want to do a performance? Why do [we] want to go up there and do some songs we haven't rehearsed that much on a cold day? And so that was kind of two votes against it. And then McCartney said come on, we really have to do it. We are a performing group, at least we used to be, and we're really good at that, let's go do it. That's what he wanted to do, and he's pretty tough when he wants to do something. But the others were . . . Ringo was going to go, but George really didn't want to go. There was a silence, and then John said, "Fuck it, let's do it." That was the vote, so we went up and did it. And then of course, they loved it. Once they started playing, the four of them together, including George, it was like they were kids back in Germany.

History may refer to a time when Harrison "quit the Beatles," but as we have seen, that incident has been unfairly blown up into the level of myth. The first musician to quit the Beatles was John Lennon, who did so the following September, albeit in a hush-hush manner that was not publicized outside the Beatles' inner circle. Lennon proved he had quit when he failed to show up for what would become the final official Beatles recording session the following January, when the group met to record overdubs for Harrison's song "I Me Mine," for inclusion on the *Let It Be* album. A few months later, on April 9, 1970, a second member of the group quit the band, when—taking the opportunity of the release of his debut solo album, *McCartney*—Paul issued a public statement that he no longer intended to work with the Beatles. On the final day of the year, McCartney filed a lawsuit against his three bandmates to dissolve their contractual bonds.

The fact is George Harrison, as unhappy as he was in the Beatles, stuck it out until the very end. George Harrison, as it turns out, never quit the band. The band quit him.

17
Standard Time

Frank Sinatra famously incorporated the Beatles' "Something" into his concert set list in the 1970s, when he would introduce it as "the greatest love song of the past fifty years." In an attempt to connect with younger listeners or to advance his hipness credibility to the rock generation, Sinatra would also call it his "favorite Lennon and McCartney song." It was a fumbled attempt, however, leaving him exposed as clueless if not something of a fraud, attributing the authorship of one of the Beatles' greatest hits to the wrong songwriter. (Sinatra finally corrected this mistake, beginning in 1978.)

George Harrison's "Something" has become as much a pop standard as any song of the second half of the twentieth century. Indeed, within a few years of its initial release on *Abbey Road* in 1969, renditions of the tune were being recorded by artists who primarily were known for their treatment of pre-rock "standards," artists such as Sinatra, Shirley Bassey, Tony Bennett, and Liberace. Popular artists, including Joe Cocker, Elvis Presley, and Ray Charles, best known for recording songs by other writers also added the song to their recording and performing repertoire. It must have pleased Harrison no end to hear a version recorded by Smokey Robinson, his longtime singing idol. Harrison also loved how James Brown turned "Something" into one of his patented funk numbers.

"Something" was a relatively long time in the making. Harrison began writing it on piano in fall 1968, during sessions for *The Beatles*, and recorded an early solo demo that September, well before he had come anywhere close to completing the lyrics. As seen in the *Get Back* documentary film, Harrison brought the song to the group in January 1969, still unfinished, and expressing frustration at his inability to come up with an object for the simile in the second phrase. Lennon jokingly suggests "a cauliflower" as a placeholder, prompting Harrison to reply with "a pomegranate"—much more romantic—for that duty. The band attempts a couple of run-throughs, during which Harrison suggests to McCartney the bassline he has in mind—McCartney does *not* reply to Harrison that he will play whatever George wants him to play or that he'll play whatever will please George—and Harrison emphasizes the song's melody and chords so the musicians can work out their parts. The run-throughs go by pretty quickly, with McCartney and Lennon providing busy and ultimately extraneous backup vocals, before Lennon redirects the group back to "the rock show." That ended rehearsals for "Something" as a potential song for the projected *Get Back* album, although it would soon resurface when the group returned to the studio to begin recording their next album.

On his twenty-sixth birthday the following month, with the final lyrics completed, Harrison recorded a new demo version of "Something," along with versions of "All Things Must Pass" and "Old Brown Shoe." With no immediate outlet for the song, Harrison began brainstorming to whom he might offer the new tune. While he wrote the number with Ray Charles and Shirley Bassey in mind, he was concurrently producing the debut album for fellow Liverpudlian Jackie Lomax, to be released by Apple, and he first considered giving it to Lomax. Harrison also approached Joe Cocker, whose vocal style was partly based on Ray Charles's, and who the previous year had enjoyed a number-one hit in the United Kingdom with a version of the Beatles' "With a Little Help from My Friends." Cocker indeed wound up recording "Something" for his second album, *Joe Cocker!*, which was released the following November, several weeks after the song made its public debut as the lead-off track on side two of the Beatles' final studio recording, *Abbey Road*.

In the meantime, the Beatles returned to the recording studio in May 1969, and as a group laid down basic tracks for the number, with overdubs—including Harrison's vocals and orchestral backup arranged by George Martin—being added in July and August. It slowly dawned on Martin and George's bandmates that in its fully realized form, "Something" was a terrific song, Harrison's crowning achievement in the Beatles, the first song they judged worthy of being issued as the A-side of a single (up until then, Harrison could only hope for his songs to appear as B-sides)—albeit one that would share A-side status with John Lennon's "Come Together." The song merited acclaim as Harrison's first Beatles song to climb to number one, over time becoming the second most covered Beatles tune behind Paul McCartney's "Yesterday." Eventually, in the digital music era, "Something" gained status as one of the most streamed songs by the Beatles, surpassed only by Harrison's other *Abbey Road* contribution, "Here Comes the Sun."

"Something" is generally regarded as a love song. Pattie Harrison claimed that George told her he wrote it for her, although late in his foreshortened life he denied this. Some, including Harrison at times, have suggested it is a love song to God, to Krishna. In either case, if it *is* a love song, it is, in typical Harrisonian fashion, one that is wracked by ambiguity and ambivalence.

Three of the most powerful phrases in the song are negatives: the singer does *not* want, he does *not* need, and he does *not* know. This is hardly the stuff of greeting-card romance. If anything, the sensibility recalls "If I Needed Someone," that earlier Harrison-penned love song betrayed at every step by the conditional mode, beginning with the very word "if." Why does the singer even bring up the possibility of leaving the object of his love? Is that supposed to be some kind of measure of devotion? When my wife comes home from work tonight, instead of telling her I love her, should I tell her I don't want to leave her? And if I did, how would that be received? One wonders why Pattie Harrison would be so eager to claim herself as the object of this curious song that, while passionate in its presentation, expresses so much uncertainty about the narrator's deep-seated emotions.

If the singer is so sure of his love—which, if we are to take him at his word, he apparently is not—why would he be reluctant to say that every day his love grows stronger, instead claiming ignorance or unwillingness or an inability to even address the question? And why does he lapse into the conditional voice when he suggests that we just hang out and see how and if his love grows? The best he can muster is that it "may" show, which implies that it may not. And what's this about us asking him in the first place? Who's asking? I didn't ask; did you? What kind of protestation of love is contingent on time? Doesn't saying that he does not want to leave her now imply that he might want to in the future? His feelings—the song's narrator's feelings—are hard to pin down.

In the end, this is no criticism of the song as love song. It is no criticism, period. What I am merely pointing out here is that Harrison at his best defies cliché or easy summary. Nevertheless, even when he raises more questions than he answers, his words—aided and abetted by music that underlines and emphasizes his emotional ambivalence—still convey deep, rich emotion. Grown-up emotion. Emotion that is fully open and honest, emotion that bears the deepest questions and uncertainties of our lives and beings. In other words, how brilliant is it to write a love song that, while fully gorgeous, romantic, and sensual, admits to the ultimate inability of us to know anything definitive about anyone, including ourselves, or even God.

Despite all this, there's something about "Something" that has captured generations of singers and listeners alike. Something that works, perhaps, on a subconscious level. Even the title suggests that it is less a statement and more a question. "Something" is something you cannot put a name to. And the many "somethings" in the song resist definition. Do people like questions better than answers? Even when it comes to love? I don't think so. We want certainty in our love. We want a meaningful pledge of lifelong faithfulness and commitment. We do not want something or other. We do not want to hear a confession of conflicted emotions or a protestation of confused love. We want to be able to hang our love on something real, something tangible, something reliable. Even Frank Sinatra noted in his introduction to the song in concert that, despite its being one of the greatest love songs "in fifty or one-hundred years," it never actually says "I love you."

Maybe that is exactly where the genius of the song lies. Maybe it is in the realization that we can never truly know how another person feels. Maybe it is in the acknowledgment that one cannot pinpoint just what it is that makes one love another. Love is beyond reason. It is elusive. It can be here one day and gone the next. I do not know if this is what Harrison meant when he wrote these lyrics. After all, he could not even say in song what it is that attracts him to the object of his affection. Before finalizing the lyrics to the song, Harrison likened her to a pomegranate. Fortunately, he eventually came up with something a little better, albeit something of a negative. There is something about her that attracts him in way that no other lover does. But even that falls short of the ultimate romantic promise. Define this "something." He cannot.

At least he cannot in words. But Harrison's guitar playing on "Something" speaks with equal or greater eloquence than the song's lyrics. After an opening drum roll, the first sound we hear is Harrison's six-note ascending hook, which defines and which recurs throughout the song, ending the song in the same manner it introduced it. The climbing phrase, played with a fluidity that anticipates Harrison's adoption of slide-guitar technique in the next year and for all the years following, gives the number its aspirational, searching feeling. His free-floating blanket of oscillating rhythm guitar lends a dreamy quality to the proceedings—as does George Martin's string arrangement—well suited to the song's meandering, investigative tone. Harrison is economical with his lead fills, using them as punctuation or as a musical reply or comment to a lyrical phrase. As Berklee guitar teacher Lauren Passarelli puts it, "No one has a touch like George did on guitar. Smooth, clean, and expressive. George played the perfect notes at the perfect time creating signature guitar parts that became intrinsic to the song and part of the composition. Very few players have ever done that as well."

After the second verse, George slightly alters the guitar hook, using it to modulate into the bridge, with its heightened vibe, as the singer cannot pin down this "something" of which he sings. The drums roll more loudly and more insistently, the strings grow more aggressive, and Harrison's delicate vocals give way to frustration verging on anger. Descending from the bridge, George's lead guitar takes over, trying to express in his instrumental solo what he is failing to nail down with his words. The first half of his solo sounds like a search mission, trying out several possibilities before zeroing in on a few notes that could offer the elusive resolve that the song and its music seek. Harrison's solo in "Something" is always included in lists of the greatest guitar solos of all time; his playing reaches a peak here, becoming just as important as the lyrics in its expression of longing. Gary Lucas told me that Harrison "invented a mode of creative slide guitar playing beginning on 'Something,' which stands out to this day as original and groundbreaking in its eschewing all blues cliches."

Shirley Bassey would indeed wind up recording "Something," making it the title track of her 1970 album; her single version of the song went to number four on the UK charts and powered a career comeback that would see her release fifteen albums in the 1970s alone. Other artists to record and perform the song have included Andy Williams, Lena Horne, Eric Clapton, Ike & Tina Turner, Isaac Hayes, Julio Iglesias, and the neo-hippie jam band Phish. Because of previously booked engagements, Bob Dylan was unable to take part in the Concert for George tribute in London on the first-year anniversary of Harrison's death, but on November 13, 2002, in recognition of the upcoming anniversary and tribute concert, he performed a sweet, heartwarming rendition of the number at New York City's Madison Square Garden, where the two had previously duetted several times, including at the Concert for Bangladesh and at the Bob Dylan 30th Anniversary Concert. Dylan sang "Something" again in concert when performing in Harrison's hometown of Liverpool on May 1, 2009. And in the years since Harrison died, Paul McCartney has regularly included "Something" in his concerts, playing a solo rendition on ukulele in tribute to his former bandmate.

One final note about "Something": the song's most descriptive, eloquent lyric comes at the end of the third line, a brilliant piece of writing that, while hardly even a real word, is a delicious and sexy pun owing entirely to the way George delivers it. On the page, it says there is something about how his lover woos him, in the sense of how she seeks his affection. But in Harrison's phrasing of the word "woo," the manner in which he stretches it out across two syllables—she doesn't just woo him, she "woo-oos" him—he almost bends and breaks the word beyond recognition, transforming its literal meaning to become a playful, onomatopoetic euphemism for sex.

Neither Frank Sinatra nor Shirley Bassey appears to have picked up on this; in their renditions of the tune, they sing the word "woo" as it appears on a lyric sheet. At least in this case, Harrison demonstrates his superior command of the art of vocal expression with the deftness, control, and intelligence of the greatest jazz singers.

Photo 1 A pre-teen George Harrison already finding his way up the guitar neck.

Michael Ochs Archives/Getty Images

Photo 2 The Beatles performing at Liverpool's Cavern Club in February 1961. (L-R) George Harrison, Paul McCartney, Pete Best, John Lennon.

Michael Ochs Archives/Getty Images

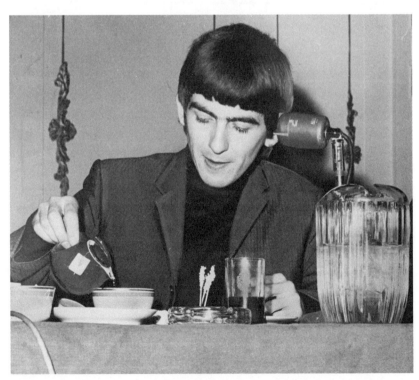

Photo 3 George Harrison enjoying tea time in New York City in February 1964.

New York Daily News Archive/Getty Images

Photo 4 George Harrison improvising a few dance steps during the shooting of the Beatles' first full-length film, *A Hard Day's Night*, in early 1964, as Ringo Starr (L), John Lennon (R), and members of the cast look on.

Bettman/Getty Images

Photo 5 George Harrison and Patti Boyd, on New Year's Day, 1966, just a few weeks before they would be wed.

Hulton Deutsch/Corbis Historial/Getty Images

Photo 6 A concerned-looking George Harrison onstage with the Beatles in Essen, Germany, in June 1966.

Photo 7 Bob Dylan and George Harrison performing together at the Concert for Bangladesh in Madison Square Garden, New York City, on August 1, 1971.

Photo 8 U.S. President Gerald Ford receives a White House visit from Billy Preston, George Harrison, and Ravi Shankar in December 1974, on a break from their cross-country "Dark Horse" tour.

Photo 9 George Harrison with his friend and mentor, Indian sitar virtuoso Ravi Shankar, in early 1975.

Michael Ochs Archives/Getty Images

Photo 10 George Harrison wryly commenting on fame in a publicity still from 1986.

Aaron Rapoport/Corbis Historical/Getty Images

18
That Ice Is Slowly Melting

Winter 1969 was especially cold and dark and seemed to linger on well past the time by which it should have taken its leave. So, when George Harrison woke up one day in April to parting clouds, it was no surprise that he played hooky from yet another series of interminable meetings with lawyers and accountants at Apple headquarters, amid the rancorous aftermath of the *Get Back* sessions and the wrangling over the direction of Apple Corps under their new, controversial business manager, Allen Klein. Instead of driving to London, he headed to Eric Clapton's place. He just needed to get away from it all, and for one afternoon, he found a way to do so.

From the evidence of what Harrison brought home with him after spending the day incommunicado, enjoying the hint of warmth in the air in Clapton's garden, playing hooky was just the tonic Harrison needed. The two friends walked and talked, and at some point, Harrison picked up one of Clapton's acoustic guitars and started strumming a new melody, working out a finger-picking pattern and a notion of a new song's lyrics, inspired by the change of seasons and the promise implied by the incipient spring season in the air. Sun, sun, sun—here it comes.

Harrison continued working on the song, fine-tuning the music and lyrics while on holiday in Sardinia in June. The Fab Four had not wasted much time after that fateful January that saw them jamming, writing songs together, arguing about how to approach the making of the album or film or TV show or all three that they were ostensibly working on with director Michael Lindsay-Hogg, with its culmination being the legendary guerrilla performance on the rooftop of Apple headquarters. They were back in the studio just a few weeks later, beginning sporadic recording sessions for their next real studio album. They did a bit of work in April and May and threw themselves into the project in a committed manner in the summer, until *Abbey Road* was completed by the end of August, just in time for a planned September release—their first proper album since *The Beatles* was released in late November the previous year.

Harrison's song, like so many he wrote and would continue to write, was structured around a duality. It spoke of the relief that comes with the change of seasons after a long, cold, lonely winter. It spoke of the renewed sense of possibility and rebirth that is the promise of spring. At its most basic level, it was simply a song about warmth replacing chill and light replacing darkness.

But it was also so much more than that. Consciously or otherwise, Harrison was channeling his own emotional turmoil into the song, grasping at hope and better times, a way out of the dark, depressive tenor of the relationships, business and otherwise, among the Fab Four. And always one step ahead of the zeitgeist—indeed, along with his bandmates, a veritable weathervane of the zeitgeist—Harrison could well have been writing an epitaph for the failed promise of the sociocultural revolution of the 1960s, albeit one disguised in the form of an ode to sunshine and renewal. It was a rare bit of sunny optimism from the dour Beatle. And in the streaming era, it would become the most popular of all Beatles songs, played at least twice as often as "Let It Be," "Yesterday," "Hey Jude," and "I Want to Hold Your Hand." How perfect that his crowning achievement as a Beatles songwriter would be the final song he would bring to the group.

One of the abundant elements that made "Here Comes the Sun" such a perfect recording was the evocative use of the Moog synthesizer. Many listeners may be surprised to learn that the Moog was even used on the track; at the time, the synthesizer was virtually unknown to the masses of pop music fans. Credit Harrison for the pitch-perfect arrangement of the Moog, used as much to create mood and ambiance while drawing little to no attention to itself. Its purpose in the recording was to approximate that of orchestral backing—which in itself was also employed in the creation of the final mix, courtesy of George Martin.

The employment of the Moog on "Here Comes the Sun" was not the very first time the instrument was used on a rock song, but Harrison was an early adopter after becoming acquainted with the new synthesizer while he was recording his experimental solo album, *Electronic Sound*, and then while he was producing an album by Jackie Lomax in Los Angeles for Apple Records. Up until that point, use of the Moog required hiring a duo of artist-engineers who would temporarily install the hefty, complex, one-of-a-kind machine in a recording studio and oversee its use. Harrison insisted on purchasing one of his own, which meant a custom model had to be built for him, transported from Los Angeles to London, and set up at his home studio, where he could experiment with it and learn its capabilities on his own time. Eventually, Harrison had it moved to the studios at EMI, where it served to add new, bright colors to what would become the Beatles' final studio album, *Abbey Road*. While the public was to remain mostly in the dark about its use on the album, the Beatles' fellow musicians realized that there was a new, versatile instrument that could expand their sonic palette exponentially. In just a short time the synthesizer—Moog and other models—became an essential part of rock music's recording and touring toolbox. "Progressive rock" artists such as Rick Wakeman, Emerson, Lake and Palmer, and electro-rock pioneers Kraftwerk built their entire sounds on the backbone of synthesizers; others, like Stevie Wonder and Cat Stevens, employed synthesizers as tools to fill out and color their already well-established musical aesthetic.

The track was masterfully produced, largely by Harrison himself, but with significant contributions by George Martin. It opens modestly and quietly with one of the most famous, recognizable acoustic-guitar figures in all of recorded history, a fingerpicked riff played high on the neck (with a capo on the seventh fret). Within a few bars of the opening, a countermelody played on synthesizer would join the guitar, and at the end of a phrase, the synth note would swoop down an octave, before Harrison began the song proper with his vocals. After the opening refrain, the full-band arrangement kicks in with bass and drums, harmony vocals (overdubbed by George and Paul), and orchestral backup. While the overall song may have come out sounding like a simple upbeat, mid-tempo folk rocker, it was in fact a complex composition, featuring at least three different time signatures varying the rhythmic patterns, which were inspired by Hindustani music. The *teentaal*, or eight-beat cycle, alternated with the *jaaptaal*, a ten-beat cycle divided 3-3-2-2, corresponding to the lyric, "Sun, sun, sun, here it comes." It was the kind of thing that Harrison had fully absorbed in his years of studying Indian music, so it came quite naturally to him. Ringo Starr initially viewed the rhythmic complexity as a challenge, once telling an interviewer, "George said, 'Hey, Ringo, I've got this song, it's in $\frac{7}{4}$ time.' I said, 'What are you telling me for? I'm $\frac{4}{4}$ or $\frac{3}{4}$, you know that.' He had gotten a bit Indian on me."[1] The addition of handclaps to the track also proved challenging to the ensemble. Yet somehow, it all came together in the end, and, while never a hit single (it was not released as a single), "Here Comes the Sun" became the most streamed Beatles song of all time. A Harrisong.

19
The Declaration of Independence

Could George Harrison have chosen a better title for his debut solo album than *All Things Must Pass*?

The album title came from the song of the same name, which Harrison began writing while the Beatles were still together. He presented the song for the group's consideration during the January 1969 *Get Back* recording sessions, and they rehearsed the track and worked on the arrangement. Harrison's instruction to them was to make the song "Band-y," a reference to the Canadian-American rock group The Band, with whom Harrison had spent time in Woodstock, New York, the previous autumn. Given that the Beatles had yet to break up, Harrison may not have originally intended the song to refer to the end of the Fab Four. But when the song finally surfaced—first in a slightly schmaltzy gospel-infused soul ballad version by Billy Preston called "All Things (Must) Pass" on his Harrison-produced *Encouraging Words* album, released on September 11, 1970, soon followed by Harrison's version the following November—the context had changed. Given its title and its position as the title track of the album, the song was forever destined to be linked to the breakup of the Beatles. (A similar thing happened to the Paul McCartney song "Let It Be," also recorded during the *Get Back* sessions, but already introduced to the group during the sessions for the White Album in September 1968. By the time "Let It Be" was released by the Beatles on the album of the same name—the group's final release—it took on the weight of an epitaph for the group.)

Likewise, by the time the world tuned into "All Things Must Pass" on *All Things Must Pass,* the title, as well as the song, accrued layers of meaning that Harrison could not have consciously intended when first writing the song. On the surface level, there is the Hindu-influenced idea of the contingency of human existence, which could be mistaken for fatalism, but which was tempered with Zen-like acceptance of the human condition. In the context of the other songs on the album, many of which addressed the same or similar themes—"Art of Dying," "Isn't It a Pity," "My Sweet Lord"—the song's philosophical inclinations are preeminent. But in the greater context of this being Harrison's first post-Beatles solo album, there is no way one cannot also read it as a statement about the inevitability of change, in this case specifically about the breakup of the Beatles, and more generally about the temporal aspects of all human efforts.

Harrison's choice of title gains further import when compared to the innocuous or egocentric titles of his former bandmates' debut solo efforts: John Lennon's *John Lennon/Plastic Ono Band*, Ringo Starr's *Sentimental Journey,* and Paul McCartney's aptly titled *McCartney* (an album title he would use twice more, with the addition of a "II" or "III"). While Lennon and McCartney's use of their names as titles for their debut albums could be seen as subtle statements of post-Beatles individualism (although Starr appeared on both Harrison's and Lennon's debut efforts), Harrison's is nothing less than a wholesale declaration of independence. And by opening his first post-Beatles album with a song cowritten by Bob Dylan, on an album musically influenced by Dylan and especially by his "backup group," The Band, Harrison telegraphed his newfound affinities—musical or otherwise.

From the moment George Harrison's *All Things Must Pass* was released in November 1970, it was more than just a record album—and a triple LP at that. It was not the first solo album released by a member of the Beatles: technically, it was Harrison's third, although the previous two—*Wonderwall Music* and *Electronic Sound*—were experimental, mostly instrumental albums. And preceding it were debut solo releases by Ringo Starr (first out of the gate) and Paul McCartney, with John Lennon's *Plastic Ono Band* getting in just under the wire with a December release, a few weeks after Harrison's.

Whatever Harrison's intentions were in titling his album *All Things Must Pass*, there was no getting around the fact that the Beatles, as a performing and recording outfit, were done. And in no small part, Harrison's album addressed this passing phenomenon from many angles. *All Things Must Pass* was to a considerable extent a concept album deeply informed by Eastern beliefs about death and dying. This was not your typical rock 'n' roll fare, although fellow rock prophets Bob Dylan and Leonard Cohen would go on to address mortality in various projects throughout the coming decades. (Aside from his many death-oriented songs, Cohen would narrate a documentary film about the Tibetan Book of the Dead.) While the lyrics on *All Things Must Pass* are infused with Hindu beliefs about meditation and chanting and reincarnation and the like, there are surprisingly no overtly Indian touches to the music. There's not a sitar nor a tabla to be heard, and nary a raga-based melody.

All Things Must Pass was also exhibit A in making the case that Harrison had been stifled as a songwriter in the Beatles, having mostly been confined to one or two tracks per album. Many of the songs on *All Things Must Pass* had been written for the group's consideration but were ultimately consigned by

Lennon and McCartney to the reject pile. Harrison had the last laugh when the band's final studio album, *Abbey Road,* spawned two of the group's all-time biggest hits, "Something" and "Here Comes the Sun." When it came time to record his first solo album, Harrison had dozens of songs from that reject pile to draw upon, songs that included "Isn't It a Pity," "Hear Me Lord," "Let It Down," and the title track. Other songs turned down by the Beatles would surface on subsequent Harrison solo albums. Even the *All Things Must Pass* cover photo was a sly commentary on the fate of the Fab Four, with Harrison seated on a stool in a field surrounded by four reclining garden gnomes, as if they had quit their day jobs. (What exactly *is* a gnome's day job?) Or as English singer-songwriter John Wesley Harding, aka author Wesley Stace, put it to me, "*All Things Must Pass* was the explosion of the repressed . . . with the vulnerable voice above the massive sound."

Harrison's choice of the Bob Dylan cowrite "I'd Have You Anytime" as the lead-off track was a shot fired across the bow, announcing right off the bat his alliance with the only other rock artist who could vie with the Beatles for artistic primacy. That the album also included a cover of Dylan's brand-new song, "If Not for You," only underlined his allegiance to a new friend and creative partner, a friendship and collaboration that would continue for decades, through the Concert for Bangladesh, the Traveling Wilburys, and beyond. Opening the album with a Dylan cowrite also connected *All Things Must Pass* to its influential predecessor and musical role model, The Band's 1968 debut album, *Music from Big Pink,* which led off with "Tears of Rage," credited to Dylan and The Band's pianist and co-vocalist, Richard Manuel.

When people talk about The Band's influence on the sprawling *All Things Must Pass* album, they are not referring to the hit single "My Sweet Lord" or the bombastic Phil Spector Wall of Sound productions, such as "What Is Life." Rather, songs like the title track and "Run of the Mill" are the ones that stand out the most as musical homages to The Band's rootsy, easygoing feel. On "Run of the Mill," Jim Gordon does a near-perfect imitation of Levon Helm's idiosyncratic drumming style; Bobby Whitlock's harmonium drone echoes Garth Hudson's organ; and Gary Wright's effervescent acoustic piano recalls that of Richard Manuel.

Harrison was not the only Beatle influenced by The Band in the wake of *Music from Big Pink,* which was released on July 1, 1968. In a semi-live version of "Hey Jude" (the vocals were performed live atop the recorded instrumental track), filmed in a studio before a live audience by Michael Lindsay-Hogg as a promotional video on September 4, 1968, Paul McCartney quotes "The Weight" by The Band at the six-minute and twenty-four-second mark, when you can hear him improvise the lyrics "Take a load off Annie . . . Take a load off

Annie . . . and put it back on me," (mis)quoting lyrics from one of The Band's best-known songs, "The Weight." Paul's second solo album, *Ram,* released in May 1971, reflected the back-to-the-roots aesthetic that underpinned much of The Band's music, although McCartney himself was living a version of this by moving to a sheep farm in Scotland.

Harrison was by no means turning his back on his former bandmates. Ringo Starr can be heard gleefully drumming throughout *All Things Must Pass,* and Harrison would go on to lend his guitar to subsequent solo efforts by Lennon and Starr. He would play a significant role in insuring that Ringo would have a thriving solo career, producing sessions for him and writing some of his biggest hits, including "Photograph" and "It Don't Come Easy," which was credited solely to Starr but is generally understand to have been written primarily by Harrison (the guitar hook alone echoes that of "Here Comes the Sun"). The album's main bassist was Klaus Voormann, who had been in the Beatles inner circle since meeting them during their first residency in Hamburg in 1960. He followed them back to London and roomed with Harrison and Starr for a time, and, given his omnipresence on early-1970s solo albums by Harrison, Starr, and Lennon, was even rumored to be a replacement for McCartney in a possible reunion or offshoot group that would have potentially also featured occasional Beatles sideman Billy Preston, who is also heard playing keyboards throughout *All Things Must Pass.*

While the cycle of birth and death and the inevitability of change were themes running throughout the songs on *All Things Must Pass,* the album was more than merely a plunge into darkness (which Harrison warned against on "Beware of Darkness") and gloom. Harrison devoted a song, "Apple Scruffs," to the (mostly) female Beatles fans who used to loiter outside the offices of Apple Corps and recording studios used by the Beatles, hoping to catch a glimpse (or more) of the Fab Four. He recorded a novelty ditty, "It's Johnny's Birthday," sung to the tune of Cliff Richard's 1968 hit "Congratulations" on the occasion of Lennon's thirtieth birthday. "Ballad of Sir Frankie Crisp (Let It Roll)," best known via its parenthetical subtitle, was a tribute to the nineteenth-century lawyer who built the castle-like Friar Park in Henley-on-Thames that Harrison bought in early 1970. The love song to his new home is peppered with faux-antiquated phrases like "Find me where ye echo lays," "Through ye woode, here may ye rest awhile," and "the fountain of perpetual mirth," lifted from signs the eccentric Crisp had posted around the house and property.

Phil Spector's big, mushy Wall of Sound powered multiple pop hits throughout the 1960s, especially what we call the "girl-group" records that the Beatles loved. This is why they turned to Spector when their regular producer,

George Martin, either was not available or when they were looking for a new sound. This is why both Lennon and Harrison engaged Spector's services on their early solo albums. Spector's production, however controversial it may have been in subsequent years, however much Harrison himself lamented the excesses of the layers of reverb and echo that nearly buried the details of the instruments and his vocals on much of *All Things Must Pass*, did not get in the way of many of these tunes (including Lennon's) becoming Top 10 hits, or having *Plastic Ono Band* and *All Things Must Pass* commonly considered among the greatest albums of the rock era.

On the other hand, *All Things Must Pass* sometimes gets a demerit for what seems like Spector's muddy, heavy-handed ways with the mixing board. A posthumous, fiftieth-anniversary remix of the album, overseen by George's son, Dhani Harrison, and released in 2021, did not set out to destroy the overall aesthetic that Spector and Harrison achieved; rather, it used state-of-the-art (as of 2020) digital technology to give a bit more "voice" to Harrison. Spector's impact on the original production may always have been overstated; during the *All Things Must Pass* sessions he was simultaneously working with John Lennon, and he was just generally a ghostly—one wants to say a *spectral*—presence in the recording studio when the tracks were being recorded. Rather than superseding the original album, the 2021 remix of *All Things Must Pass* helps a listener appreciate Harrison's accomplishment, while also—with its dozens of demos and outtakes and jams—opening a window on the creative process of making one of the greatest albums of all time, certainly the best solo album by a former Beatle and an album ranking with the best of the Beatles and Bob Dylan and The Band and Phil Spector, all of whose influence can be heard directly or indirectly on the way toward the creation of the unique sound that was George Harrison's.

Entire books have been written about the music that was released in 1970 and 1971, two years of remarkable, career-topping creativity not only by Harrison but also by many of his peers and colleagues. Albums in 1970 that vied for popularity alongside *All Things Must Pass* included Van Morrison's *Moondance*; Neil Young's *After the Gold Rush*; Miles Davis's *Bitches Brew*; Simon & Garfunkel's *Bridge over Troubled Water*, Joni Mitchell's *Ladies of the Canyon*, Crosby, Stills, Nash & Young's *Déjà Vu*; James Taylor's *Sweet Baby James*; Derek & the Dominos' *Layla and Other Assorted Love Songs* (in reality an Eric Clapton album)—and something by George's old group called *Let It Be*. The following year saw chart-toppers that included *Who's Next* by the Who, *Every Picture Tells a Story* by Rod Stewart, *Sticky Fingers* by the Rolling Stones, *Pearl* by Janis Joplin, *Abraxas* by Santana, *Tapestry* by Carole King, *Ram* by a singer-bassist named McCartney, and *Imagine* by some guy named

Lennon. The music made over the course of these two years was a summation of all that had gone on in the 1960s with a focus on the future, a promise of new, creative heights that never did come to fruition, as the 1970s saw musical styles and trends fracture—for better or worse—into a thousand subgenres, with no center holding it all together, as the Beatles had in the 1960s.

Released in late November 1970, *All Things Must Pass* crept to the top of the album charts in both the United Kingdom, where it spent eight weeks at number one, and in the United States, where it held the top post in Billboard's Hot 100 LP charts for seven weeks between January 2, 1971, and February 20. Curiously, this heavily Hindu-oriented album was knocked out of its perch by *Jesus Christ Superstar*, one of the original "rock operas," on February 27. The musical album, cowritten by Andrew Lloyd Webber and Tim Rice, and whose protagonist was not the title character but his closest friend (and ultimate betrayer), was reportedly inspired by Rice's obsession with the Bob Dylan song "With God on Our Side" and the phrase "You'll have to decide whether Judas Iscariot had God on his side." Thus was Dylan, still in a period of seclusion with only rare forays into the recording studio and even rarer appearances onstage, still exerting his influence over popular music in a manner comparable only to the Beatles.

20

Hare Krishna, Yeah Yeah Yeah

Imagine a number-one pop hit across the globe sung in significant part in Sanskrit and Hebrew and, for nearly a third of its playing time, consisting entirely of chanting the names of Hindu gods. A pop song that is essentially a prayer. A single that within weeks of its release in late fall 1970 had sold over a million copies and parked itself atop the US pop charts for four weeks—five weeks in the United Kingdom and nine and ten weeks in France and Germany, respectively. A single that would sell five million copies before the end of the decade and double that over the course of the next few decades; a song that would re-enter the pop charts, reaching number one again in the United Kingdom, in the month's following the singer's death in 2001.

On paper, "My Sweet Lord"—which also topped the charts in Ireland, Australia, the Netherlands, Norway, Switzerland, Australia, and New Zealand, and was the first number-one hit by a former Beatle in both the United States and the United Kingdom—was an unlikely candidate for the toppermost of the poppermost. A simple prayer of longing for the mystical experience of the Godhead, musically inspired by the Edwin Hawkins Singers' gospel rendition of an eighteenth-century Christian hymn, "Oh Happy Day," the song grabbed Western listeners with its refrain of "Hallelujah"—a Hebrew word common to Judaism and Christianity, meaning "praise God"—morphing into "Hare Krishna," a Sanskrit term with approximately the same meaning.

Yet somehow "My Sweet Lord" spoke loudly and vividly to millions of radio listeners at a time when songs in the Top 10 tended toward such lightweight fare as "Knock Three Times" by Tony Orlando and Dawn and "I Think I Love You" by the Partridge Family. "My Sweet Lord" displaced "Tears of a Clown" by Smokey Robinson and his group, the Miracles, at the top of the charts, which certainly must have meant a lot to George Harrison, to be in the same league as his beloved soul idol, to whom he repeatedly paid tribute in song and interviews over the years.

"My Sweet Lord" opens with an army of strumming acoustic guitars, slowly building to a full-fledged orchestral, rock 'n' roll Wall of Sound courtesy of the technique's original architect, producer Phil Spector. It also introduces what will soon become Harrison's trademark slide-guitar sound. "It's one of the greatest songs ever written," Wesley Stace says. "The strength of that sentiment and the wonderful arrangement and the strength of those acoustic guitars strumming so big, and the interlocking riffs, the way it grows . . . It never fails to bring tears to my eyes. That's the song that does it because that's the sound of a spiritual man's thoughts."

Harrison's unlikely megahit was a gentle manifesto, a mission statement of sorts, encapsulating in just a few lines the deep theology underpinning the album *All Things Must Pass* in a highly personal confessional. The song, powered by Harrison's plaintive vocals and the wailing of his slide guitar, is a nakedly direct plea for a mystical experience. "I really want to see you" is the concept that lies behind all mystical traditions, Eastern and Western alike. In the Hebrew Bible, Moses begs God for a glimpse of his countenance, to which God replies, "No man sees my face and lives." Christian mystics long practiced asceticism and meditation on the crucifixion as a path toward oneness with God. For Harrison, the longing for a glimpse of the Lord and to sit by God's side is the ultimate manifestation of Hindu devotion and the belief that a being's soul is reincarnated (*samsara*) many times—perhaps thousands of times (hence, "it takes so long my Lord")—before achieving perfection, or *moksha*, at which point reincarnation ceases and the soul merges with the divinity. As American singer-songwriter Sarah Beth Driver told me, "I wouldn't call myself a religious person, but listening to certain George songs is like church for me. . . . No one else wrote a prayer and put it in a pop song and it was a huge hit. That's crazy."

This is indeed heady stuff for a pop song. But Harrison translates the basic concept in just a few short, repetitive phrases, made up of an original prayer combined with Hebrew and Vedic chant to create a musical meditation or tool for seeking enlightenment. The commercial success of this superficially uncommercial song speaks to its universal power and allure. This did not happen in a vacuum—the Hare Krishna chant had already made several appearances in popular song and culture, most notably in the 1967 rock musical *Hair*; in a 1968 recording by the Fugs, featuring poet Allen Ginsberg; and in the song "We Will Fall" on the Stooges' eponymous 1969 debut album. Harrison himself had a hand in setting the stage for the chant's popularity, having produced the 1969 "Hare Krishna Mantra" single by the Radha Krsna Temple for Apple Records, which went to number twelve on the UK charts. But even that was predated by the appearance of the term "Hare Krishna" in the Beatles' 1967 song "I Am the Walrus." Ultimately, it was Harrison's and the Beatles' popularization of Hinduism through their music and their high-profile visits to India that built the foundation for the ubiquity of the "Hare Krishna" chant and, more generally, for all things "Eastern" in Western popular culture.

For the first half of "My Sweet Lord," Harrison sticks to "Hallelujah" as a choral response during the refrain. Halfway through, he switches over to "Hare Krishna" and "Hare Rama," drawing a spiritual connection between West and East, Christianity and Hinduism. Toward the end of the song, Harrison expands the chant to include the Guru Brahma mantra, "GururBrahma GururVishnu GururDevo Maheshwaraha Guru Saakshaat ParaBrahma Tasmai Sri Gurave Namah," a devotional prayer of respect.

"Perhaps the thing that makes it so fascinating is the foreignness of those background phrases," says Wesley Stace. "There was something very cabalistic almost, I mean, alchemical about it. It really dragged you in in a way that you wanted to know where the mystery and the glory was coming from."

Harrison wrote "My Sweet Lord" in fall 1969 and brought it to Billy Preston when Harrison coproduced Preston's *Encouraging Words*, Preston's second album for Apple Records. The Edwin Hawkins Singers were touring the United Kingdom at the time, and Harrison snagged the California-based ensemble to lend backup vocals to the track, which boasted a much stronger gospel-influenced R&B feel than Harrison's subsequent version. While Preston's rendition featured great keyboard work by the singer, his phrasing lacked fluidity and conviction—it was more of a performance *of* conviction rather than a convincing performance. Also, Preston's version made room for the phrase "Hare Krishna" only twice, both times sung by the Hawkins singers and not by Preston. (That same album also includes a somewhat schmaltzy rendition of "All Things Must Pass.") In hindsight, it is surprising that Harrison was willing to allow Preston to "scoop" himself, although Preston's tracks wound up being suitably overlooked. (For the record, Preston's album also includes a deliciously funky, inventive version of the Beatles' number "I've Got a Feeling.")

What fans around the world undoubtedly responded to in "My Sweet Lord" was how it sounded and the way it made them feel, as Stace and Driver both suggest. The song opens with an army of acoustic guitars being strummed in sync—by the likes of Harrison, Eric Clapton, members of Badfinger, and Peter Frampton, still a relative unknown despite his membership in English rock groups including the Herd and Humble Pie. After eight measures of guitars, a new chord is played on a zither-like instrument, followed immediately by Harrison playing the song's hook on slide guitar, introducing the entirely new sound that would become his post-Beatles trademark. The sound of Harrison's slide owed virtually nothing to the sound of slide guitar as played up until then by blues-based guitarists. In Harrison's hands and with his unique touch, the slide spoke, or sang, like a human voice with a slight Indian accent.

Harrison's slide-guitar sound was immediately distinctive and personal, expressing his "voice" as much as his voice. "Most people just slide around and get a nice effect, but they're not going for any particular melody and notes," says guitarist Lauren Passarelli about Harrison's slide technique. But Harrison used his slide as a tool rather than as a crutch. "He was playing specific melodies in tune using standard tuning with a medium weight glass slide and harmonizing it," continues Passarelli. "George was very sure of what he wanted to play and when. He had his own melodic sense. Everything he comes up with had his own signature piece. . . . It's his touch. You can't make this stuff up. You can't get that with an effects pedal or an amp or a special guitar."

Over the course of the next year or two, dozens of cover versions of "My Sweet Lord" were recorded by the likes of Nina Simone, Johnny Mathis, Andy Williams, Peggy Lee, Edwin Starr, and Marion Williams. Over the decades, the song has been performed and recorded by John Mayer, Raul Malo, Richie Havens, Julio Iglesias, the Golden Gate Quartet, Boy George, the Wailing Souls, Bonnie Bramlett, and Brian Wilson of the Beach Boys.

In 1975, the Chiffons, an African-American "girl group" founded in the Bronx, New York, in 1960, recorded their jazzy version of "My Sweet Lord," substituting a flute solo for Harrison's slide-guitar intro. The Chiffons were best known for their 1963 number-one hit, "He's So Fine," written by Ronald "Ronnie" Mack, who sadly died at age twenty-three just a half year after his song topped the charts. The track, which also cracked the Top 20 in the United Kingdom, was produced by members of the New York City–based doo-wop group the Tokens—best known for their 1961 number-one hit, "The Lion Sleeps Tonight." The Tokens, who owned their own publishing company, Bright Tunes, also played on the recording, along with their Brill Building songwriter friend, Carole King, who contributed piano. (Later that summer, the Chiffons would have a Top 5 hit with King's "One Fine Day.")

The Chiffons' 1975 version of "My Sweet Lord" omitted the "Hare Krishna" chant and all the other Vedic references, sticking to "Hallelujah." They also cheekily interpolated the phrase "He's so fine, wish he were mine," from "He's So Fine," into their rendition. Why cheekily? Because in February 1971, while Harrison's "My Sweet Lord" ruled the charts and the airwaves, Bright Tunes had filed a lawsuit alleging that in writing his hit tune, Harrison had "plagiarized" Ronnie Mack's "He's So Fine." Never mind that the key vocal riff of "He's So Fine" was "doo-lang doo-lang doo-lang," or that "He's So Fine" had a middle-eight section that bears no resemblance to any part of "My Sweet Lord," or that the entire recording is utterly different from "My Sweet Lord" in feel and vibe and mood. Or that nothing sounding like Harrison's slide-guitar hook—the essential musical element that defined "My Sweet Lord" and that to this day is one of the most memorable and recognizable hooks of the rock era—exists in "He's So Fine." The resemblance of the first three descending notes of the opening phrase, "He's so fine," to Harrison's three-note opening phrase, "My sweet Lord," was enough to get a hearing before a judge for Bright Tunes, albeit not before five years of legal dithering and filings and postponements and delays and countersuits and negotiations and behind-the-scenes machinations of Harrison's business manager, Allen Klein, who continued to represent Harrison and Apple (as well as Lennon and Starr) beyond the breakup of the Beatles.

But not for long. In part due to Klein's mishandling of the tax implications of the funds raised by the Concert for Bangladesh project, which saw Harrison having to pay a heavy penalty on the proceeds from the live album and film in England—plus Klein's grabbing a significant portion of the Bangladesh proceeds for himself as a commission—Harrison fired Klein in March 1973. Lennon and Starr also had their own beefs with Klein, prompting all Fab Three to fire Klein, leading to lawsuits and counter-lawsuits that took much of the remaining decade to bring to closure.

Before being fired, Klein had suggested that Harrison simply buy the copyright to "He's So Fine" as a way around the plagiarism lawsuit and be done with it. Once Klein no longer represented Harrison, however, he secretly switched sides, using his knowledge of the negotiations up to that point as well as the access he had to Harrison's financials to outbid the latter for the rights to "He's So Fine." Klein then turned around and sued Harrison for copyright infringement (at a much higher rate than the $150,000 he had initially negotiated with Bright Tunes on Harrison's behalf). This measure alone became the subject of suits and countersuits, Klein having been accused of betraying his former client in a manner so outrageous that to this day the case is taught in law schools.

Never mind that the entire plagiarism issue should have been thrown out of court. In August 1976, Federal Judge Richard Owen, of the Southern District of New York, cleared Harrison of intentionally plagiarizing "He's So Fine," writing, "Did Harrison deliberately use the music of 'He's So Fine'? I do not believe he did so deliberately." Nevertheless, Judge Owen found Harrison guilty of "subconscious plagiarism," a crime for which there was no precedent in law. Claiming some kind of supernatural powers to read into Harrison's psyche, the judge wrote, "[H]is subconscious knew it had worked in a song his conscious mind did not remember." So, Harrison wound up sort of guilty, sort of not.

By Judge Owen's byzantine calculations, Harrison had earned $1.6 million from "My Sweet Lord"; he even attributed fifty percent of the sales of the *All Things Must Pass* album to the success of the "My Sweet Lord" single (at a time when people still bought 45-rpm singles by the millions). Judge Owen almost totally dismissed the value of Harrison's lyrics as a factor in the song's popularity: "How much of the income is attributable to the text, to the selling power of his name? Although this is not an area susceptible to precise measurement, I conclude that three-fourths of 'My Sweet Lord's success is due to plagiarized tune and one fourth to other factors, such as the words and the popularity and stature of George Harrison in this particular field of music." In Judge Owen's estimation, "Hare Krishna, Hare Rama" was the equivalent of "Doo-lang doo-lang doo-lang." To say nothing of the fact that Harrison's song was about spiritual pursuits while Ronnie Mack's tune was about puppy love. Or that "My Sweet Lord" opened with strumming acoustic guitars and a completely original hook played on electric guitar in Harrison's patented slide style, in contrast to the Chiffons' song, which had a cold open featuring the "Doo-lang doo-lang doo-lang" vocals. In his decision, Judge Owen wrote, "In this case I conclude that the much-touted 'hook,' an introductory musical motive used by Harrison, was a minimal factor." Although Owen was an amateur composer, he clearly was no pop music critic.

In spite of the gross overvaluation of the revenue generated by "My Sweet Lord" and the wholesale undervaluation of all that was unique to George Harrison about the track, Owen saw fit to discount Klein's claims against Harrison, limiting the latter's penalty to the same $587,000 Klein paid for the rights to the tune, in exchange for which Harrison would then own the rights to "He's So Fine." On appeal, Klein's insistence that he was due the full $1.6 million as a profit on his investment was laughed out of court when, in a hearing before the United States Court of Appeals for the Second Circuit in February 1981, Judge Richard Cardamone admonished Klein, declaring that the case was "not only novel, but unique," a polite way of saying that Klein's underhanded tactics in betraying his former client to his adversary was a gross violation of his fiduciary responsibility to Harrison, and that Klein should not profit a single penny from the deal. By order of Judge Cardamone, Klein's company ABKCO sold the song's copyright to Harrison for the same $587,000 Klein had paid for it. Nevertheless, the complete legal fiasco dragged on for decades, only finally being fully resolved in the 1990s.

It is hard to calculate the psychic damage the "My Sweet Lord" plagiarism debacle had on Harrison and his creative process. He spoke about how from then on he constantly doubted himself when writing songs, wondering if he might be picking up bits and pieces of previous melodies. He said he could not listen to the radio without hearing a song and thinking it sounded like a different song.[1] Harrison had written "Sue Me, Sue You Blues" in 1971 in response to the legal wrangling that commenced with the breakup of the Beatles; he could not have predicted how much worse his legal problems would become.

Nevertheless, Harrison always had his sense of humor and his equanimity to fall back upon, which is exactly what he did in one of his bigger solo hits, "This Song," a comic replay of the whole debacle, included on his 1976 album, *Thirty Three & 1/3*. "This Song" is a knowing, cheeky protest song that wears its influences on its sleeve, providing a ready-made defense against any charges of plagiarism—"This song came to me unknowingly." He gets in his dig at Allen Klein in the phrase "This song has nothing bright about it," a reference to Bright Tunes, and reassures the listener that his "expert" vetted the tune and assured him that it was "OK." Harrison even mocks himself for recycling his own riffs, singing "This song could be you," punning on his previous, similar Motown-inspired song, "You." He also engaged the services of his Monty Python pal Eric Idle to insert, in a high-pitched squeal, "Could be 'Sugar Pie Honey Bunch,' no, more like 'Rescue Me,'" referring to hits by the Four Tops and Fontella Bass, respectively.

"This Song" is no tossed-off novelty, either. In addition to Eric Idle, Harrison employed an A-team of backing musicians, including keyboardist Billy Preston, Preston's drummer Alvin Taylor, bassist Willie Weeks, and saxophonist Tom Scott. Together they laid down one of funkiest tracks of Harrison's solo career. The vibe of gleeful abandon belies the black comedy of the number, powered along as it is by Richard Tee's honky-tonk piano and colored by Scott's R&B-fueled saxophone solo. Harrison even duets with himself, answering wordless vocals with slide-guitar lines. In the end, "This Song" is one of the smartest, funniest, catchiest tunes of his—or anyone's—musical career.

In a footnote to the whole sordid saga of Allen Klein versus George Harrison, the latter replaced the former with an American attorney named Dennis O'Brien, who came highly recommended by Harrison's friend, the actor Peter Sellers. O'Brien steered Harrison's ship through the treacherous legal and financial waters he faced throughout the 1970s. In 1978, the two formed a production company, HandMade Films, for the express purpose of financing *Monty Python's Life of Brian*, after the comedy troupe lost the support of EMI Films, the original backers. As we will explore elsewhere, HandMade would go on to enjoy a decade-plus string of commercial and critical successes as one of England's premier independent production companies. After the company had run its course and shut down in 1991, Harrison discovered that his most trusted adviser and business partner had been using company funds—meaning Harrison's money—as a personal credit card. A court ordered O'Brien to reimburse Harrison to the tune of $11 million, plus several million in damages. O'Brien declared bankruptcy, and Harrison never saw a penny from yet another manager who fleeced him.

Oy, my Lord . . .

21
What I Feel I Can't Say

I recall hearing "What Is Life" for the first time when it became a Top 10 hit in early 1971 and feeling an instant sense of recognition, as if the song were an "oldie," a song that had been around for years. I still have that feeling fifty-odd years later; no matter how many times I have listened to it—hundreds if not thousands of times—it sounds instantly fresh, brand new, but also timeless, as if it predated itself. Perhaps that is a function of the confluence of influences that went into making the track. It is a perfect pop single—channeling Motown and early rock 'n' roll, even as it creates an entirely new sound, bright and effervescent, soulful and anthemic, and incredibly catchy, its multiple riffs circling in and around one another, building a glorious celebration of the power of music to express a gleeful combination of love, lust, and gospel-like prayer. "My Sweet Lord" may have been the greater commercial success on its way to becoming Harrison's iconic solo number—what with its introduction of George's new slide-guitar sound that would characterize and define his music for the duration of his career and its reliance on the hypnotic power of chant—but "What Is Life," at least musically, was the much more detailed architectural triumph, the best realization of Harrison's collaboration with Phil Spector. Indeed, it may well rank as Spector's all-time greatest production, applying his 1960s girl-group and blue-eyed-soul arrangements to a more sophisticated, adult, hard-rocking approach, a climactic pop gem that belies the song's ponderous title.

"What Is Life" does not deliver on the promise of the song's title, but how could it? Although there is no question mark at the end of the title, the song indeed poses a question: *What is my life without your love?* The "you" to whom the question is directed is vague, unclear, and ambiguous, but it is generally considered to be both an individual—Pattie Harrison, most likely—and, given the overall spiritual context of *All Things Must Pass*, a divinity. Not that it even matters: the point is it is a love song, and if there *is* an answer to the question Harrison poses, it is love itself, not the object of one's love. And the manner in which the song is delivered bespeaks ecstasy, in the sense of intense joy and delight combined with the sort of rapture fostered by prophetic or mystical exaltation.

The song grabs attention from the outset, opening with the catchy lead-guitar riff—played solo—that recurs throughout the song. Harrison was a master craftsman of the opening hook, many of which led off Beatles songs, but here he is at the height of his powers. There is catchy, there is memorable, and there is transcendent. The opening riff of "What Is Life" is transcendent in its shape and its urgency, and that perhaps is what accounts for the feeling I get when I hear it, the feeling that it has been around forever. It is as if George had tapped into some universal wavelength, something Jungian, something that functions on an unconscious level. Maybe it is mathematical; maybe it is scientific; maybe Harrison stumbled upon a mystical formula. Wesley Stace says the opening guitar riff "assaults your ear—that's a nasty sounding, great guitar tone and it interlocks like Lego pieces. It's so perfect."

The guitar's fuzz-laden tone and its descending ostinato with an upward curlicue at the very end, set the scene for what is to come. The second time around, Carl Radle's bass guitar joins Harrison's lead guitar, doubling the same riff. The third time around, rhythm guitar—perhaps played by Eric Clapton—offers a chordal variation on the lead line while creating its own riff (from which the Doobie Brothers built their entire sound), working in tandem with the lead to fuel the song's engine. Fourth time around, drums and horns join the mix. This building-block approach to the opening measures of the track creates drama; the full band plays out the riff for several measures before a quick pause from which the song proper launches with Harrison's vocals. Harrison introduces a new hook on fuzz-toned guitar that flies in and around his voice, playing a kind of countermelody. After a return to the opening riff during the song's middle eight, John Barham's orchestra replaces the lead guitar, recapitulating the countermelody as the song crosses into operatic rock territory.

"What Is Life" does not stand alone on *All Things Must Pass*. In its soul-rock approach, it is of a stylistic piece with "Wah-Wah," "Awaiting on You All," and "Art of Dying." None of these songs could have been properly realized by the Beatles, although Harrison's "While My Guitar Gently Weeps" may have hinted at what was yet to come. That is not the case with the title track, which was the subject of lengthy rehearsals during the *Get Back* sessions, or with "Isn't It a Pity," "Let It Down," "Beware of Darkness," "I Dig Love," and "Hear Me Lord." In this sense, there are several different albums contained within *All Things Must Pass*—which, after all, was an unprecedented, three-LP set as originally released—the other being songs more influenced by The Band, including "Behind That Locked Door," "Run of the Mill," "Ballad of Sir Frankie Crisp (Let It Roll)," the Dylan co-write "I'd Have You Anytime" and the cover of Dylan's "If Not for You," and the title track, clearly modeled on the sound of The Band.

But "What Is Life" is a pure pop confection, the kind that time cannot erase. It is not an earworm—not in the sense of a tune that you cannot shake but want to. There is nothing to shake off here, as it is a joy-fueled rocket. Why would anyone want to resist the palpable pleasure that it offers, the clarion call—echoed by the track's horns—to wake up to the power of physical, romantic, and spiritual love. Wesley Stace also credits the opening line with setting up the song's alluring dynamic. "'What I feel I can't say'—there you have it in the first line," says Stace. "A lot of George Harrison is the unutterable thing that he understands but cannot enunciate. . . . . It's a great first line, and it's very Harrisonian." Indeed, in this sense it harks back to his *Revolver* tune, "I Want to Tell You," in which the singer has a head full of things to say but all the words just slip away.

"What Is Life" peaked at number ten the week ending March 27, 1971. It was a time of great creative ferment in pop music. The Top 10 that week included songs by the Temptations ("Just My Imagination"), Ike and Tina Turner ("Proud Mary"), and Marvin Gaye ("What's Going On"), quite the trifecta of R&B-pop crossover success. That same week, outlaw country songwriter Kris Kristofferson placed two songs in the Top 10—Sammi Smith's country-pop version of his "Help Me Make It Through the Night" and Janis Joplin's chart-topping rendition of his "Me and Bobby McGee." The rest of the Top 10 was filled out by commercial pop confections by the Carpenters, the Osmonds, and the Partridge Family.

The following week, "What Is Life" fell to number fourteen, swapping places with Paul McCartney's "Another Day," his first single as a solo artist, an outtake from the recording sessions for his album *Ram*. Like many of McCartney's songs, "Another Day" was melodically inventive. Whether the song belonged to the first group of creative singles, alongside "Just My Imagination," "What's Going On," "Me and Bobby McGee," and "What Is Life," or with the commercial pop numbers by the Carpenters, the Osmonds, and the Partridge Family, remains a matter of taste.

22

My Friend Came to Me

After some preliminary footage orienting viewers to the humanitarian crisis that impelled the two benefit concerts held at Madison Square Garden in New York City on August 1, 1971, the concert portion of the documentary film *Concert for Bangladesh* opens with a set of music by a dynamic instrumental quartet. The musicians have obviously been playing together for a long time; you can see it in how they intensely, almost telepathically, communicate with one another through their playing. They engage one another with call and response—they "trade fours" as jazz musicians do, a form of highly controlled group improvisation that requires intense listening skills. Once they have gotten going, the music becomes an interlocking groove, the four musicians seamlessly navigating the hills and valleys of the piece, through subtle changes of speed, rhythm, volume, and texture. Filmed in close-up, the set allows viewers to imagine themselves sitting onstage beside the musicians, who drive the engine of the composition through their phenomenal group interplay, reading one another's eyes and gestures, turning this way and that way with seemingly psychic understanding of the musical terrain. If the musicians were not Indian, if the instruments were not Indian instruments, if the music was not based in centuries-old Hindustani classical music, one might easily imagine this fabulous foursome—whose whole is far greater than the sum of its parts—as the Beatles, perhaps in a parallel or alternative universe. The music is exciting, passionate, almost shocking at times in its speed and intensity. In a word, it rocks.

Ravi Shankar, the sitarist, nominal leader, and most famous of the group, melts right into the ensemble, just one of four wheels needed to propel the musical vehicle forward, along with Ali Akbar Khan on sarod (a guitar-like instrument), Kamala Chakravarty on tambura (a long-necked, four-string instrument that produces a drone), and Alla Rakha on tabla (a hand drum, often played in pairs). All four are virtuosi, and together they form a sort of Hindustani classical supergroup, albeit musicians who wholly subsume themselves to the music and telegraph great joy in doing so.

In the film (and on the *Concert for Bangladesh* live album) the quartet plays for about fifteen minutes. At the original concerts (there were two, an afternoon and an evening show), they reportedly entertained the audience for three times as long. The crowd was eager and appreciative. After a minute of hearing the musicians warming up, they burst into applause, to which Ravi Shankar famously and politely replied, "If you appreciate the tuning so much, I hope you will like the playing even more." By the end of the number, the audience was ecstatic; in hindsight, it is no wonder that Harrison decided to take a Shankar-organized ensemble of sixteen Indian musicians—including Alla Rakha—on the road with him when he toured North America in late 1974. Harrison would also produce *Shankar Family & Friends,* an album featuring a fusion of Hindustani music with elements of rock, jazz, and funk, recorded mostly in spring 1973 and released on Harrison's label, Dark Horse Records, in September 1974.

The quartet's appearance opening the concerts that were intended to raise funds for victims of war, flooding, and famine in Bangladesh reminded audiences and performers alike why they were all assembled for what was the first superstar charity concert. They also set the tone for the evening, which, given the fame and renown of some of the performers, was remarkably devoid of ego and star turns. Harrison seemed intent on squelching this sort of thing from the outset, carefully curating the lineup to feature friends and collaborators who, he knew, would respond in the spirit required to make the concert both entertaining and meaningful. Indeed, official concert promotion promised "George Harrison and Friends," tantalizing potential concertgoers as well as the general public—who were these "friends," exactly?

Behind the scenes, this meant calling on some obvious pals: Billy Preston, whom Harrison had brought into the Beatles recording sessions for what became the *Let It Be* album and with whom he continued to work with in varying capacities—including signing him to Apple Records and producing his album *That's The Way God Planned It*—and Leon Russell, on whose eponymous 1970 debut album Harrison played, along with Fab Four bandmate Ringo Starr. Eric Clapton also was onstage at the Bangladesh concerts, but he mostly blended into the background, seemingly in no condition to take center stage and perform any of his own songs.

With word leaking out that Ringo Starr would be participating, the rumor mill was all abuzz with talk of a possible Beatles reunion taking place at the goodwill event. This was nixed early on when it became clear that Paul McCartney could not possibly appear with his former bandmates amid lawsuits that enmeshed the formerly Fab Four at the time, legal proceedings that largely pitted McCartney against the other three Beatles and their manager, Allen Klein. As for a three-quarters Beatles get-together, John Lennon initially accepted Harrison's invitation to take part. But when Lennon made his participation contingent upon his appearing alongside his current musical partner, Yoko Ono, he was disinvited, thereby ending any more talk of an almost-Beatles reunion. Half the Beatles would be there, the "economy-class" Beatles (not counting "Fifth Beatle" Billy Preston), but even having George and Ringo onstage performing together live for the first time since 1966 was a great thrill. Members of Badfinger, the first group signed to Apple Records in 1968, filled out the instrumental ensemble, along with guitarist Jesse Ed Davis and longtime Beatle friend and *All Things Must Pass* bassist Klaus Voormann, who ably held down the bottom end for most of the show alongside drummer Jim Keltner. Leon Russell brought a few members of his own touring band to back him on his own set, and saxophonist Jim Horn assembled a colorful brass section nicknamed "the Hollywood Horns."

The film version of the concert was drawn mostly from the evening performance, with a few exceptions from the afternoon show, so what is seen in the movie does not correspond exactly with the set list of either show. Nevertheless, following the opening set by Ravi Shankar and company, the rock portion of both concerts kicked off with "Wah-Wah," one of several tunes from *All Things Must Pass*—released the previous autumn—that Harrison performed over the course of the day. Harrison's voice was commanding and clear—more so than it was on *All Things Must Pass*, where it sometimes competed with Phil Spector's Wall of Sound production, which included drenching it in reverb. Harrison came out on stage in a beautiful white suit, his guitar strapped around the midsection of his torso as it was in his Beatles days, and in marked distinction from the way Clapton wore his guitar, slung down around his waist. Throughout the performance, Jesse Ed Davis would prove to be Harrison's secret weapon, filling in the notes and chords that Clapton failed to play.

After "Wah-Wah," Harrison greeted the crowd with a hearty "Hare Krishna!" before launching into "My Sweet Lord," his global number-one hit from the previous winter. Harrison donned his acoustic guitar for the number, ceding the electric slide-guitar duties to Davis and Clapton. The band lay back until the song's second bridge, making for a dramatic entrance midway through the song, which was as much a mood-setter as it was a triumphant statement of independence on Harrison's part, albeit delivered with all due humility. The audience, however, responded with torrid enthusiasm.

Harrison continued with another *All Things Must Pass* number, "Awaiting on You All," with its invocation to listeners to chant the names of the Lord, before handing over the spotlight to Billy Preston, whose gospel-based soul on "That's the Way God Planned It" perfectly blended with Harrison's musical aesthetic and spiritual message. Indeed, Harrison had produced and played guitar on the studio version of the song on the album of the same name in 1969. (Clapton also played guitar on the studio recording, with his ex-bandmate from Cream, Ginger Baker, on drums and Rolling Stones guitarist Keith Richards on bass.) After making most of his way through the song seated at his Hammond organ, Preston got up from his keyboard and kicked it up another notch, singing and dancing from center stage.

The next artist up also sang a song originally produced by Harrison. Without any verbal introduction, Harrison's instantly recognizable lead-guitar intro evoked a huge roar from the crowd, as the spotlight shone on the other former Beatle in the ensemble, and Ringo Starr sang "It Don't Come Easy," his Top 5 hit from just a few months earlier. As with Billy Preston's number, the song blended in perfectly with Harrison's—indeed, Harrison was the song's secret, uncredited author—and Ringo's disarmingly humble vocals and fun-loving presence spread joy throughout the arena. So what if he fumbled a few lyrics? Even that was such a Ringoesque move that he could hardly have planned a better way to ingratiate himself with the crowd (although, to quote Billy Preston, perhaps that's the way God planned it).

George followed Ringo with another *All Things Must Pass* number, "Beware of Darkness," a slow, moody song, befitting its title, but one that packs an emotional wallop. If the strength of Harrison's Liverpool accent was any measure of his personal commitment to a lyric, to American ears it did not get any stronger than it did on this number—when George sang, "Watch out now, take care" it sounds as if he were singing "take curr." After introducing the members of the ensemble, Harrison gave the crowd another treat they came hoping to hear—the first of three Beatles tunes he would play. He strapped on his electric guitar and delivered an impassioned version of "While My Guitar Gently Weeps."

Leon Russell gave George a break with a musically satisfying interlude, with a medley featuring a cover of the Rolling Stones' "Jumpin' Jack Flash" enveloping a version of the Coaster's 1957 hit "Young Blood," a classic rock 'n' roll tune written by Doc Pomus, Jerry Leiber, and Mike Stoller. "Young Blood" was an apt choice: the song was in the Beatles' nightclub repertoire in the days they played the Cavern Club, and a June 1963 live version recorded for the Beatles BBC program *Pop Goes the Beatles* is included on the 1994 compilation *Live at the BBC*, released in 1994. It also happens to have been one of the few songs in the Beatles' early repertoire that belonged to George Harrison as lead vocalist. The Beatles played the song at almost twice the speed of the Coasters' original, and devoid of the saxophone that in the Coasters' version originally danced throughout the number with the lead vocal, Harrison performed double duty, accompanying his vocals with a lead-guitar line that snaked through most of the song. While in their carnality "Young Blood" and "Jumpin' Jack Flash" may have strayed from the otherwise heavenly or spiritual focus of most of the material heard in the concert, Russell's gospel-drenched piano playing and his preacher-like testifying did not stray too far from the overall vibe of the proceedings.

At this point, Harrison doffed his white jacket to reveal a billowing, saffron-colored long-sleeved buttoned-down shirt. The rest of the ensemble disappeared while Harrison, alone at a microphone with his acoustic guitar, flanked only by Badfinger acoustic guitarist Pete Ham, played another of the Beatles' greatest hits, "Here Comes the Sun," marking its first-ever live performance.

Then, looking down at the running sheet he had taped to his guitar, George hesitated for a moment, peered off into the wings, and saw a body and a guitar making its way onstage, at which point he said to the audience, "I'd like to bring on a friend of us all . . . Mr. Bob Dylan." It is hard to capture fully the feeling at Madison Square Garden and the import and impact of Dylan's appearance. Harrison's friend and occasional songwriting partner had not performed publicly in any meaningful way since his one-off set at the Isle of Wight Festival, backed by The Band in 1969, and he had not toured before that since late spring 1966, when, during a brief hiatus from his world tour with The Band—then known as the Hawks—he suffered a devastating motorcycle accident near his home in Woodstock, New York, and took the opportunity provided by the need to recuperate to settle down and withdraw from the concert stage and the public eye, opting to spend his time tending to his ever-growing brood of children (he would have five in all, including his wife's daughter from a previous marriage, whom Dylan adopted) and hanging out with the Hawks, writing and recording informally in a basement studio at a house nicknamed "Big Pink" where some of them were living.

Dylan remained mostly in seclusion since 1966, occasionally releasing quiet albums mostly out of step with the music of the time and leaving fans and the merely curious to wonder if he would ever perform again. Dylan's appearance at the Concert for Bangladesh was just as intriguing and exciting as that of the Beatles reunion that did not take place (and which would have overshadowed the entire meaning of the event if it had).

While Dylan had privately agreed to take part and support his friend's effort, his participation was not an absolute certainty until Harrison saw him walk out onto the stage at the afternoon show. When Dylan had arrived at Madison Square Garden the night before for sound check, amid all the lights and sound equipment and technicians scurrying all over the place and dozens of musicians, singers, performers, and hangers-on, he had panicked. The reality of what he had agreed to do had sunk in, as had his doubts and discomfort about appearing at such a high-profile event with all eyes on him, and he told Harrison he was no longer sure he could perform. Harrison reportedly looked Dylan in the eye and reminded him that his own role in the concert was even more of an unlikely leap than Dylan's; unlike Dylan, Harrison had never performed in public as a front man, either playing solo or leading a band. He had never stood up before an audience of twenty thousand and spoken to them directly. Still, Dylan would not commit to returning to the Garden the next day. When Harrison saw him walk out onstage, seemingly pumped up and ready to perform, he breathed a huge sigh of relief. Dylan, flanked by Harrison on guitar, Leon Russell on bass, and Ringo Starr, off to their side, playing the role of Mr. Tambourine Man, performed a remarkably intimate and soulful five-song set that included such career-defining numbers as "Just Like a Woman," "A Hard Rain's a-Gonna Fall," "Mr. Tambourine Man," and "Blowin' in the Wind." Dylan and Russell had just a few months earlier been together in a New York City recording studio, where Dylan asked Russell to produce a session for him, out of which came the single, "Watching the River Flow," which was included on Dylan's *Greatest Hits, Vol. II* release in November 1971. (That session also included Concert for Bangladesh band members Jesse Ed Davis on guitar and Jim Keltner on drums, and produced "When I Paint My Masterpiece," which also found a home on Dylan's *Greatest Hits, Vol. II.*)

Dylan's appearance toward the end of the concert and his commitment to his performance elevated the excitement level of the event into the stratosphere. It was a generous act of friendship, finding the future Nobel Prize winner choosing to emerge out of his self-imposed isolation not on his own terms or for his own purposes but simply to help out his friend for a worthy cause. This was not a strategic career move found in any rock manager's playbook. It was plain and simple: the voice of a generation, the hidden Olympian, the God who would not show his face even to Moses, surprised everyone— probably no one more than himself. Beatles reunion be damned; no one had ever seen or expected to see anything like Dylan and half the Beatles playing onstage together.

What came after Dylan's five-song set was a denouement of sorts, but this denouement was also one of the greatest climaxes of any rock concert, superstar benefit or otherwise. In the evening concert, Harrison followed Dylan's appearance with his third Beatles song of the night, "Something." Like Ringo before him, Harrison muffed some of the lyrics, but again, this was the first time the song was performed live, and with Pattie Harrison, the ostensible muse of the song, watching from the wings, George gave an inspired performance.

For the final number, the band kicked everything up a notch and launched into Harrison's brand-new single written expressly for the event: "Bangla Desh," commonly referred to as "rock's first charity single." Recorded less than a month before the concerts, "Bangla Desh" was one of Harrison's all-time best songs, a heavily R&B-influenced rock number that explodes with urgency befitting the purpose of the tune. It is a masterpiece of lyrical economy, in just a few words encapsulating the tragedy of Bangladesh and the need for everyone listening to pitch in to help the starving, the afflicted, and the dying. A delicious pun went to heart of the matter: "Won't you give some bread, get the starving fed." The plaintive quality of Harrison's vocals suited the song's pleading message; an ideal example of form as content. Vibewise, the song would have fit swimmingly on *All Things Must Pass*, and it features many of the same musicians who played on that album. Phil Spector coproduced the track, dialing down the *All Things Must Pass*–style echo and reverb that some, Harrison included, found excessive. Harrison added subtle guitar fills that underline his vocals, which are double tracked for a fuller sound, and he occasionally adds overdubbed vocal harmonies. The song's middle eight is mostly given over to instrumental passages by Russell on piano and Jim Horn on saxophone, and then George plays slide guitar for a few measures, but the track is mostly propelled by piano and horns.

The "Bangla Desh" single became a Top 10 hit in the United Kingdom and elsewhere in Europe and peaked at number 23 on *Billboard*'s Hot 100. The whole sequence of events—the single, the concerts, the live album, and the concert documentary—not only eventually raised millions for humanitarian relief but are widely credited with having made "Bangladesh" a household name at a time when the news media and politicians were still referring to the newly independent nation as "East Pakistan."

Watching the *Concert for Bangladesh* today, one is struck by the coherence of the music—despite the variety of performers—and the humility of the players, perhaps Harrison above all. The weight of the world—or at least, the weight of fans' expectations of a former Beatle—was upon his shoulders, to say nothing of his roles as organizer and frontman of a concert, neither of which he had ever been before. After months of almost nonstop preparations for the concert and a week of rehearsing late into the night in the lead-up to the performance, plus the lingering uncertainties that lasted well into the concert itself—Would Eric Clapton be able to take the stage? Would Bob Dylan even show up?—found Harrison exhausted by the time he walked onto the stage at Madison Square Garden. Not that anyone would have known that to see him and hear him.

While much of the drama behind the scenes was unknown to the vast majority of attendees, with hindsight one cannot help viewing the concert itself as a triumph of perseverance on Harrison's part. And his musical colleagues and friends seemed equally driven to make the performance not just a musical success but a profoundly meaningful event. The opening set by Ravi Shankar's quartet grounded the performance, setting a tone for the evening of dignity, respect, and unsurpassed virtuosity. It also lent a spiritual context to the proceedings, one that carried through the entire event, powered in part by Harrison's overtly religious *All Things Must Pass* songs but also in the gospel-influenced musical arrangements and backup vocals by the six-member choir. The concert never strayed far from its meaning and purpose, intentionally or otherwise, which gives it its enduring power well into the twenty-first century.

23
The Constitution

It was a full two and a half years before George Harrison followed up *All Things Must Pass* with his next studio album, *Living in the Material World,* which was released in late May 1973. Not that Harrison had been twiddling his thumbs, basking in the glory of his groundbreaking solo debut, all that time. Precisely the opposite. He had been busy and distracted, as had all the members of the Fab Four, by intra-band legal disputes, as they attempted to extricate themselves from their obligations to one another as Beatles, and eventually from the clutches of the manipulative Allen Klein. Fresh off the making of *All Things Must Pass,* Harrison threw himself into helping promote the Ravi Shankar documentary, *Raga,* and producing efforts for other Apple recording artists, including Lon & Derrek Van Eaton, a spiritually oriented American brother duo from Trenton, New Jersey, and Cilla Black. Harrison also lent his guitar to albums by former bandmates John Lennon and Ringo Starr, as well as to a handful of friends, including *All Things Must Pass* keyboardist Gary Wright, saxophonist Bobby Keys, and Harry Nilsson, for whom he played slide guitar on the singer-songwriter's notorious (and unplayable on radio) single, "You're Breakin' My Heart." Summer and fall 1971 saw Harrison busy with planning for the Concert for Bangladesh and overseeing its corollary projects in the form of the live triple album and concert film. In early 1972, Harrison made another trip to India. He took some time off to rest and regroup in mid-1972, before heading back into the studio to begin recording the songs that would make up his second studio album, *Living in the Material World.*

Where *All Things Must Pass* was loud, eclectic, and sprawling, *Living in the Material World* was much more compact, controlled, and intimate. Where George sounded like a (relatively) happy seeker on *All Things Must Pass*, its follow-up gave voice more to the believer. If *All Things Must Pass* was his Declaration of Independence, *Living in the Material World* was his Constitution, in which he laid down the law. Some felt it went overboard, sounding like the work of a preacher, a lecturer, an evangelist, or a scold. But Harrison was in tune with the times as well as writing from a heartfelt, emotional place.

The album opens with "Give Me Love (Give Me Peace on Earth)," a cousin to "My Sweet Lord" that, like its predecessor, was a repetitive prayer that captured the ears of listeners on its way to the top of the pop charts, where it knocked former bandmate Paul McCartney's syrupy ballad "My Love" from the number-one position on *Billboard*'s Hot 100. The song swims along on the current of Harrison's melodic invocation to God, propelled by his shimmering acoustic guitars, leaving room on top for Harrison's plaintive vocals and his eloquent slide-guitar fills, as he begs God to "Keep me free from birth" and "Help me cope with this heavy load"—to break the cycle of reincarnation and ascend to an astral plane or another dimension. Klaus Voormann and Jim Keltner lock in together on bass and drums, respectively, and remain locked in, allowing for a few extra measures here and there in between verses and choruses to stretch out fluidly without skipping a beat. When Nicky Hopkins finally joins in on piano at the one-minute mark, the song gains traction, and, with Keltner adding a cymbal here, a tom there, piece by piece, until he is playing the whole kit, the song ascends even higher. Harrison's mid-song slide solo drives the song ever upward before the whole thing peaks with George singing, "Om . . . my Lord."

The prayerful bliss and transcendence that "Give Me Love" promises are immediately subverted by the bilious "Sue Me, Sue You Blues," which, instead of speaking to Harrison's spiritual life, spoke to the harsh reality of life in the material world—specifically the legal muck in which the post-Beatles found themselves mired. "Bring your lawyer and I'll bring mine, get together, and we could have a bad time," sings Harrison. For this number, he replaces the otherworldly sound of his electric slide guitar with the raw, biting tones of an acoustic resonator guitar, the better for notes and chords to decay downward, as if falling into a pit. In its portrayal of a legal system that feeds upon itself, Harrison leavens the finger-pointing aspect of the tune away from his former bandmates to make a more general point about the "material world," where, as his pal Bob Dylan put it, "money doesn't talk, it swears." Unfortunately for Harrison, the song would prove prescient and enduringly relevant—for much of his remaining life he would be embroiled in lawsuits that had nothing to do with justice but everything to do with money.

"Sue Me, Sue You Blues" made its public debut not on *Living in the Material World* but on guitarist Jesse Ed Davis's 1972 album, *Ululu*. A Native American from Oklahoma, Davis traveled in musical circles that included Levon Helm and Rick Danko of The Band (he recorded a version of The Band's "Strawberry Wine" on *Ululu*), Taj Mahal, Gene Clark of the Byrds, Jackson Browne, Arlo Guthrie, Emmylou Harris, Jackie DeShannon, and fellow Oklahoman Leon Russell. As mentioned previously, Davis played with Russell on Bob Dylan's

1971 one-off single "Watching the River Flow," and through Russell, who produced the Dylan session, Davis wound up as one of the army of guitarists in the house band for the Concert for Bangladesh. In addition to performing on Harrison's 1975 album, *Extra Texture*, Davis also played on projects by John Lennon and Ringo Starr, went on to become a touring member of the Faces, and contributed guitar to albums by the likes of Eric Clapton, Rod Stewart, Steve Miller, Harry Nilsson, Willie Nelson, and Leonard Cohen. In 1987, Davis was a member of Taj Mahal's band when the audience at the Palomino Club in North Hollywood, California, included Bob Dylan, John Fogerty of Creedence Clearwater Revival, and George Harrison, the three of whom joined Davis onstage and ran through a spontaneous set of rock 'n' roll classics by the likes of Carl Perkins, Buddy Holly, and the Everly Brothers.

Davis's version of "Sue Me, Sue You Blues" placed the song in a heartland, boogie-rock setting that made plenty of room for metallic, blues-based guitar solos by Davis. His vocals are an indistinctive blend of Russell's and Harrison's. Davis does not bring much passion to the song; it lacks the dark, tension-filled piano riff powering Harrison's menacing version.

The organ- and piano-drenched title track (courtesy of Gary Wright and Nicky Hopkins, respectively), the final song on side one, jumps out at a listener as a deep, soulful rocker, retracing in both words and music Harrison's career and spiritual arc in brighter, lighter, and more humorous tones than those in "Try Some, Buy Some," which covers similar territory. "Living in the Material World" marks the return of Indian instruments on a Beatles and George Harrison studio album for the first time since *Sgt. Pepper's Lonely Hearts Club Band*, with tabla, tamboura, and sitar coloring the middle eight as Harrison sings about "the spiritual sky." It also marks the return of the Beatles, from Ringo Starr's perfectly galumphing rhythms on drums (doubled by Jim Keltner) to lyrical invocations of John, Paul, and, in a delicious pun, Ringo, when Harrison sings, "Though we started out quite poor, we got 'Richie' on a tour." (Starr's given name is Richard Starkey, and his intimates call him Richie, not Ringo.) It's also a masterpiece of vocal phrasing; Harrison transforms the awkward title into a mellifluous vocal riff. An instrumental verse features a gorgeous call-and-response duet between Harrison's slide guitar, heard here at the epitome of Harrison's eloquence on the instrument, and Jim Horn's flaming, jazzy tenor saxophone.

This time out, George explains his beliefs on a more practical level; he alludes to the cycle of a spirit's earthly incarnations, with the ultimate goal of advancing to a higher spiritual plane. He does suggest that there is a clear hierarchy between the two levels, with the materialism of earthly existence bogging down the individual in frustration, wherein senses are never gratified nor satisfied. Nevertheless, the song puts a more optimistic spin on earlier numbers on the same topic, including "Art of Dying" and "Hear Me Lord." In his memoir, Harrison credits the influence of A.C. Bhaktivedanta Swami for "the realising 'we are not these bodies,' we are *in* these material bodies in the physical world."[1]

Another song that Harrison had sitting around for a few years before recording *Living in the Material World* was "Be Here Now," borrowing its title and concept from the 1971 book of that name by Baba Ram Dass (born Richard Alpert in Boston, Massachusetts, in 1931). The book recounts Alpert's own spiritual journey, from his work as a psychologist to his early 1960s experiments with fellow Harvard University researcher Timothy Leary on the psychotherapeutic effects of psychotropic drugs and the role they might play in mystical experiences. Alpert and Leary were dismissed from their positions at Harvard in 1963, and they spent the next four years continuing their experiments independently, with an enhanced focus on the relationship between mind-altering drugs and altered states of consciousness. Alpert began traveling to India and studying Hindu concepts around the same time as Harrison. Alpert's *Be Here Now* became one of the "bibles" of the Sixties counterculture, containing a collection of free-verse reflections on various spiritual traditions and a "manual for conscious being" called "Cookbook for a Sacred Life," offering specific guidance on techniques that included yoga, conscious breathing, and meditation for readers looking to integrate practices that would aid in connecting them with Eastern mystical beliefs.

It's no surprise that Harrison would find in the book inspiration for his own spiritual life as well as for his own songwriting, especially as a way to put forth his own Eastern-derived lessons. "Be Here Now" was written around the time of the Concert for Bangladesh, and Harrison would pick the song up again the following year when he began recording for *Living in the Material World*. Its musical setting was vaguely reminiscent of "Blue Jay Way" and "Here Comes the Sun," although it was dialed down a few beats from the latter to make the music more meditative in keeping with the song's message: that the past and future are illusory and that the only state of being that matters is the present. It is a concept familiar to anyone who has ever taken a yoga class (the *asanas,* or poses of yoga, practically require one to "be here now" in the moment in order to execute them correctly) and that in more recent times has been referred to more broadly as "mindfulness." Harrison sings, "A mind that wants to wander 'round a corner is an unwise mind," sometimes referred to in yoga practice as "monkey mind." Through sheer focus on one's breath, one quiets the monkey mind and replaces it with qualities of stillness and being in the moment.

Although Harrison's core band of Klaus Voormann, Gary Wright, Nicky Hopkins, and Jim Keltner all appear on the track, they mostly stay out of Harrison's way, allowing his languorous, hypnotic vocals and acoustic guitar to lure listeners into the very dreamlike state the song conjures. Wright plays a pedal point—a sustained drone—on organ, and Hopkins's piano provides delicate filigrees and decorative counterpoint. Voormann's bass punctuates Harrison's vocal phrases and works with Keltner's percussion to lend a tabla-like feeling to the rhythm. The song may not be a proper raga, but it evokes a raga-like mood, with Harrison's finest vocal melisma dancing above a modal undercurrent. Near the very end of the song one can hear the faint sounds of a sitar surfacing—it may have been there underneath all along. One of Harrison's most profound and evangelical songs is thus delivered in one of the most quiet, gentlest performances of his career, one that is also, most appropriately, timeless—the most intimate performance on his most intimate album.

Britpop avatars Oasis—who were never shy about their debt to the Beatles and to Harrison in particular—titled their third album *Be Here Now*. Released in 1997, the album was full of musical and lyrical references to Beatles songs. The title track—not the Harrison song but an original composition—bears no musical relationship to Harrison's song; it is more of a slow-churning tribute to the Rolling Stones with a nod to American Southern rock—but it does invoke the Beatles in the line "Sing a song for me, one from 'Let It Be.'" (The Oasis song also nods to North American rock band Steppenwolf in the line "Be my magic carpet ride," namechecking one of the group's greatest hits, 1968's "Magic Carpet Ride," although the only sonic relationship between the two is the guitar feedback that opens the Steppenwolf song and closes the Oasis number.)

Living in the Material World also included "The Light That Has Lighted the World," a complaint about being judged—and criticized—for changing and for finding comfort in a spiritual tradition. "I've heard how some people have said that I've changed, that I'm not what I was, how it really is a shame," Harrison sings in the opening lines of the song, a ballad driven largely by Nicky Hopkins's piano accompaniment. It is another gentle song, more of a plea for understanding, a statement of sincerity, and a track that eerily prefigures "I Believe in You," one of the initial statements by his friend Bob Dylan, after the latter adopted the guise of a "born-again Christian" on his 1979 album, *Slow Train Coming*. Dylan sings more from an injured victim's point of view— "they look at me and frown, they'd like to drive me from this town, they don't want me around, 'cause I believe in you"—than Harrison does, although not by much. Harrison's acoustic guitars shimmer throughout the number, and he answers a piano interlude with a tidy and eloquent slide-guitar solo. Hopkins's gospel chords on piano lend a churchly feel to the number, enhanced by the organ-like chords that Gary Wright plays on harmonium in the background.

Much like "Try Some, Buy Some," Harrison originally wrote "The Light That Has Lighted the World" with the idea that another artist, in this case Cilla Black, would record it. Black—whose birth name was Priscilla White—was an English pop singer from Liverpool who gained renown right around the same time as the Beatles, whom she first met while she was working at the Cavern Club. Black was soon performing in clubs around Liverpool, and the Beatles became her champions, persuading Brian Epstein to manage her. Within weeks of formalizing their ties in September 1963, Epstein got Black signed to a deal with the Beatles' label, Parlophone, under the direction of Beatles producer George Martin. Her first single, "Love of the Loved," was written by Paul McCartney (credited to Lennon-McCartney). The Beatles had included the song in their live shows, but the group never properly recorded the tune, which cracked the UK Top 40 in October 1963 in Cilla Black's version. Just a few months later, Black's rendition of the Burt Bacharach–Hal David composition "Anyone Who Had a Heart"—a hit for Dionne Warwick in North America and elsewhere in January 1964 (her first Top 10 hit in the United States)—spent three weeks at number one on the UK charts in late February and early March, when it vied with hits by the Dave Clark Five, Cliff Richard, and the Rolling Stones. (Fortunately for Black, the Beatles left a gap between hits at the time, "I Want to Hold Your Hand" having topped the charts in November 1963 and "Can't Buy Me Love" soon to take the top spot on April 1, 1964.) Black would go on to record a number of hit singles, including several more Lennon-McCartney songs—"Yesterday," "For No One," and "The Long and Winding Road" among them—over the course of the next decade, all while remaining in the Beatles' orbit.

In May 1971, Black was part of a contingent that included Harrison and Ringo Starr and their wives and went on holiday to the south of France. It was on this trip that the two former Beatles collaborated on a song called "Photograph," which was originally intended for Black to record. Recognizing that he and George had come up with a potential hit single, Starr claimed the song for himself, although Black would go on to record her own version a few years later. An early version of "Photograph" was recorded during the *Living in the Material World* sessions. Starr then rerecorded the final version in Los Angeles in early 1973, using the same instrumentalists, including Harrison, who appeared on *Living in the Material World,* with the addition of Bobby Keys, whose saxophone solo became an elemental part of the recording. The final track was given the Wall of Sound treatment with orchestral and choral arrangements courtesy of Jack Nitzsche, who had provided those services to

Phil Spector on many of the latter's hit songs in the 1960s. "Photograph" became a huge number-one hit for Starr and the third in a series of three singles cowritten (officially or otherwise) by Harrison, the others being 1971's
"It Don't Come Easy" and 1972's "Back Off Boogaloo," both of which were
also produced by Harrison. Although Harrison was also responsible for much
of the work that went into "Photograph," including supplying the backup
musicians, Richard Perry was the producer of record for the song and for
the *Ringo* album on which it found a home. (Perry would go on to great success as the producer of albums by pop and soft-rock artists, including Barbra
Streisand, Andy Williams, Carly Simon, Art Garfunkel, and Leo Sayer.)

Harrison had been helping Ringo write songs going back to their days in
the Beatles. One of the revelations of Peter Jackson's 2021 film, *Get Back*, was a
scene showing Ringo at the piano in the recording studio, saying, "I wrote this
last night." He begins playing the song we know as "Octopus's Garden," but he
has yet to flesh it out. George comes over to him and suggests several different
avenues the song can take musically. In a radio interview in August 1977,
Ringo acknowledged his songwriting debt to Harrison. "I'd write a single, or
he'd write it with me," said Starr. "I can start a thousand songs but finishing
them I always find very hard. So, George would help me finish it. You know,
I only know three chords, and he'd stick four more in, and they'd all think I was
a genius. 'Oh, he's playing F-diminished, is he?' I don't even know what it is."[2]
The band Oasis would go on to quote "Octopus's Garden" lyrically and musically on no fewer than three different songs, including the title track to their
compilation album *The Masterplan*, which also includes a live concert version
of "I Am the Walrus."

Harrison began writing "The Light That Has Lighted the World" as a B-
side to go along with "When Every Song Is Sung," which he originally wrote
for Welsh singer Shirley Bassey, who had a hit with a version of his Beatles
song "Something." The Bassey recording never panned out, nor did a version
Harrison himself recorded during the *All Things Must Pass* sessions. He produced a version with Ronnie Spector for her solo album that was never completed, and Apple recording artist Mary Hopkin also had a go at the tune, as
did Leon Russell. The song finally saw its first official release when Ringo Starr
recorded a version, retitled "I'll Still Love You," for his 1976 album *Ringo's
Rotogravure*. Cilla Black finally did get around to recording a version of the
song in the mid-1970s, but it surfaced publicly only in 2003, when it was included on a compilation album, *Cilla: The Best of 1963–1978*.

For our purposes, the point is that once "The Light That Has Lighted the
World" lost its connection to "When Every Song Is Sung," Harrison was free
to reorient the composition from a song about the changes brought about

by success to the changes brought about by a spiritual awakening. Although Harrison pointed out in *I Me Mine,* whether changes are brought about by success, growth, religion, or any other cause, change in and of itself is not a "sin." "The whole of life is a change,"[3] wrote Harrison, pleading the case that he so eloquently explores in the song.

Whether it was addressed to Pattie Harrison or God, "Don't Let Me Wait Too Long" was more than just an update of "Blue Jay Way," another song of longing for the return of a friend or loved one. For one, it demonstrates that Harrison had fully absorbed whatever arrangement and production lessons there were to learn from Phil Spector while they were working together on *All Things Must Pass.* The composition and arrangement are classic Spector, with the track's girl-group vibe made Harrisonian and its big-beat, Wall of Sound production evocative of Spector's early-1960s hits. Ringo Starr is on hand to provide the double-drum attack with Jim Keltner, and Pete Ham and Tom Evans of Badfinger reprise their acoustic-guitar-army approach, strumming along with Harrison the way they did on much of *All Things Must Pass.* The lyrics are straightforward: it is a love song expressing longing, with just a hint of a spiritual dimension in the line "Now only you know how to lay it down like it came from above," a sentiment not unknown in decades of pop tunes that explore the mystery of love by contextualizing it with a higher power. Although no singer or songwriter necessarily needs be a devotee to talk about the love of another being "heaven-sent," for Harrison to express this aspect in one phrase of what otherwise is a bright pop-rock tune that should have been a hit is no great stretch. The greatest mystery is why the song was not released as a single, as it likely would have been a worthy follow-up to "Give Me Love"—it verily pops out of the speakers in between the gorgeous ballads "The Light That Has Lighted the World" and "Who Can See It" and makes the case for Harrison as hitmaker (as does the title track).

"The Lord Loves the One (That Loves the Lord)" encapsulates the strengths and weaknesses of *Living in the Material World.* Musically, it's a delicious, funky, mid-tempo, swampy rocker that makes great use of Harrison's slide guitar to punctuate the melody. For the intro, Harrison recycles an acoustic-guitar riff from his Beatles *Let It Be* composition, "For You Blue." The song's initial ascending chord progression suggests a positive mood before a left-ward turn underlines the contingency of the law of karma, introduced with the line "the law says whatever you do is going to come right back on you."

Here is where Harrison becomes the Constitutional scholar, warning listeners to live by that law: "The law says if you don't give then you don't get loving." Perhaps his intention was merely to place Hindu concepts into a relatable, catchy pop tune. But with references to "leaders of nations [who are] acting like big girls with no thoughts for their god who provides us with all," he comes across as bitter and churlish, to say nothing of crudely sexist— what in the world does it mean for politicians to "act like big girls"? The song gives voice to one of Harrison's least attractive tendencies: that of the funda- mentalist preacher. Even if he implicates himself in this ritual of bad faith, acknowledging the potential hypocrisy of his outlook, he still comes across as a scold, once again prefiguring the similar conundrum that would afflict Bob Dylan just a few years later when he would similarly assume the mantle of a preacher.

To Harrison's credit, he acknowledges all this in his memoir, *I Me Mine*, where he writes, "Some people have thought that in certain songs like this one . . . I was implying that I was 'holier than thou.' I do not exclude myself and write a lot of things in order to make *myself* remember."[4] At the very least, Harrison put his money where his mouth was: he assigned the publishing roy- alties for all but two tracks on *Living in the Material World* to his newly formed Material World Foundation, which he set up to evade the financial morass he incurred when funds raised from his Bangladesh charity efforts got held up by taxation offices in both the United States and the United Kingdom.

Written immediately in the days following the Concert for Bangladesh, "The Day the World Gets Round" is a huge sigh of disappointment, an ex- pression of Harrison's realization that those who really hold the power—the wealthy and world leaders—could not be relied upon to bring about much- needed change, even if that just meant to provide humanitarian aid in a sit- uation such as that afflicting the refugees from flood, famine, and war in Bangladesh. Musically, the song nods to the Beatles' "Across the Universe," with an *All Things Must Pass*–like string section, arranged by John Barham. Although the song's creation may have been rooted in Harrison's frustration over the limits of what those like him could accomplish to bring about justice and provide for basic human dignity on a global scale, he does not succumb to self-pity or bitterness; rather, he offers hope and portrays a time when the pre- vailing world order could be overturned—in his poetic formation, "the day the world gets round." In (perhaps surprisingly) Western terms, he paints a vision of a messianic era. As he put it in *I Me Mine*, "If everyone would wake- up and do even a little, there could be no misery in the world."[5] Amen to that.

(Incidentally, on his first solo album, 2009's *A Sideman's Journey*, bassist Klaus Voormann would revive "The Day the World Gets Round," with lead vocals provided by Yusuf, aka Cat Stevens. The spiritually minded Stevens, whose acoustic-guitar-based sound in the early 1970s owed more than a little to Harrison's "Here Comes the Sun," would also contribute a version of "All Things Must Pass" to Voormann's effort, which is worth seeking out for a Paul

McCartney/Ringo Starr duet on a Fats Domino tune and Bonnie Bramlett's version of "My Sweet Lord." Stevens would also go on to record a version of "Here Comes the Sun" upon signing with Dark Horse Records in February 2023, released within days of what would have been Harrison's eightieth birthday.)

Living in the Material World boasted some of the best vocal performances of Harrison's career. A highly personal lament beseeching understanding for his desire to be seen as an individual human being and not a thing—to be seen as George Harrison and not "a Beatle"—"Who Can See It" is also a musical tribute to Roy Orbison. While Harrison was no Orbison, he acquitted himself marvelously, adeptly swooping into the highest registers his voice box allowed. One can only fantasize about how the two of them might have sounded duetting on the number, had Orbison not died so soon after the Traveling Wilburys' debut album was released, squelching any chance of the group performing in concert and, perhaps, drawing upon appropriate songs like this one from their solo repertoires.

The album concludes with the aptly titled "That Is All," which opens with the phrase "That is all I want to say." As with any number of Harrison's love songs, the object of his love could be either God or an earthly lover—or both. My bet is on his wife Pattie. After ten songs about many aspects of spirituality and materialism, it only makes sense that Harrison would bring it all back home with a song of devotion to his beloved in a gorgeous, "Something"-like ballad, with ethereal slide guitar and a stately, orchestral arrangement once again courtesy of John Barham. The song ends on a curious note (or two): Harrison's vocal melody never resolves—it just ends in the middle of a musical phrase—and the final guitar figure likewise is more of an ellipsis than a conclusion, as if to say, "to be continued."

Subsequent reissues of *Living in the Material World* in the early twenty-first century would include several bonus tracks, giving a home to the "Bangla Desh" single, that single's B-side, "Deep Blue," and "Miss O'Dell," a novelty paying tribute to Beatles associate and Apple employee Chris O'Dell, who lived at Friar Park for a time as Harrison's assistant and Pattie's friend. Despite the easygoing, jaunty feel of "Deep Blue," an informal, folk-blues number on which Harrison plays acoustic guitar and dobro with minimal accompaniment by Klaus Voormann on bass and Jim Keltner on drums, the song was written in response to Harrison's frequent trips to visit his ailing mother, dying of cancer, in a hospital near Liverpool during the sessions for *All Things Must Pass*. The song's imagery, including "suffering in the darkness" and the incessant repetition of the title, portrays a state of emotional depression—understandable, given the circumstances at the time, but suggestive of a familiarity with the feeling beyond those immediate circumstances. "Miss O'Dell" is even more informal—a lighthearted, jokey tribute to the title character (whom former boyfriend Leon Russell immortalized in his song, "Pisces Apple Lady"), given a very Dylanesque treatment, replete with Harrison on harmonica as well as guitar, again joined only by Voormann and Keltner. One distinguishing feature of the recording is how Harrison breaks out in laughter not once, not twice, but three times. The laughter, in this case, came at his own expense, not Chris O'Dell's.

Contrast *Living in the Material World* with Paul McCartney's April 1973 release, *Red Rose Speedway* (credited to "Paul McCartney and Wings"). While the McCartney album spawned the US megahit "My Love," which occupied the number-one position on *Billboard*'s Hot 100 for four weeks, any but the most fanatical McCartney fan would be hard put to name a single other song from the album: "Big Barn Bed"? "Little Lamb Dragonfly"? "Single Pigeon"? The most adventurous number on the album was a new arrangement of "Mary Had a Little Lamb," which presumably caught McCartney thumbing his nose at critics who accused him of churning out the musical equivalent of children's nursery rhymes. If that was their critique, he would throw it right back in their face and literally record one. (This also anticipated the strategy behind 1976's "Silly Love Songs," which found McCartney laughing all the way to the top of the pop charts with a riposte to his critics.) McCartney biographer Philip Norman said the nursery rhyme "would take Wings' credibility as a rock band to rock bottom."[6] Even McCartney, with all the power that accrued to him after a decade's worth of hits, could not convince EMI to release *Red Rose Speedway* as the double album he had originally intended; he wound up having to whittle it down to a single album.

A few months after the release of *Living in the Material World*, John Lennon went into a New York City recording studio to lay down tracks for *Mind Games,* which would be released in late fall. Just as with Harrison's album, *Mind Games* marked Lennon's first solo album without the services of Phil Spector as producer. It was also Lennon's first solo album not to include participation by any of his former bandmates. (Although the studio portion of his June 1972 album, *Some Time in New York City*, lacked contributions by any other former Beatles, it did include two live tracks, recorded in December 1969 in London, on which Harrison played.) Other than the title track—a very Beatles-esque production that Lennon began writing in 1969 and that cracked the Top 20 in both the United States and the United Kingdom—the other songs on *Mind Games* were second-rate Lennon, and the album was roundly condemned by critics as aimless and confused.

Ringo Starr, on the other hand, spent the spring and half of summer 1973 in recording *Ringo*, which would be his first solo album of pop-rock songs. *Sentimental Journey*, his 1970 solo debut, saw him focusing on pre-rock "standards," and *Beaucoup of Blues*, released less than a half year later, was a country-flavored effort recorded in Nashville. *Ringo*, on the other hand, established the titular artist as a solo force to be reckoned with—although one of the distinguishing characteristics of the album is how much he relied on a little help from his friends, including all three of his ex-bandmates. Other musicians who lent a hand included guitarists Marc Bolan of T. Rex and Steve Cropper of Booker T. & the M.G.'s, keyboardists Billy Preston and Nicky Hopkins, saxophonists Tom Scott and Bobby Keys, and Harry Nilsson on vocals (perhaps foreshadowing the "All-Starr Band" lineups Ringo would begin touring with in 1989 on a near-annual basis into the 2020s). The album produced three hit singles—"Oh My My," "You're Sixteen," and "Photograph"—and featured songs by John Lennon ("I'm the Greatest") and Paul McCartney ("Six O'Clock"), and two songs cowritten by Harrison, including "Photograph" and "You and Me (Babe)," the latter cowritten by Beatles assistant Mal Evans, plus "Sunshine Life for Me (Sail Away Raymond)," a country-flavored track with a hint of "old Irish folk song"[7] written by Harrison, with instrumental accompaniment by members of The Band plus string virtuoso David Bromberg. With the upbeat feel of an Irish jig, the song, which also has a dour, very Harrisonian outlook, is easy to overlook, in which the refrain is "It's a sunshine life for me, if I could get away from this cloud over me." Even when he was writing for Ringo, George could not help investing the number with his trademark ambivalence. ("American Pie" singer-songwriter Don McLean recorded the song the following year in a raw, stripped-down version prominently featuring the banjo, underpinned by tabla in what was presumably a nod to Harrison's authorship.)

24

Running on a Dark Racecourse

Dark Horse was in no small way George Harrison's "divorce" album, released just a month and a half before Bob Dylan's *Blood on the Tracks*, widely hailed as one of Dylan's greatest albums and an incisive portrait of the breakup of a marriage. The main difference between the two albums was that Dylan's found the voice of a generation at the top of his game, with a collection of songs loosely connected thematically and performed with a level of passion that had not been heard from Dylan since 1966's *Blonde on Blonde*, whereas *Dark Horse* was a mixed bag at best. It displayed a Harrison sounding beaten up and battered around, struggling to get through songs of self-pity and bitter invective when he was not just biding his time with filler like his New Year's Eve novelty, "Ding Dong, Ding Dong," and the opening track, "Hari's on Tour (Express)," an instrumental number based on a jam session at Friar Park featuring Harrison and Tom Scott's jazz-rock outfit, the L.A. Express, who were in England touring with Joni Mitchell.

This is not to say that there were not some gems amidst the dross of *Dark Horse*. The bouncy, rocking title track served as an updated manifesto as well as an answer song to critics, to former bandmates, and to his then-wife, Pattie Harrison, who had left Harrison for Eric Clapton in July 1974. (Harrison addressed the Pattie-Eric situation directly elsewhere on the album, including in a rewrite of the Everly Brothers' "Bye Bye Love," with its reference to "Old Clapper.") Like many of the songs on the album, "Dark Horse" was somewhat marred by Harrison's vocals, weakened and raspy due to a lingering case of laryngitis, leading some to refer to the song, album, and subsequent tour as "Dark Hoarse."

But at its best, Harrison's occasional hoarseness worked with the songs, lending additional character to his voice, and adding a sense of vulnerability to his performance suiting the material. More generally, calling himself a "dark horse," with the connotation of constantly being underrated and underappreciated, gave new meaning and focus to his work; it served to recontextualize his professional and personal lives with a new self-narrative. Whether it was as a Beatle or a solo artist or a lover or a husband, he seemed to be suggesting, he was "a blue moon," as he sang in the song, something that only occasionally or rarely shows up, not unlike a "dark horse." The smart money does not bet on a dark horse, as dark horses win only once in a blue moon. It is all about being underestimated, and after two number-one albums, two number-one hits, and the triumph that was the Concert for Bangladesh—to say nothing of his success with the Beatles—Harrison had had enough of being bet against. Thus, by the time he gets to the final track on the album, "It Is 'He' (Jai Sri Krishna)," a prayer to a god who sees "who we really are," Harrison found a way to tie his newfound sense of self with his Hindu worldview.

Inspired by Bob Dylan's barnstorming *Before the Flood* concert tour with The Band in early 1974 and then Joni Mitchell's *Miles of Aisles* tour later that same year and desiring to spread the gospel of Ravi Shankar and Indian music once more, Harrison put together a North American concert tour—the first by a former member of the Beatles—for the end of the year. The tour would borrow the name of the new album, as would Harrison's new record label, Dark Horse, which would be distributed by A&M Records, which provided an up-front investment of $10 million. Harrison himself was still under contract to Apple/EMI, to whom he still owed delivery of another album. So, his *Dark Horse* album did not appear on his own label—whose first few signings included the band Splinter and Ravi Shankar—nor did his follow-up album, *Extra Texture*, which finally fulfilled his contractual obligations to EMI. Thus, his late-1976 album, *Thirty Three & 1/3*, was Harrison's first album released on his home label, which remains operational to this day, now run by Harrison's son, Dhani Harrison. (Other artists signed to Dark Horse include the late Joe Strummer of the Clash, Ravi Shankar, and Cat Stevens, a.k.a. Yusuf.)

Partly because of his own hesitancy to put himself in the spotlight as a frontman—the same ambivalence that plagued him going into the Concert for Bangladesh—and partly because of his desire, as he did at the Bangladesh concert, to share the spotlight with other artists, most notably Ravi Shankar and his ensemble of Indian musicians, as well as Billy Preston and the L.A. Express—Harrison arranged the concerts as a kind of East-meets-West rock 'n' roll revue, blending Indian music, jazz, funk, and Harrison's brand of pop-rock music, sometimes all in the course of a single song. Having been initially inspired by Dylan's tour with The Band, Harrison helped set up a kind of feedback loop; one year hence, Dylan would hit the road and front a rambling folk-rock carnival called the Rolling Thunder Revue, featuring a succession of performers in addition to the headliner, including Joan Baez, Ramblin' Jack Elliott, and Roger McGuinn, plus occasional guest artists who would show up here and there for a night or three, including Joni Mitchell, Roberta Flack, Ronee Blakely, Stephen Stills, and Ringo Starr.

When Harrison began his tour in Vancouver on November 2, 1974, he was still hoarse, but the crowd's innate enthusiasm for seeing a live performance by a former member of the Beatles and their openness to the semi-experimental nature of the Dark Horse concert experience overcame any disappointment. And as the tour rolled on, Harrison's voice strengthened. With a slight tweaking of his set list to include a few more Fab Four numbers, at the prodding and insistence of legendary tour promoter Bill Graham, the audiences and the reviews grew even more enthusiastic. The national music press was critical of both Harrison's performances and the *Dark Horse* album, but local reviewers tended toward the ecstatic in their accounts of the concerts. Harrison was not immune to criticism; indeed, he may well have been his own harshest critic. It would be several decades before Harrison would embark on another concert tour, and even that would be a short, two-week stint in Japan, at the instigation of and largely directed by Eric Clapton.

Otherwise, apart from a very few one-off performances, Harrison eschewed the concert stage for the rest of his life. His highest-profile live appearance was at Bob Dylan's 30th Anniversary Concert Celebration on October 16, 1992, at Madison Square Garden in New York City, where Harrison was one of the final artists to take the stage to pay tribute to his mentor and friend, turning in an impassioned version of Dylan's "Absolutely Sweet Marie" and sharing verses with Tom Petty, Neil Young, Eric Clapton, and Dylan himself on the latter's "My Back Pages," the song with the aptly immortal couplet, "I was so much older then, I'm younger than that now." For one moment, Harrison, Dylan, and the rest of them probably felt it and believed it.

25

The Ghost of Ronnie Spector

The term "palimpsest" originally referred to medieval written documents—typically of papyrus or parchment—that contained faint evidence of earlier markings that were incompletely erased (in earlier times, scraped off and washed), remaining somewhat legible underneath the new writing. The word is now used to denote anything reused that carries traces of past use: a building (e.g., Angkor Wat, originally constructed as a temple devoted to a Hindu god, later remodeled as a center for Buddhist worship, yet still retaining traces of its Hindu past), a city, even memory itself is a kind of palimpsest. Paintings by Rembrandt sometimes show hints of previous paintings, and contemporary scanning technology allows greater access than what the naked eye reveals to what lies beneath the top layer of paint.

In older times, palimpsests were unintentional, the result of the scarcity or dearness of the raw materials—the parchment, the canvas—and the impossibility of eradicating all traces of the past. Modern artists, however, have embraced the palimpsest and have consciously made it part of their work, replicating the evidence of earlier use of their media as part of the artwork in and of itself, using the technique to create additional layers of meaning beyond the surface layer of their creations.

The concept of the palimpsest and the conscious employment of the tradition has leaped beyond visual art to be embraced by literary and sonic artists. Literary critics speak of the "suppressed narratives" hidden within the work of nineteenth-century female writers and, in more modern times, of the palimpsestic nature of works by D.H. Lawrence, Umberto Eco, and Ian McEwan. With the advent of recording on tape in the twentieth century, a whole new world of sound palimpsests was born, recapitulating the history of the original written palimpsests. In its early years, recording tape was used multiple times—a recording could have been made for one-time broadcast and then taped over for subsequent programs. Also, tape could be reused when a recording was deemed insufficient, sonically or creatively, and a new version was recorded over the one being disposed of. But rerecording over tape was not an all-or-nothing proposition; remnants of earlier recorded sounds, however faint, could sometimes be heard in the new recording using the same tape, analogous to the incomplete scraping of writing on ancient parchment. Mostly this was not a desired effect, but some composers and recording artists have incorporated such sonic palimpsests into their work, finding it provides additional atmosphere or dimensionality.

Which brings us to the case of George Harrison and the ghost of Ronnie Spector. Veronica Yvette Bennett, born in August 1943, in New York City, is best known as the cofounder and leader of the female vocal group the Ronettes, whose hits included such seminal soul-pop tunes as "Be My Baby," "Baby, I Love You," and "Walking in the Rain." These and a few other songs saw the Ronettes come out of nowhere—they were only just signed to a deal with Philles Records in 1963—to give the Beatles a run for their money on the American pop charts in 1963-1964. The Ronettes toured England in January 1964; their opening act was a London-based band called the Rolling Stones. On one of their first nights in England, the Ronettes—Veronica, her sister Estelle, and their cousin Nedra Talley—went to a party where they met George Harrison, Ringo Starr, and John Lennon. In her memoir, Ronnie Spector recalls Harrison praising her voice: "We loved it the first time we heard you."[1] She was surprised to learn that the Fab Four were big fans of the American "girl groups." Plus, according to Spector, they knew every Motown song. Ronnie also recalls John Lennon putting moves on her, which she deflected, still a virgin at the time and in love with the Ronettes' producer, Phil Spector.[2] Meanwhile, Harrison disappeared into a room with Estelle.[3] The foursome went out on a few "double dates" subsequently; Spector recounts how all Lennon and Harrison wanted to talk about was what soul legends like Ben E. King were like in person.[4]

Ronnie also recalls going to a nightclub with George one night, when the two of them sang along to the song "Mockingbird," trading off the verses just as Inez and Charlie Foxx did on the original recording, which was a big hit at the time. As the sun began to rise, they wound up at George's apartment. Harrison had no fresh food in his flat, "but his cupboard was filled with canned stuff—peas and potted meats, and every kind of soup in the world. So we opened every single can in his cupboard and made this enormous breakfast. And then we couldn't stop laughing as we tried to eat this crazy breakfast of potted ham, pickles, corn, and turkey noodle soup."[5] When the Beatles went to the United States the following month, the Ronettes were discreetly sneaked into the Plaza Hotel to pay them a visit.

By 1965, the Ronettes were voted the third top vocal group in England, just behind the homegrown Beatles and the Rolling Stones. Their hits were cowritten by Phil Spector and the husband-and-wife songwriting teams of Jeff Barry and Ellie Greenwich ("Be My Baby," "Baby, I Love You") and Barry

Mann and Cynthia Weil ("Walking in the Rain"). But the big news about the Ronettes was their producer, Phil Spector, Ronnie's future husband, who developed his trademark Wall of Sound production style on recordings by the Ronettes. He enveloped the group's vocals in a monumental blanket of sound built upon large ensembles of Los Angeles–based studio musicians (who later became known collectively if informally as "the Wrecking Crew"), with individual instruments such as guitars, keyboards, and drums doubled and even tripled, plus lush backing provided by a small orchestra. Added to this was a heavy dose of reverb—an effect produced by sending the live sound played in the studio into a separate room outfitted as an echo chamber equipped with speakers and microphones, before sending the echo-laden sound back to the control room, where it was captured on tape. Hence, Spector's Wall of Sound, imitated by many but never fully replicated, as it was the product of the single-minded, grandiose, eccentric—some would say mad—musical visionary.

The Beatles, as did most everyone, loved that sound and those records, so much that eventually they succumbed to its allure and engaged Spector to overdub and mix the recordings that became the *Let It Be* album. These were some of the only studio recordings that the Beatles' longtime producer George Martin had not supervised. The original aesthetic intended for these recordings was to capture a live-in-the-studio sound, with recording overseen by engineer Glyn Johns, who had long worked in the studio with the Rolling Stones. Johns took a stab at mixing the tracks, but the Beatles were unhappy with the results. John Lennon then handed the tapes over to Spector and asked him to have a go at them. The resulting album was a mishmash, with some Spectorian productions bumping up against raw, stripped-down tracks, including several recorded during the famous rooftop concert at Apple headquarters. Paul McCartney was especially unhappy with the lush orchestral and choral overdubs that Spector added to his song "The Long and Winding Road"; in one of the papers filed in his lawsuit to disband the Beatles, McCartney even listed this musical atrocity as one of his reasons for breaking up the group. George Martin allegedly said that the recording credits should have read, "Produced by George Martin, over-produced by Phil Spector." In 2003, McCartney finally got his preferred version of "The Long and Winding Road" released as part of the album *Let It Be . . . Naked,* which largely eliminated Spector's overdubs and presented the album with the stripped-down aesthetic originally envisioned for the project.

Lennon and Harrison, nevertheless, went on to work with Spector on some of their early solo projects, and he wound up staying in London for the better part of a year, when he was nominally head of A&R (artists and repertory, a fancy name for talent scout) at Apple Records. Spector is credited as producer or coproducer of Lennon's *John Lennon/Plastic Ono Band, Imagine, Rock 'n' Roll,* and *Some Time in New York City.* Harrison turned to Spector to help him with *All Things Must Pass* and *The Concert for Bangladesh.* While the two were working together on the former, they hatched the idea of recording a Ronnie Spector solo album for Apple Records, using many of the same musicians who were already working on Harrison's solo debut.

Recording in early 1971, they tried a handful of tracks before the effort was abandoned, mostly because of Ronnie's frustration with the material George and Phil presented to her, plus Spector's notoriously erratic behavior and his jealousy of John Lennon, who started hanging around the recording sessions, even contributing a lick or two on piano. One of the only numbers brought to completion was the Harrison-penned song "Try Some, Buy Some." The track was released by Apple as a single in April 1971, but failed to catch on. Ronnie was not surprised. She first heard the tune only when she arrived at the studio to record the number. As Ronnie recounts, "George started playing. He banged out the slow melody on the piano and sang along in a high-pitched chant. The first verse didn't exactly grab me. It was written in the voice of a guy who kept talking about how he wanted to try some and buy some. Exactly what it was he was trying to try and buy wasn't exactly clear. Religion? Drugs? Sex? I was mystified. And the more George sang, the more confused I got."[6] By the time George got to the second verse, Ronnie stopped him and said she didn't think she could do the song. "I don't understand a single word of it," she told him. Harrison replied, "That's okay. I don't either."[7]

Ronnie did, however, finish recording the track, after which they moved onto the next song, slated for the B-side of the single. It was "an even weirder song"[8] called "Tandoori Chicken." The neo-rockabilly track, equally inappropriate for the soul singer, recounted asking the singer's "pal" named "Mal"— presumably a reference to Beatles assistant Mal Evans—to fetch a takeaway order of tandoori chicken and a "great big bottle of wine." That pretty much sums up the song in its entirety. "My husband produced 'My Sweet Lord' for George Harrison and 'Instant Karma' for John Lennon, but when it came time to record me, what did he pick? A song about Indian chicken. . . . My big comeback on Apple Records turned out to be nothing but a joke,"[9] writes Spector. That spelled the end of the recording project, and Phil gave Ronnie a ticket back home to California.

Ronnie Spector was right about "Try Some, Buy Some" being the wrong song for her. One can hear the recording on the compilation *Come and Get It: The Best of Apple Records.* Despite the producers' best efforts to salvage the track, Ronnie seems lost or buried in the Wall of Sound: her rhythmic phrasing is out of sync with the rest of the music (probably not her fault); her vocal interpretation is reflective of her confusion and non-understanding of what the song is about; and not even the generous serving of "woah oh-oh oh-ohs" rescue the track, which with its mandolins and harps is indeed down-right weird—and not in a good way. Ultimately, the singer is not even present; she is just an interchangeable musical afterthought. Spector also recorded a Harrison-penned ballad called "When Every Song Is Sung," which wound up resurfacing in a slightly different version as "I'll Still Love You" on Ringo Starr's 1976 album, *Ringo's Rotogravure*.

When it came time to record his 1973 album, *Living in the Material World*, George Harrison revisited "Try Some, Buy Some," rebuilding a new version atop the basic rhythm track of the original recording, stripping out Ronnie Spector's vocals and replacing them with his own, and adding new instru-mental elements, remixing the entire number so that it sounds almost like an entirely new take. The introspective, hymn-like song was personal and inti-mate, much more suited to be sung by Harrison, with his pleading, yearning vocals the perfect delivery mechanism for a song about the struggle between the false panaceas of money and drugs and the very real achievement of spir-itual ecstasy. Where there was a total disconnect between singer and song in the original Ronnie Spector version, Harrison's rendition is invested with hard-earned, deep-seated pathos. Two years after Harrison died, David Bowie paid tribute to Harrison—honoring George's intentions and adding his own otherworldly qualities—when he remade the song for his 2003 album, *Reality*. As in Harrison's rendition, Bowie's cover also included his own, stylized ver-sion of Ronnie Spector's woah-oh-oh-ohs.

But the story of Ronnie Spector's ghost did not end there. In addition to "Try Some, Buy Some" and "Tandoori Chicken," Spector had also recorded another Harrison song—an upbeat, Motown-inspired love song called "You." The latter song was much more in the vein of Ronnie's hit singles with the Ronettes than "Try Some, Buy Some," and one imagines that had the re-cording been seen all the way through to completion and issued as a single, it might have provided the elusive comeback hit both Spectors had been hoping for ever since the Ronettes had disbanded in 1967. One gets the slightest hint of what this might have sounded like through the palimpsest of Ronnie's vocals that remains on George Harrison's version of the track, released in 1975 as the opening number and lead single of his album *Extra Texture (Read All About It)*.

For his own version, Harrison went back to the original recording he made with Spector in 1971—much the way he did with "Try Some, Buy Some"—stripping out her vocal track, replacing it with his own vocals, and adding some colorful overdubs—particularly tenor-sax riffs by Jim Horn and dreamy synth-keyboards by David Foster. Having been originally recorded for Ronnie Spector, the backing track was played in a key better suited to Ronnie's vocals. Unfortunately for Harrison, that did not match up with his own range, and he therefore had to strain to reach the high notes as he wrote them. In an early demo version, Harrison can be heard referring sarcastically to his "Billy Eckstine" voice, a reference to the mid-twentieth-century African-American jazz and pop singer who boasted a deep, rich bass-baritone. Pushing his voice to the limit, however, wound up adding a note of tenderness and vulnerability—almost desperation—to Harrison's protestations of love. George was well acquainted with sliding into a falsetto voice, a strategy employed by all the Beatles vocalists, and he made good use of that skill, too.

"You" opens with George counting down the beat, "One . . . one two three four" above an ambient sound—perhaps David Foster's string synthesizer that provided the sound of the orchestral backing of the tune (forsaking the real orchestra Harrison employed for the *All Things Must Pass* sessions). After a few beats of hand percussion, drums fire up the ignition in advance of the bass, guitars, and saxophone that launch the number before even hitting the ten-second mark. George answers his own one-syllable vocal phrases with guitar lines that swaddle them in ribbons, almost like another voice. Harrison is a one-man guitar army, strumming acoustic guitars and charging forward on electric, aided by a keyboard brigade comprised of Leon Russell on piano, Gary Wright on electric piano, and David Foster on organ. The middle eight modulates to a minor key, albeit briefly, before the song returns to the main chord progression of the verse, here featuring Jim Horn's sax solo before returning to the refrain and Harrison's vocals. As the song approaches its conclusion at the three-minute and fifteen-second mark, Harrison turned the knob up on what remained of Ronnie Spector's guide vocals, her wordless (and timeless) incantation of "woah oh-oh oh-oh," echoing her outro from "Be My Baby." It was a subtle gesture, perhaps a nuance easily overlooked, but it adds a whiff of nostalgia to this timeless bit of pop music. A palimpsest, both literally and figuratively.

"You" was inscrutably only a minor hit—topping out at number twenty in the United States and number thirty-eight in the United Kingdom (although in Canada it cracked the Top 10)—even though it leaps out at a listener as a jazzy, soul-pop delight. Harrison's 1975 version enhanced the already significant Motown-like feel of the song; the bridge he composed for the song was built on a riff recalling the bassline of the Four Tops' saxophone-drenched 1965 hit, "I Can't Help Myself (Sugar Pie Honey Bunch)"—a fact Harrison cheekily acknowledged a few years later in "This Song," his riposte to the plagiarism lawsuit that followed in the wake of "My Sweet Lord," on which Eric

Idle of Monty Python screeches in a silly, high-pitched voice, "Could be 'Sugar Pie Honey Bunch.'" All this proved is that Harrison had great taste and his ear tuned to mid-1960s soul music. The entire genre serves as a conceptual palimpsest underneath so many of his solo recordings, and he was eager to emulate the sound of the music he loved while giving it his own, unique twist.

The sheer joy and passion George invested in "You" was a welcome turn of events after a couple of albums of what some felt were rather dark, glum tunes. For sure, "Give Me Love (Give Me Peace on Earth)" and "Dark Horse" were terrific songs, but neither was as deliberately celebratory as "You," whose simple message was as basic as I love you, you love me, oh how happy we can be. The lyrics drew upon a very different wellspring from that of the one that inspired "Dark Horse." The lyrics to "You" were so simple, if not downright silly (in the best possible way), that one can hear echoes of the music and lyrics in Paul McCartney's megahit, "Silly Love Songs," released the following year, whose refrain, "I love you"—which also figures prominently in Harrison's song—could be a pun on "I love 'You,'" a reference to the Harrison tune.

An airplane ride gets you from one place to another, hopefully on time, and if you are lucky without any untoward events or discomfort. A spectacular view, however, might make it memorable. The view that Harrison provides from "You" is spectacular; it crams so much that is fun and infectious and alluring about pop music into one song that it sounds as if it had always been there. It has an instantly recognizable quality to it, one full of happiness and movement and delirium—just a perfect bit of pop that just happened to have been made by one of the most serious songwriters and musicians of the rock era. Harrison knew he had such a great riff that he included "A Bit More of You"—a forty-five-second instrumental reprise of "You"—as the opening track of side two of *Extra Texture*. (I'm still waiting for Dark Horse Records to release "A Whole Lot More of 'You.'")

George and Pattie Harrison saw their marriage come to a de facto end in summer 1974, after one too many indiscretions on both of their parts, including George's affair with Ringo Starr's wife Maureen. (George and Pattie were finally legally divorced in June 1977.) By fall 1974, Harrison had already taken up with the woman who would become his next wife, Olivia Arias, a staffer at A&M Records, and Pattie soon succumbed to Eric Clapton's years-long pursuit of her affection, most famously telegraphed in his song "Layla." George still apparently had demons to exorcise, and what was equally as remarkable as the presence of dark, melancholic numbers on *Extra Texture* was the lack of tunes about spirituality or, for that matter, songs about love—other than "You," which, as we have seen, was written five years earlier, possibly with Pattie in mind, or perhaps just with silly love in his heart.

26

Could Be "Sugar Pie Honey Bunch"

If you had to name a single George Harrison solo album that was his most "normal" album—"normal" in the sense of a pop album with songs in a variety of styles and moods, "normal" in that it lacked an overarching theme, "normal" in that it was full of accessible music that was well produced and well recorded, "normal" in that it was fun and soulful and loving without being too far out or weird, without being too challenging or provocative, then *Thirty Three & 1/3* would probably be the one. This 1976 album marked a new beginning for Harrison in numerous ways, not the least that it was his first solo album not to bear the imprint of Apple Records but instead to belong to his own Dark Horse Records, now being distributed by Warner Brothers Records (after the dissolution of his distribution deal with A&M Records). As owner of his own label, Harrison felt freer than he had in the past to do what he wanted, to make the sounds he heard in his head come alive, and to put as much of his past behind as he could.

It may be surprising that given his newfound freedom, Harrison chose to record and release such a *normal* album. But the normality of *Thirty Three & 1/3* was of course relative; this was still a George Harrison album, and one by a former member of the Beatles. The world, meaning record buyers, radio programmers, and music critics alike, would not easily ignore an album by one of the Fab Four—at least not yet (they would, sadly, in due time). And if *Thirty Three & 1/3* was no *All Things Must Pass*, nothing ever would be. That was just something everyone would have to get used to. Lightning was not going to strike again, at least not in the same place or even in the same neighborhood, and it was time to listen to Harrison with new ears and, if not with lowered expectations, at least on his own terms.

Since *All Things Must Pass*, Harrison had been an erratic recording artist. He still produced the occasional hit single or brilliant deep cut—think of "Give Me Love (Give Me Peace on Earth)," the title track to *Dark Horse*, and "You," to name just three—but there was often something that marred each effort: the preacherliness of *Living in the Material World*, the hoarseness of his voice on, ironically, *Dark Horse*, and the sense of chaos and indirection that plagued *Extra Texture*. But with *Thirty Three & 1/3*, all such concerns were gone. It was a well-made album, in some ways sounding even better than *All Things Must Pass*—at the very least, the production did not draw attention to itself. The songs were mostly upbeat, or at least positive in their outlook. Love songs rubbed up against a few comic novelties; it featured some of Harrison's most soulful singing of his career; the delightful melodies must have been the envy of Paul McCartney; and he even found room for a couple of spiritual tunes and a cover of a pre-rock standard, Cole Porter's "True Love," that had been in the Beatles repertoire when they were playing nightclubs in the early 1960s. While largely keyboard driven, the numbers on *Thirty Three & 1/3* featured plenty of Harrison's eloquent licks and solos on slide guitar. And the funky nature of much of the material was no doubt partly the product of the musicians he assembled for the effort, a core group comprising primarily Black musicians from America who had come up the ranks by playing R&B music, including Billy Preston, bassist Willie Weeks, drummer Alvin Taylor, and keyboardist Richard Tee.

Thirty Three & 1/3 picked up where Harrison had left off with *Extra Texture* in his excursion into American soul music, from the song "Pure Smokey," which was his tribute to his soul-singing idol Smokey Robinson, to "This Song," his satirical retelling of the "My Sweet Lord" plagiarism debacle, which openly flaunted its similarity to classic 1960s R&B songs, including "I Can't Help Myself" by the Four Tops and "Rescue Me" by Fontella Bass. Serving as his own producer with assistance from saxophonist Tom Scott, Harrison left behind any lingering vestige of Phil Spector's Wall of Sound approach to the album. Instead he favored a keyboard-driven live-band feel, no doubt enhanced by the fact that recording was done at FPSHOT (Friar Park Studios, Henley-on-Thames), Harrison's home studio at Friar Park. The songs were all written and recorded in keys that suited his voice, and all the recorded tracks were original to these sessions—none of which was entirely the case on previous albums.

That is not to say that all the songs were new and fresh off his pen. As late as 1976, George Harrison still had not exhausted his back catalog of unrecorded songs, including those that had not made the cut for *All Things Must Pass* and even some going back further to his Beatles days. The opening track, "Woman Don't You Cry for Me," dated back to late 1969, and was considered for inclusion on *All Things Must Pass*. The same goes for "Beautiful Girl," which harked back to the same time, and which Harrison originally considered giving to Doris Troy for her eponymous LP that he produced for Apple Records. When that did not pan out, he cut a demo for *All Things Must Pass*. (Session outtakes of "Woman Don't You Cry for Me" and "Beautiful Girl" were included in the fiftieth-anniversary edition of *All Things Must Pass*.) "See Yourself" dated back even further: Harrison began writing it in 1967 in the wake of the public outcry over Paul McCartney's public admission that he had taken LSD. If the song had begun its life as an indictment of McCartney's perceived hypocrisy, by the time Harrison got around to recording it for *Thirty Three & 1/3* its tone had softened to be more understanding and forgiving of human frailty in the face of adversity, and to focus more on one's own responsibility than to cast blame on others, as hinted at in the song's title.

"Pure Smokey" was not the first time Harrison paid tribute to his soul-music idol, Smokey Robinson, in song. His previous album, *Extra Texture*, included "Ooh Baby (You Know That I Love You)," a tribute to Robinson inspired by his group the Miracles' "Ooo Baby Baby." The song "Crackerbox Palace," for which Harrison made a music video filmed inside and in the gardens of Friar Park, slyly references a naughty joke from Mel Brooks's *Blazing Saddles* by Madeline Kahn as Lili Von Shtupp; the song cracked the US Top 20. "Learning How to Love You" featured a rare acoustic-guitar solo, one that recalls the one he played in the 1964 Beatles song "And I Love Her."

Harrison was excited enough by *Thirty Three & 1/3* to participate in promotional efforts for the album. Besides the "Crackerbox Palace" video, which, like one for "True Love," was directed by Eric Idle, he also made a video for "This Song," which made its premiere on the American TV variety show *Saturday Night Live*, on November 20, 1976. Fellow singer-songwriter Paul Simon was hosting the program that night, and Harrison joined Simon for duet performances of "Here Comes the Sun" and Simon's "Homeward Bound." Harrison also submitted to radio, TV, and print interviews, and, most surprisingly, appeared for photo ops with former British prime minister Edward Heath (he of "Taxman" fame) and then-US Secretary of State Henry Kissinger, to whom he gave a copy of Yogananda's *Autobiography of a Yogi*. Anything for a laugh.

Even though his two previous albums had spawned Top 20 hits (the title track of *Dark Horse* and *Extra Texture*'s "You"), *Thirty Three & 1/3* outsold both of its predecessors. But rather than build upon the momentum of this modest, unlikely success, Harrison would wait nearly two and a half years to release a follow-up. If *Thirty Three & 1/3* was a mostly outward-facing album featuring jazzy melodies and soulful arrangements, *George Harrison*—recorded over a long period in 1978 and released just a few days before his birthday in February 1979—was an inward-focused album that mostly dispensed with the jazz and the soul. With just a few exceptions, the songs lacked depth, conviction, and inventive melodies. While the choice of the eponymous title suggested to listeners that this was the real Harrison, it found the singer-songwriter dithering and without direction. It has its pleasant moments: "Here Comes the

Moon," an obvious answer-song to his own "Here Comes the Sun," boasts gorgeous acoustic-guitar playing (as one would expect) and some heavenly, Beatles-esque harmonies. The album's surprise hit, "Blow Away," showcases Harrison on both seamless acoustic and slide guitar and is heavily colored by Neil Larsen's keyboards; it could easily have fit on *Thirty Three & 1/3*. The tune "Not Guilty," which Harrison had had lying around since 1968, was another standout on *George Harrison*, and is dealt with in greater depth in Chapter 28.

"Soft-Hearted Hana," on the other hand, is a vaudevillian ditty about a psychedelic drug trip that sounds like something off an early Paul McCartney solo album (but not in a good way), with Harrison plucking a rootsy dobro, replete with crowd noises and an extended outro that varies in speed in order to enhance the trippy feeling. The end result sounds dated both musically and thematically. Trying a listener's patience, the song "Faster"—Harrison's ode to his beloved Formula One motor racing—opens with a full half-minute of the sound of race-car engines revving before the song proper begins. One gets the impression right out of the gate that Harrison wrote the tune as a sop to all his racing friends who were constantly pestering him about when he was going to write a song about them. "Faster than a bullet from a gun," Harrison sings, as if he were introducing a sportscast; to underline the connection, sounds of cars racing to and fro keep popping up throughout the track. Songs like "Dark Sweet Lady," "Your Love Is Forever," and "Soft Touch" belie their origins, having been written in Hawaii and other tropical vacation spots where Harrison and his then-girlfriend and future wife Olivia Arias had spent much of the past year, with musical accents deriving from those holiday hotspots. Harrison took to these musical influences, and to the ukulele, in a similar manner to which he had taken to Indian music and the sitar fifteen years earlier. While in the end it is a matter of taste, this one seems harder to acquire. Given that *George Harrison* was coproduced by big-time record producer Russ Titelman, whose credits included Randy Newman, James Taylor, Ry Cooder, and Rickie Lee Jones, it comes as something of a surprise that Harrison's eponymous album was not as compelling as his self-produced *Thirty Three & 1/3*.

27

George Goes to the Movies

When Ravi Shankar told his friend George Harrison about the plight of his Bengal countrymen in 1971 and his desire to stage a benefit concert to raise $20,000 in humanitarian aid, Harrison stopped what he was doing during that busy time in his solo career and focused all his energies on producing an all-star concert to raise ten or one hundred times that amount. And with the Concert for Bangladesh, which began out of the desire to do a favor for a friend, Harrison succeeded in doing just that, exceeding Shankar's wildest dreams in a project that created the template for all such charitable events to come, wherein pop and rock stars leverage their celebrity for a wide variety of social and humanitarian causes.

A few years later, another friend would casually confide in Harrison about a problem he faced, only to see Harrison turn around and solve the problem for his friend by taking on the burden of the problem as his own. This time around, the problem was not a humanitarian crisis but trouble that his friend faced in financing a creative project. On the verge of beginning filming of *Monty Python's Life of Brian*, the studio backing the project, EMI Films (the film arm of EMI, the record label that released the Beatles albums), withdrew its funding after the company's leader took a look at the script and decided the potential damage to the company's reputation from a movie that, in his view, mocked Christianity, was simply not worth the hassle. When Harrison's good friend Eric Idle, a member of the Monty Python's Flying Circus comedy troupe, related his tale of woe to Harrison, the latter assured him he would come up with a solution that would allow the filming to proceed as scheduled. Harrison wound up raising the four million dollars needed by taking out a second mortgage on his beloved home, Friar Park. Idle would later joke that it was the most anyone had ever paid for a movie ticket; in his typically understated fashion, Harrison would simply explain that he ponied up the cash because he wanted to see the film.

Harrison had the last laugh on EMI. After its release in 1979, *Monty Python's Life of Brian* was a huge international hit, grossing $21 million in the United States alone. Harrison's investment, motivated purely out of friendship for Idle and love for all that Monty Python represented—they were sometimes referred to as the Beatles of comedy—proved to be a shrewd one. Egged on by Harrison's business partner and manager, Denis O'Brien, this was to prove to be only the first of such efforts. The two formed their own production company, HandMade Films, which was at first primarily supporting more film projects by Monty Python, but which over the next dozen years or so would be responsible for the release of about two dozen films, including such critical and commercial successes as *Time Bandits*, *The Long Good Friday*, *Mona Lisa*, and *A Private Function*.

From a young age, Harrison, like many of his peers, loved movies almost as much as he loved music. Soon after the Beatles broke big, they ventured into film, acting in their two farcical romps—*A Hard Day's Night* (1964) and *Help!* (1965)—directed by Richard Lester. In 1959, Lester had worked with two of the Beatles' comedy heroes, Peter Sellers and Spike Milligan, on *The Running Jumping & Standing Still Film*, a short, surreal sketch-comedy film that wound up being nominated for an Academy Award. (Curiously, Beatles producer George Martin had worked with both Sellers and Milligan on comedy albums before signing the Beatles to the Parlophone label, in part because of his feeling that they shared something of the anarchic spirit that characterized these cutting-edge comedians. Martin also worked with the comedy troupe the Goons, featuring Sellers and Milligan, whose irreverent, satirical approach was hugely influential on both the Beatles and Monty Python.)

The two Lester features proved tremendously influential, emphasizing the antic side of the Beatles, putting their wit fully on display and helping to create and cement their individual personalities while establishing themselves as celluloid heroes. The musical set pieces in each film anticipated the widespread use of the medium as musical promotion vehicles nearly two decades before MTV made music videos essential tools in the marketing of popular music. Additionally, the two feature films were released concurrently with albums of the same names. While these "soundtrack" albums included some of the songs used in the movies, they also were treated as stand-alone Beatles studio albums and are generally counted as such.

With its close-to-true-to-life portrayal of the Fab Four and its totally-on-the-mark representation of the phenomenon of Beatlemania—the term was an early working title for the film—*A Hard Day's Night* has been called the original "mockumentary," a term applied to later movies such as *This Is Spinal Tap*, *A Mighty Wind*, and the 1978 TV film *All You Need Is Cash*, which portrayed a fictional but very Beatles-esque group called the Rutles, a film that includes a cameo appearance by one George Harrison, playing a TV journalist conducting a streetside interview in front of "Rutle Corps" headquarters.

For George, the first two Beatles films would prove influential above and beyond anything that happened on camera. It was on the set of *A Hard Day's Night* where Harrison first met an up-and-coming model named Pattie Boyd. In November 1963, Boyd had appeared in a television commercial for Smith's crisps. The TV ad was directed by an equally up-and-coming director named Richard Lester. Done and done, or so they thought. A few weeks later, Boyd's agent rang her about another casting call. For a model like Boyd, it was just another day in the life, nothing to get too excited about. When her turn came, she was surprised and pleased to find Richard Lester among those assembled in the casting room. Seeing Lester merely affirmed her assumption about the gig, that it was for another commercial placement. Soon after the audition, Boyd's agent called to tell her she got the role. Except the role was not another commercial. Pattie Boyd had been cast in a top-secret project about which she could not tell a soul. She was to appear in a new film starring the Beatles.

On her first day on the set, Pattie met the four Beatles. She sussed them up quickly: John Lennon was brash, Paul McCartney was cute, and Ringo Starr was endearing. As for George Harrison, he was simply the best-looking man she had ever seen. She wound up sitting with him at lunch, but the two shy and introverted Pisces spoke barely a word to each other. At the end of a long day, as the two were saying their farewells upon returning to London, Harrison turned to her and asked her if she would marry him. Speechless, the best Boyd could muster up was a nervous laugh, meant to break the tension. George then asked, if she would not marry him, would she consider having dinner with him? Still feeling nervous, Boyd mumbled something about her boyfriend, suggesting the three of them get together some time. Somewhat deflated, Harrison said goodbye and took his leave.

But that was not the end of it. The two were back together again on set about ten days later. Harrison asked after her boyfriend. She told him the truth: she had dumped him. Harrison asked her out to dinner again. This time she said yes. They went to a fancy restaurant at a private club, chaperoned by Beatles manager Brian Epstein, which was a good idea, as the young, nascent couple—George had only just turned twenty-one; Pattie was still nineteen—would have otherwise probably just sat there throughout dinner looking at their hands. Epstein played the charming, refined host, keeping the two entertained with his polished conversation and observations about food, wine, and the London dining scene. Even though Pattie and George just sat there listening to Brian most of the evening, the date was a smashing success. In less than a week, Boyd brought George home to meet her family on the occasion of her twentieth birthday. This time around, George was his effervescent self, as charming with Pattie's family as Epstein was with the two of them, sharing funny stories from the front lines of life as a member of the Beatles. Since Boyd was already something of a semi-celebrity herself, a very public courtship began. By summertime, Harrison had purchased his first house, Kinfauns, in Esher, Surrey, and shortly after, Boyd moved in with him. George was often away for extended periods of time on tour with the Beatles, but the two found ways to maintain their ties. They became engaged on December 25, 1965, and married the following month. The wedding was an intimate affair with their families in attendance. Brian Epstein served as George's best man, and Paul McCartney was the only other Beatle in attendance. It was not lost on the newlyweds that they likely would never have met had it not been for that package of Smith's crisps.

Likewise, making the movie *Help!* proved to be a game changer for Harrison and by extension for the Beatles. It was on the set of *Help!* that Harrison first laid eyes on Indian instruments, including the sitar. A scene for the film took place in an Indian restaurant, where a few Indian musicians provided ambient music. Liking what he heard and intrigued by the instruments, Harrison picked up the sitar on a break from filming—it was the closest instrument to a guitar, with a neck and strings—and tried (unsuccessfully) to make sounds with it. The story could have ended there, but in ensuing weeks and months, he kept hearing about Ravi Shankar. On a trip to Los Angeles in August 1965, the Beatles were hanging out with members of the Byrds, including David Crosby and Jim McGuinn, later to be known as Roger McGuinn. The musicians were swapping tunes and licks, and McGuinn played something that grabbed Harrison's attention. McGuinn explained it was based on a number by Ravi Shankar, with whose music both McGuinn and Crosby were already familiar. Crosby launched into an enthusiastic explanation of Shankar and his music, and building on what he had already absorbed on the set of *Help!*, Harrison resolved to learn more about the music, the instrument, and this guy Shankar.

Another curious thing happened on the set of *Help!*, which was mostly filmed on location in the Bahamas. One day, the Fab Four were on a beach, when an Indian swami approached each one of them and gave them copies of his book, *The Complete Illustrated Guide to Yoga*. Nothing came of this strange encounter immediately, but in hindsight, Harrison could not help feeling it was a sign of some sort.

Upon returning to London, Harrison purchased a cheap sitar from an Indian gift shop. On October 21, in a recording session for the group's next album, *Rubber Soul*, the group worked on John Lennon's song, "Norwegian Wood." Rather than add electric guitar to the track, Harrison, who had yet to learn how to properly play the instrument, composed and played a guitar-like hook on sitar at Lennon's suggestion. The success of the recording instantly launched an entirely new genre, "raga rock"; in its wake, sitar and Indian influences could be heard in songs by the Rolling Stones, the Yardbirds, the Byrds, and Donovan. More than just popularizing the sonorities of Hindustani classical music and the work of Ravi Shankar, "Norwegian Wood," and Harrison's subsequent raga-rock efforts with the Beatles, including "Love You To" and "Within You Without You," opened listeners' ears to a wide variety of non-Western pop music and attempts to create new fusions of rock with a variety of African and Asian sounds. Writing in the *New York Times* a few weeks after Harrison's death, minimalist composer Philip Glass—himself a student of Indian music and a collaborator with Ravi Shankar—eulogized Harrison as an icon of world music. Glass wrote, "George was among the first Western musicians to recognize the importance of music traditions millenniums old, which themselves had roots in indigenous music, both popular and classical. Using his considerable influence and popularity, he was one of those few who pushed open the door that, until then, had separated the music of much of the world from the West."[1]

All this due to the presence of a sitar on the set of *Help!*

Besides other Beatles films and videos, including *Magical Mystery Tour*, *Let It Be*, and his posthumous appearance in *Get Back*, Harrison did not pursue further work in front of the camera, outside of a few cameo appearances in Monty Python–related projects and HandMade Films productions. (Ringo Starr and John Lennon appeared in dramatic roles in feature films wholly outside the Beatles domain). This is not surprising, given what we know about Harrison's shyness. But the camera loved him in *A Hard Day's Night* and *Help!* In a conversation with director Richard Lester published in *the Guardian* in October 1999, Academy Award–winning filmmaker Steven Soderbergh said, "I happen to think that George was the best actor of the four of them by far. I don't think there's any question." To which Lester replied, "I don't think that there's any question either." Soderbergh added, "It's amazing, there's not a line he doesn't nail," which Lester agreed with.[2]

So when Harrison found himself as the almost-accidental owner of a film company (a 2019 documentary film about HandMade Films was titled *An Accidental Studio*), he was not entirely green to the medium. He had at least been on film sets and observed the process of making movies. Having worked with O'Brien for most of the 1970s, he felt he had a business partner he could trust. And while not entirely hands off, he convinced his musician friend Ray Cooper to come on board as the company's creative director, suggesting "Why don't you be me at the office?" For over a decade, Cooper fielded script proposals and oversaw the making of the films. He functioned as Harrison's eyes and ears, consulting with Harrison, who maintained veto power over all projects. He also served as a counterbalance against O'Brien, who had his own dreams of growing HandMade Films into a global entertainment conglomerate, far beyond anything Harrison envisioned or desired. For Harrison and Cooper, HandMade was driven by an idealism similar to that which initially fueled the Beatles' Apple Corps. It was meant to be a boutique production house focused on artist-driven projects they deemed worthy of support.

At first, the yin and yang duality of Harrison and O'Brien, mediated by Cooper, worked well. With a close eye on budgets, working primarily with emerging directors and actors, the company was able to produce a series of critically acclaimed movies that turned a profit. Those profits were continually plowed back into the company, and for a while the unlikely team of Harrison and O'Brien were hailed as saviors of a moribund British film industry. Harrison scoffed at the notion, saying, "I'm far too humble these days to think of saving anything—I can't even save myself."[3] Eric Idle was said to have referred to the duo fondly as "Bialystock and Bloom," the lead characters of the Mel Brooks comedy *The Producers*—which happened to have been Harrison's favorite film. Here he found himself living out the fantasy life that so entertained him that he supposedly could recite the entire script by memory. For O'Brien's part, he was all too aware of how the success of *Life of Brian* brought them frighteningly close to the plot of *The Producers*; he had arranged the finances in such a way that he had expected the film to lose money, which would have been advantageous to Harrison's tax situation at the time.

Harrison reveled in the success of *Life of Brian*. As with the Concert for Bangladesh before, he was able to help his friends in a big way. His vision of HandMade Films was largely one of producing more Monty Python films and projects, including spin-offs by individual members of the troupe, such as *Time Bandits*, directed by Terry Gilliam, cowritten by Michael Palin, and starring John Cleese. Despite the essential roles the three of them played, the film was not a proper Monty Python project, although O'Brien, much to everyone's chagrin, including Harrison's, tried to blur the distinction in the marketing of the film. In any event, HandMade scored big yet again, watching their $5 million investment bring in $42 million in gross box office receipts.

In the meantime, O'Brien succeeded in bringing Monty Python under his wing as their manager. It turned out to be a short-lived match made in hell, with O'Brien assuming total control over their business. A series of spurious deals, some made without their knowledge, caused the members of the comedy group to quickly grow disillusioned with O'Brien. Both Gilliam and Idle brought their concerns about O'Brien's competence and integrity to Harrison, which only infuriated O'Brien when he caught wind that they were badmouthing him behind his back. Despite his disastrous run with Allen

Klein, Harrison implicitly trusted O'Brien, and without his intervention on their behalf, the members of Monty Python chose to disassociate themselves from O'Brien's managerial clutches, only two years after *Life of Brian*. This also meant that they would no longer make films for HandMade. Their next film, *Monty Python's The Meaning of Life*, was another huge critical and commercial success, even winning the Grand Jury Prize at the 1983 Cannes Film Festival, without any backing from HandMade. Despite the break, Idle and Palin remained on friendly terms with Harrison, and the two, as well as John Cleese, eventually wound up working with HandMade on their own projects, including Palin's *A Private Function* and *Privates on Parade*, which starred Cleese.

Although its output was diverse, a catalog of comedy, romance, drama, and crime—sometimes all wrapped into one—films by HandMade were unified by a common approach. The films tended to be genre-bending, character-driven stories boasting smart scripts and cinematic realism. The movies were very English: most took place in the British Isles and were populated by English talent both in front of and behind the cameras, including such writer-directors as Neil Jordan, Bruce Robinson, and Richard Loncraine. They boasted moody soundtracks, often composed by Michael Kamen, a relative unknown on his way to becoming one of the biggest names in Hollywood film scoring. They eschewed big-name Hollywood stars in favor of serious, hungry actors. Bob Hoskins was the most notable—his career was basically created at and perpetuated by HandMade. Actors Robbie Coltrane, Cathy Tyson, Zoë Nathenson, and Richard Grant also received early career support from HandMade. Over time more bankable names were added to the casts, including Sean Connery and Maggie Smith, lured by the cachet of HandMade and its reputation for artistic integrity, but even actors like them were drawn primarily from British stage and film. It was not until O'Brien attempted to go all-stops Hollywood with the big-budget, 1986 romantic comedy, *Shanghai Surprise*—featuring the then-husband-and-wife team of Sean Penn and Madonna—that the tide began to turn at HandMade. Despite Harrison's cameo appearance as a nightclub singer and his rare contribution of a few original songs to the soundtrack, the movie was a fiasco every which way and nearly wrecked the company. Because of O'Brien's overreach, HandMade got too big for its britches and was punished in kind by reviewers and at the box office.

To paraphrase Robbie Robertson, it was the beginning of the beginning of the end of the beginning. Though HandMade would persevere for another five years, with O'Brien opening offices in New York City and Los Angeles in an ill-fated attempt to turn HandMade into a big-time Hollywood studio, it was spinning out of control both creatively and financially. A few more movies were successful, including *Withnail and I* and *Nuns on the Run*, which brought Eric Idle back into the HandMade fold as lead actor, but it grew increasingly apparent that O'Brien was playing fast and loose with the company's finances. "In November 1988, Ray Cooper and film accountant John Reiss (hired, ironically, by Denis O'Brien) visited George Harrison at home at Friar Park to tell him they'd discovered that Denis O'Brien was robbing him blind," according to a history of HandMade Films.[4] "Harrison was almost like a walking credit card for O'Brien that the American used whenever HandMade's coffers went bare."

At first, Harrison refused to believe that the man in whom he put all his trust, the same man who had rescued Harrison from the clutches of Allen Klein, could possibly have betrayed him. But slowly the truth emerged, and Harrison could no longer deny it. In the wake of the *Shanghai Surprise* debacle, which was mostly O'Brien's doing, steering HandMade in a direction totally foreign to its unofficial credo, Harrison sought to become more involved in the day-to-day operations of the company, but was deterred by O'Brien every step along the way.

Finally, when banks refused to make any more loans to the company, O'Brien could not hide the disastrous state of the company's finances from Harrison. The company shut down operations in 1991 and was sold for parts to a Canadian outfit in 1994. Meanwhile, there was still the matter of O'Brien's alleged fraud and negligence, and in 1995, Harrison sued O'Brien in a Los Angeles court to recover the $25 million he was owed. O'Brien was ordered to provide restitution to Harrison to the tune of $11 million, plus millions in damages. O'Brien filed for bankruptcy, and the drawn-out legal battle continued for the rest of the decade. Harrison never recovered any of his funds from O'Brien, and it was only the financial windfall of the mid-1990s Beatles *Anthology* project that saved him from losing Friar Park, his beloved home and the selfsame asset that Harrison had originally risked to finance *Monty Python's Life of Brian*, which had led to the creation of HandMade Films in the first place.

28

Why Peggy Lee Matters

A few months after his eponymous solo album was released in February 1979, George Harrison sat for a freewheeling interview with *Rolling Stone* magazine, in which he said his song "Not Guilty"—which he had written in 1968 and which was almost included on *The Beatles*, but which only publicly surfaced in a remade version on *George Harrison*—would suit the pop-jazz singer Peggy Lee.[1] This was no throwaway dismissal of the song or the artist, who had some history with the Beatles. Until then, "Not Guilty" had enjoyed a mysterious reputation, mostly because everyone knew it existed, but few had ever heard it. When finally released for the first time officially on *George Harrison*, it displayed, according to musicologist Walter Everett, Harrison's "interest in unusual chord colors, at a new level of sophistication similar to jazz methodology."[2]

From very early in their careers, the members of the Beatles were attuned to Peggy Lee, even though her music represented a style they considered old-fashioned, unhip, and to some extent the kind of music they were looking to roll over (along with Beethoven). A young John Lennon could nevertheless not help being entranced by Lee's moody ballad "Johnny Guitar," the title track for the 1954 Western starring Joan Crawford, for which Lee penned the lyrics, the first line of which was "Play the guitar, play it again my Johnny." He heard it, and he did. And in their Hamburg club days, the Beatles were drafted to back up Lu "Wally" Walters—the second vocalist in Rory Storm and the Hurricanes—on a few recordings, including his version of Lee's signature tune, "Fever."

The Beatles again connected with Peggy Lee via her 1961 version of "Till There Was You," a song originally written and recorded by Meredith Willson in 1950. Willson recycled the tune for his Broadway musical *The Music Man*, in 1957. The first hit version was recorded in 1959 by Anita Bryant, a beauty-pageant winner who scored a few pop hits before becoming best known as the brand ambassador for the Florida Citrus Commission. (Bryant later gained notoriety as an outspoken opponent of gay rights, which pretty much spelled the end of her career as an entertainer.) But it was Peggy Lee's version of "Till There Was You," a minor hit in the United Kingdom in early 1961, that first caught the ear of Paul McCartney, who added the tune to the Beatles' live repertoire when they were still performing in clubs in Hamburg and Liverpool in 1962. "Till There Was You" was one of the fifteen numbers the Beatles played on New Year's Day, 1962, as part of their in-studio audition for Decca Records.

The Beatles recorded a version of "Till There Was You"—the only proper show tune they ever released—the following year for their second album, *With the Beatles*. Their bossa nova arrangement, influenced by Peggy Lee's subtly Latin-styled rendition, featured twin acoustic guitars picked by John Lennon and George Harrison. Harrison's lead playing colored the tune throughout, and he created a convincing flamenco-styled solo to bring the song to its conclusion, ending on a surprising major-seventh chord that did not exist in Lee's version. While its show-tune origins may have made "Till There Was You" a novelty in the Beatles' repertoire, it offered fans—and especially parents of their fans—a hint that the group was more than merely a rock 'n' roll band. Musically speaking, the song said that the Beatles contained multitudes, as they would prove time and again in ensuing years with songs based in other traditions, including vaudeville, folk, jazz, and a variety of ethnic music. Thus, it was not surprising that "Till There Was You" was one of only three songs the Fab Four played in the first of their four appearances on the American TV variety program, *The Ed Sullivan Show*, in early 1964. As for Peggy Lee herself, she would return the favor in 1965, when she recorded her own sultry rendition of "A Hard Day's Night" for her album *Pass Me By*.

Peggy Lee also played a bit role in George Harrison's song "Blue Jay Way," which he wrote on a night in August 1967 in Los Angeles, while waiting late into the night for Derek Taylor and his wife to arrive for a visit. The house Harrison rented for his stay belonged to Lee's manager, Ludwig Gerber. (Some accounts have the house belonging to entertainment lawyer Robert Fitzpatrick, but he was more likely the go-between who found the house for Brian Epstein.)

Given the Beatles' long history with Peggy Lee, which included her 1970 cover of Harrison's "Something," it is no surprise that George thought that "Not Guilty" might be suitable for Peggy Lee. Indeed, "Not Guilty" boasted a bit of that "Fever" feeling. It probably did not hurt that Lee was also a Maharishi-trained adherent of Transcendental Meditation. Paul McCartney gave Lee "Let's Love," a song he had written with his wife Linda, which Lee recorded in 1974, with McCartney producing. It became the title track to her fortieth album.

Harrison first presented "Not Guilty" to the group in May 1968, in the sessions that took place at his home in Surrey, which produced what are now known as the Esher demos (which were included on the fiftieth-anniversary rerelease of *The Beatles* in 2018). Years before the band got bogged down in lawsuits stemming from the breakup of the group, Harrison warned in the song, "no use handing me a writ." As for the song's title, the ultimate irony was that this was the verdict passed on Harrison's would-be assassin, who stabbed the singer nearly to death during a home invasion at Friar Park on December 30, 1999. There was no question that the man on trial, Michael Abram, was the one who attacked Harrison and his wife, Olivia. Nevertheless, he was found "not guilty" by reason of insanity.

The original, 1968 version of "Not Guilty" boasted jazzy chord progressions and changing time signatures, both of which were brought to the forefront in Harrison's 1979 solo version, albeit at the expense of the original electric guitar solo that so heavily colored the version cut by the Beatles. In the remake, the guitar solo was replaced by Harrison scat-singing over the chord changes played on keyboards. Fans had to wait until 1996, when the *Anthology 3* archival Beatles compilation was released, to hear "Not Guilty" as it was originally intended for the White Album. The *Anthology 3* version includes a blistering guitar solo at the end of the number, which turned out to be an edited version of the original track. When *The Beatles* was reissued in 2018, it included a version that ran a full minute longer than the *Anthology 3* version, containing Harrison's complete guitar solo. This version is labeled "Take 102," which indicates how much work Harrison and the Beatles put into the song that was ultimately not included on *The Beatles*.

It does not take a forensic detective to figure out why "Not Guilty" was left off the White Album. While musically it fit right in with the overall sound and aesthetic of the album, the song itself, written upon Harrison's return from India, betrays a self-defensive mindset in the wake of the group's hurried exit from the Maharishi's ashram in Rishikesh over allegations against the guru of sexual improprieties. In the song, Harrison sought to deter any blame that might accrue to him for being the main exponent of the Maharishi and the group's residency in Rishikesh. The lyrics also pointed to internecine squabbling over the number of songs Harrison was allowed on each album, although his pointed barbs were tempered by poking fun at himself and his image ("making friends with every Sikh") and by his insistence that ultimately he would remain a team player ("I won't upset the apple cart," a sly allusion to the Beatles much-beleaguered business arm, Apple Corps).

In a sense, "Not Guilty" was a sequel to "Only a Northern Song," another critique of the Beatles' business arrangements and Harrison's status in the group, recorded a year earlier during the sessions for *Sgt. Pepper's Lonely Hearts Club Band* but ultimately left off the finished album. The fact that Lennon and McCartney saw fit to veto the inclusion of "Not Guilty" on *The Beatles* is quite understandable, even as it would have strengthened the scattershot album, especially if it had replaced one of a handful of barely justifiable weak songs that did make the cut (e.g., "The Continuing Story of Bungalow Bill," anyone?).

Harrison's 1979 "remake" of a song that had never been released was on an album that included a new song with a nod to the Beatles, "Here Comes the Moon," his answer song to his own "Here Comes the Sun." A remake of his song "Circles"—like "Not Guilty," a song first introduced to the Beatles at Esher for White Album consideration but never recorded by the Fab Four— was also intended for *George Harrison*, but the singer was unhappy with the track, which he revisited and wound up including on *Gone Troppo* a few years later.

George Harrison's "Not Guilty" was given an entirely different treatment from the guitar-heavy track recorded for *The Beatles*. Instead of rock, Harrison mined the jazzier aspects only hinted at in the original version. Keyboards replaced Harrison's guitar as the main sonic propellant, not an entirely unusual approach for Harrison in the latter half of the 1970s and the early 1980s. In this case, however, the track boasted the distinctive sound of the Fender Rhodes electric piano, a favorite of jazz musicians in particular, including Herbie Hancock and Chick Corea, as well as Beatles sideman Billy Preston, Stevie Wonder, and Donald Fagen of Steely Dan. Harrison drafted Neil Larsen to play the Rhodes; Larsen was a popular jazz session musician, playing on jazz-rock fusion efforts alongside the likes of Michael Brecker, Robben Ford, and Steve Gadd, eventually settling in as a recording and touring member of Leonard Cohen's band. Harrison did not even play electric guitar on the track; he played acoustic guitar, albeit treated with enough effects to make it sound like a third keyboard (the second one played by Steve Winwood, which lent the tune a hint of orchestral backing). Harrison's regular rhythm section of bassist Willie Weeks, drummer Andy Newmark, and percussionist Ray Cooper filled out the band for this track. And instead of ending the song with a guitar solo, Harrison scat-sang the outro, further emphasizing its jazz feel. The song did indeed have a "Fever"-ish feel to it, so it is no wonder that Harrison thought of Peggy Lee as a potentially reliable interpreter. Unfortunately, Lee never did find her way to covering the song.

29

In the Eyes of the Lonely One

Imagine you are a member of the most popular rock band of all time, the group that veritably defined what it means to be a rock band. Your music rules for the better part of a decade and is so powerful and influential that it becomes a key signifier of the decade, far beyond just music, penetrating all aspects of culture on a global basis. When the next decade rolls around and the group has disbanded, you become one of the most popular and critically acclaimed solo artists of the era and your biggest hit becomes one of the most popular singles of all time, firmly establishing itself in all lists of the best songs ever and being honored with a place in the Grammy Awards Hall of Fame.

Then imagine the calendar turning on the next decade. Your reputation still precedes you; how could it not? The reigning styles of popular music have changed quite a bit from your well-established sound, with the charts now full of disco and New Wave music. Perhaps the hits no longer flow as easily from your songwriter pen, although just recently you cracked the Top 20 with a bouncy, cheery pop tune that sits comfortably in your overall oeuvre. But you are not inclined to go chasing after the latest musical fads, as one of your former bandmates does to great commercial success. You know your lane, your strengths, and your weaknesses, and you have always done your best work when you sing from your heart and your soul. You still have a loyal fan following, and you always will, given your proven track record. You are as beloved by the world as much for your refusal to cave to the latest trends as you are for the beauty and sincerity of your music.

You take your time between albums; your output slows because you want to maintain the standards and high quality for which you are known after twenty years or so as a recording artist. The group to which you once belonged typically released two albums per year; up until recently, you put out one album a year as a solo artist, but now you are fine with waiting a year or two (or even three) in between albums. You also take your time with working on them; you are in no hurry. You record your music at your state-of-the-art home recording studio, calling on longtime friends and collaborators to help craft the settings for your new tunes. When you are finally satisfied with your latest batch of songs, you deliver the finished product to the record company that distributes the recordings you make for your own, boutique record label.

You have known criticism and rejection throughout the years, especially when you were a member of a band that included two of the world's greatest songwriters. But in your solo work, you are not accustomed to being asked to revise your songs or to write something entirely different.

When Warner Brothers Records initially rejected George Harrison's 1981 album, *Somewhere in England*, it marked a low point in his career and only added to Harrison's disgust with the music business. The swinging of the pendulum from respecting an artist's creative freedom and development at one extreme to measuring an album's worth according to a nebulous calculation of its potential sales—always a guessing game even among the most experienced of "hit men"—at the other extreme was never part of the bargain, for George Harrison or many others of his ilk who once enjoyed the respect and even the indulgence of record-company A&R executives more attuned to the long game than to tomorrow's bottom line. Nevertheless, when his record company pushed back on what he delivered as his ninth studio album, Harrison did exactly what was asked of him, withdrawing four of the targeted tunes and coming up with four replacements, two of which, even though they were written to satisfy the record company, would give George the last laugh.

One of the four songs originally recorded for 1981's *Somewhere in England* that his record company insisted he remove and replace, "Tears of the World," is one of George Harrison's most overtly political songs, an indictment of world leaders and big businessmen for their failure to combat militarism and environmental destruction. It is also one of Harrison's most depressing, pessimistic songs, finding "no way out" from a "hopeless" situation. For a song with the word "tears" in the title and in which the word itself appears multiple times, Harrison aptly, cleverly, and subtly paraphrases lyrics from his Beatles tune, "While My Guitar Gently Weeps," when he rhetorically asks, "Where's your love been sleeping? Has your heart been weeping?" Despite the song's theme and mood, Harrison cloaked it in a bouncy, mid-tempo, funk-based arrangement, peppered with saxophone, galloping percussion, and plenty of tasty slide-guitar licks—hardly an "uncommercial" packaging despite the weightiness of the lyrics. Harrison's vocals express deep, soulful commitment and a rarely heard (from him) measure of sneering disgust. "Tears of the World" eventually surfaced on *Songs by George Harrison 2*, the second of two limited-edition book-and-CD packages featuring lyrics to sixty Harrison songs plus four previously unreleased tracks, including a rare live version of the instrumental "Hari's on Tour (Express)," which was the opening number on Harrison's 1974 North American tour as well as the lead-off track on the contemporaneous *Dark Horse* album. Eventually, and somewhat unaccountably, "Tears of the World" also found a home as a bonus track on a remastered version of his 1976 album, *Thirty Three and 1/3*.

"Flying Hour," a bouncy, mid-tempo, synth-driven pop tune, was originally recorded during the sessions for George Harrison's eponymous 1979 album but wound up as part of the original sequence submitted for *Somewhere in England*. Cowritten by Bad Company guitarist Mick Ralphs, one of several musician friends who lived in or near Henley-on-Thames and participated in frequent informal musical get-togethers at Friar Park, the tune was inspired by one of the many inscriptions left by the property's original owner, Sir Frank Crisp, which fit perfectly with Harrison's "be here now" sensibility. Given the proper promotion, the song had hit potential; at the very least, it did not deserve banishment from *Somewhere in England*. The other songs booted off *Somewhere in England* were "Sat Singing," a song about meditation playing on the Sanskrit term *satsang*, referring to Hindu devotion, and "Lay His Head," a dreamy love song. "Flying Hour," "Sat Singing, and "Lay His Head" all appeared on the first volume of the *Songs by George Harrison* package, along with a rare live version of Harrison's Beatles number, "For You Blue," in a jazzy, swinging arrangement, from his 1974 tour.

Apparently, the record label was not bothered that the album as originally submitted included not just one but two renditions of Hoagy Carmichael songs: "Baltimore Oriole" and "Hong Kong Blues." The latter contained some unfortunate "Oriental" instrumental elements, including the predominant use of a gong and a lyrical reference to a "colored man." In 1939, when Carmichael wrote the tune, that sort of language and musical idiom may not have provoked a second thought. By 1981, George Harrison, of all people, should have known better, given his immersion in Indian culture. Today, these lapses render the song practically unlistenable. Nevertheless, the Carmichael songs passed muster with Warner Brothers and remained on the album as it was released. Nor were the record-company honchos bothered by "Save the World," the album's other indictment of the military-industrial complex, with references to the "rape" of the planet, destruction of the rain forest, and the "armament consortium" of "half-wits" leading us to hell on earth. At least on this number, as opposed to "Tears of the World," Harrison offers a glint of hope, reminding listeners that God lives in their hearts.

Harrison dutifully if somewhat mischievously did as requested and recorded four new numbers for the album. In the interim, John Lennon had been murdered in New York City in December 1980. Harrison reworked a song he had written for Ringo Starr into "All Those Years Ago," a tribute to the slain Beatle, featuring all three surviving members of the Fab Four and delivering Warner Brothers the hit single for which they were willing to trash an entire George Harrison album. The song spent three weeks at number two on the US charts, denied the top slot by the Kim Carnes smash, "Bette Davis Eyes," which spent a non-contiguous nine weeks at number one and was the biggest hit single of the year. Still, "All Those Years Ago" was Harrison's biggest hit since "Give Me Love (Give Me Peace on Earth)" in 1973; it helped the world, including his former bandmates, mourn Lennon.

The other three numbers Harrison added to the album were "Teardrops," "That Which I Have Lost," and, remarkably, "Blood from a Clone," a veritable tirade against the music business that is clearly addressed to the Warner Brothers executives who told Harrison to get back to the drawing board and write songs with more commercial potential. How they judged "Blood from a Clone"—which finds the singer beating his head on a brick wall and likening record company executives to Nazis—to pass muster when the original four songs did not is curious and, perhaps, a tribute to their lack of ego (or possibly to their stupidity). But good for them; it was a catchy, upbeat number, a fusion of ska rhythms and New Wave touches, that piled as much scorn on clueless music business executives as the deleted "Tears of the World" piled on feckless world leaders. And for a final punch line, the song was sequenced so that it was the opening track on the album as submitted and released. (Around the same time, Harrison wrote another stinging indictment of the music business, "Wrack My Brain," which he gave to Ringo Starr, who enjoyed a Top 40 hit with the tune the following autumn. The single was produced by Harrison, who also contributed a lively guitar solo to the number.)

Beatles author and Paul McCartney biographer Allan Kozinn puts the *Somewhere in England* debacle into perspective, tracing it back to Harrison's place in the Beatles. "I suspect that the impression of George as a sideman and a second-drawer Beatles composer caused problems for him later as well," Kozinn told me.

> Think of *Somewhere in England*, where he had to suffer the indignity of his album being rejected by Warner. He did what he had to do, i.e., he reworked it, recording some new songs, not least being "All Those Years Ago." But I've always been struck that one of his new songs was "Blood from a Clone," which is basically an indictment of the pop scene as it was then. It's as if he's saying, "You want me to rework this album—okay, here's a new tune about what crap the music business is, and it's the opening track!"

The up-tempo "Teardrops," coproduced by Ray Cooper, sounds like a musical tribute to Elton John, with hints of "Crocodile Rock," "Philadelphia

Freedom," and "Don't Go Breaking My Heart," among other numbers by the piano man. Credit Cooper, who had been a longtime member of John's band, with steering Harrison in the direction of a contemporary-sounding potential hit, one that also foreshadowed Harrison's adoption of some of the sonorities of ELO (Electric Light Orchestra), which saw their full flowering (for better or worse) on his 1987 "comeback" album, *Cloud Nine*, co-produced by ELO founder Jeff Lynne. "That Which I Have Lost" was a wordy, country-infused ditty capturing a state of mind that is one part self-pitying and another part searching for spiritual salvation, recalling some of the best work Bob Dylan produced on his 1978 *Street-Legal* album.

No wonder Harrison grew increasingly fed up with the music business around this time. By the time he returned to the recording studio in summer 1982 to lay down the tracks for *Gone Troppo*, an album not without its moments of charm, his mind was seemingly elsewhere. His film production company, HandMade Films, was churning out hits by then, and his attention was otherwise largely focused on tending to his beloved gardens at Friar Park and participating fully in the upbringing of his young son, Dhani, who was born just a few years previously in 1978.

(In a further irony, Harrison had written and recorded "Mo," or "Mo's Song," a tribute to Mo Ostin, the Warner executive responsible for bringing Harrison to the label, in 1977. As it turned out, Ostin was the one responsible for making Harrison redo *Somewhere in England*. The song remained unreleased until 1994, when it was included on a promotional-only tribute album to Ostin on the occasion of his retirement. Harrison was apparently willing to let bygones be bygones.)

The *Somewhere in England* debacle presaged a trend wherein several of Harrison's peers would face similar situations in having perfectly good—or even great—albums rejected by labels that were single-mindedly focused on mining them for hit singles. In 1982, Neil Young left his longtime label, Reprise, to sign with the upstart Geffen Records, founded by David Geffen, who had once managed the Crosby, Stills, Nash & Young supergroup. Young's first album for Geffen was the highly experimental, heavily electronic *Trans*, which was released in January 1983. The album, awash in synthesizers and processed vocals, sounding more like ELO than Neil Young, mystified critics and the public alike. When Young submitted the follow-up to Geffen, a previously recorded country-flavored album called *Old Ways*, the label refused to release it. Geffen turned around and sued the artist for, in essence, violating his contract by submitting records that did not sound like Neil Young. Apparently label owner David Geffen had never heard or had forgotten about classic Neil

Young country-influenced albums such as *Harvest* and *Comes a Time*. Geffen lost the lawsuit, and *Old Ways* was released in 1985 in a revised format.

Canadian singer-songwriter Leonard Cohen was the victim of one of the most notorious major-artist rejections when Columbia Records rejected his 1984 album *Various Positions*. Label president Walter Yetnikoff famously summoned Cohen to his New York City office, where, as the legend goes, he told Cohen, "Look, Leonard, we know you're great, but we don't know if you're any good." Never mind that the album contained such soon-to-be Cohen standards as "Dance Me to the End of Love" and the megahit "Hallelujah"— Yetnikoff refused to release it. The album came out the next year on a small, independent label. It took the likes of Bob Dylan, who began playing "Hallelujah" in concert in the late 1980s, as well as John Cale and Jeff Buckley, both of whom recorded versions of the song in the early 1990s, for it to gain popularity, culminating in its use in the 2001 animated movie, *Shrek*, making it a worldwide hit. When Columbia Records rereleased Cohen's complete catalog on CD in 1990, *Various Positions* was back in the fold.

Tom Petty's debut solo album, *Full Moon Fever*—produced by Jeff Lynne in the wake of his success with George Harrison on the 1987 album *Cloud Nine* and *The Traveling Wilburys Vol. 1* in 1988—was initially rejected by his label, MCA, in 1989, after label chief Irving Azoff complained that it did not contain any potential hit singles. Petty stuck to his guns, and eventually the label relented and released it as is. The album turned out to be a huge critical and commercial success, going five-times platinum in the United States and spawning three hit singles: "Free Fallin'," "Runnin' Down a Dream," and "I Won't Back Down," on the last of which George Harrison played acoustic guitar and sang backup vocals. Petty got his revenge on MCA when he jumped ship and signed a deal with . . . Warner Brothers.

In early 2001, popular American alt-rock outfit Wilco submitted *Yankee Hotel Foxtrot* to its label, Reprise Records, which summarily rejected the album and reverted the rights to the recording to the band free of charge. After briefly streaming the album for free on their website the following September, Wilco signed with the artist-friendly label Nonesuch, which finally released the album in April 2002. *Yankee Hotel Foxtrot* would go on to become critically regarded as the band's greatest achievement and prove to be its greatest commercial success. The irony is that Nonesuch was a subsidiary of Warner Music, as was Reprise, so Wilco got paid twice by Warner for the same album.

Being the first major rock artist to have an album rejected by a record company was a dubious distinction for George Harrison. Thus, it was no surprise that he would follow up *Somewhere in England* the very next year with the mostly underwhelming, indifferent *Gone Troppo*, which sounded like the "contractual obligation" album it was. "Here I go again" are the first words Harrison sings on *Gone Troppo*. The lead-off track on the 1982 album, "Wake Up My Love," is a synth-driven, New Wave–style number that sounds nothing like George Harrison; even his voice is buried in the mix. Harrison presumably front-loaded the album, which would be his last before a five-year recording hiatus. Like some weird fusion of the music of Van Halen, Duran Duran, and Elton John, the song, in which the singer admits to "barking like some hound," is a generic appeal to romantic and spiritual love as a cure for what ails him. In a very un-Harrisonian move for the master of a proper coda, Harrison does not bother to construct an ending to the song, but rather just lets it fade out, as if he could not be bothered to come up with a final musical statement.

Which is partly why "That's the Way It Goes," the very next number on *Gone Troppo,* reassured listeners that Harrison had not entirely gone troppo. It is immediately recognizable as a George Harrison song both musically and lyrically. Harrison's slide guitar is fully and deliciously present right from the outset, providing an introductory hook that establishes the tonality of the song as well as its mood. The guitar goes on to dance around Harrison's vocals and peppers the number with several evocative instrumental interludes, some of which even hint at Indian and Hawaiian sonorities. (Harrison was spending a lot of time living in Hawaii while writing the songs for *Gone Troppo*.) His vocal phrasing is highly syncopated, and the song's rhythms occasionally venture off course, another signature element of Harrison's best work. As for the lyrics, Harrison is back in *Living in the Material World* territory, castigating a series of straw men with concise portraits of their clueless materialism and concluding that they are all spiritually blind. Welcome back, o hectoring prophet! We've missed you.

"Greece" is a mostly instrumental travelogue—travel being one of the nominal themes of the album. It boasts a catchy, bouncy melody and a handful of guitar parts that variously evoke Hawaiian guitar and the Greek bouzouki. The lyrics, such as they are, are two verses of geographical wordplay, including a nod to his comedy avatars: "I came Acropolis on Monty Pythagoras." It is a pleasant enough ditty with music that merited and would have gained from real lyrics. Then again, one must be careful about what one wishes for: the title track boasts another catchy melody with tropical touches and lyrics to suit. The only problem is that those lyrics are written in a kind of faux pidgin English, which may have seemed clever at the time but now sinks under the weight of the colonialist attitude they betray. The only redeeming quality is that the song title, also a bit of pidgin English, refers to one who has gone mad, as in crazy, due to the tropical heat.

Contrast this with Harrison's heartfelt "Mystical One," another breezy, upbeat melody that directly addresses the duality of withdrawing into tropical relaxation and taking spiritual stock of oneself. From the first line, "They say I'm not what I used to be," we are drawn back into the world of Guru George and his cosmic balancing act. Is the mystical one of the title—the one who has returned to make him more real and melt his heart away—Krishna or his wife Olivia? Either works, and there is no reason to insist they must be mutually exclusive. Harrison's spiritual pursuits were always tied up in love, whether it was love for a deity or the spiritual quality of romantic love. Harrison's wisdom was to know that they can be one and the same, and this is plainly stated here in a manner that harks back to *All Things Must Pass*—even in his pointed use of the slide guitar. Similarly, "Unknown Delight" is an ode to the mystical power of a child to emanate love, to enrapture all those with whom he comes into contact—I write "he," because presumably the song was inspired by his son, Dhani, who was about four years old when the song was released. Harrison emphasizes the connection between love of a child and love of God by reviving the trebly guitar sound of "Something," even throwing in a note-for-note quotation from the classic in a turnaround between verses.

Gone Troppo also includes a remake of the Stereos' 1961 doo-wop hit, "I Really Love You," with lead vocals almost entirely turned over to American gospel singer Willie Greene, a member of Ry Cooder's vocal ensemble. The rest of *Gone Troppo* is a mixed bag but not without its charms. It is a case study in how essential the guitar was to Harrison's sound. Over the years, he had grown fonder of using keyboards for songwriting purposes, to the point that sometimes he did not even bother to add guitar parts to his songs. And as in "Wake Up My Love," which mostly forsook guitar in favor of layers of keyboards, his songs suffered for it. Harrison had long ago established his guitar as an equal partner to his voice, the two often duetting with each other, often in dialogue, sometimes in commentary.

Gone Troppo concludes with "Circles," which Harrison began writing fourteen years earlier while in Rishikesh, studying meditation at the Maharishi's ashram. Once they all had returned from India, the Fab Four assembled at Harrison's house, Kinfauns, where they made demo recordings—the so-called Esher demos—of the many songs they had written in Rishikesh, "Circles" included. The track, along with all the Esher demos, finally saw official release as part of the fiftieth-anniversary box set of *The Beatles,* released in 2018. It was a rare demo not accompanied by acoustic guitar; instead, it featured Harrison's voice with organ accompaniment, accentuating its mystical qualities. From the outset, the song explored reincarnation (it even used the word) and the continual birth-rebirth journey of the soul. The song could have easily fit on

All Things Must Pass, but for whatever reason Harrison first hauled it back out in 1978 during the sessions for his eponymous 1979 album. It still didn't make the cut, and Harrison gave it another shot in the 1982 sessions for *Gone Troppo*. By this point it had gained a few more verses and along the way had picked up a bassline (played by Harrison) reminiscent of the one powering the Beatles' "I Want You (She's So Heavy)." Although there were multiple keyboards on the track, including Harrison's synthesizer, the finished effort had the vague sheen of a late-era Beatles number, with gospel-influenced organ and keyboards courtesy of Billy Preston and sinuous, twin guitar leads played in an *Abbey Road* throwback style. Everything goes "round and round," indeed.

Gone Troppo would mark Harrison's farewell to public-facing music-making for the next five years, with just a few rare exceptions. In 1985, Harrison contributed a rendition of an obscure Bob Dylan song from 1968 called "I Don't Want to Do It" for fellow UK songwriter and guitarist Dave Edmunds, who was music supervisor for *Porky's Revenge*, the third and final film in the *Porky's* series. The superstar soundtrack featured an all-star cast of rock legends, including Carl Perkins, Willie Nelson, Jeff Beck, and Robert Plant and Phil Collins as a duo they called the Crawling King Snakes, mostly recording early rock 'n' roll classics such as "Do You Want to Dance," "Stagger Lee," "Blue Suede Shoes," and "Love Me Tender." Harrison had been experimenting with the Dylan song for many years; a solo demo version from 1970 surfaced on the fiftieth-anniversary box set of *All Things Must Pass*, proving once again that the latter was the gift that kept giving.

Also in 1985, Harrison took part in a concert paying tribute to one of his all-time musical idols, Carl Perkins, alongside musician friends such as Ringo Starr, Eric Clapton, and Dave Edmunds. The following year, Harrison recorded a few songs for *Shanghai Surprise*, the HandMade Films production starring Madonna and Sean Penn. Although a soundtrack album was never released, the tracks have surfaced on various compilation albums and as bonus tracks on CD reissues. As the decade passed the halfway mark, slowly but surely Harrison was dipping his toes back in the musical waters. When he made a complete landing on shore with his next album, the world sat up and took notice. Harrison may have been down for a while, but he certainly was not out.

30

You've Got to Leave to Come Back

You can be forgiven if you have never heard of the songwriter Rudy Clark, although you might kick yourself to learn that his pen produced hit singles as varied as "The Shoop Shoop Song (It's in His Kiss)," a girl-group number that Betty Everett took to the top of the R&B charts in 1964 (later remade into a hit by Cher in 1990), and "Good Lovin'," cowritten with Artie Resnick and a number-one hit for the Young Rascals in 1966. Clark also helped pen "Everybody Plays the Fool," a top-three hit for the Main Ingredient in 1972, and such colorfully named tunes as "Waddle, Waddle," "Do the Monkey," and "Shirl Girl," a hit for Wayne Newton, aka "Mr. Las Vegas," in 1963.

But if you are the kind of person who reads liner notes religiously, you might recognize the unheralded Black American songwriter's name as the author of several numbers recorded by James Ray, a virtually unknown R&B singer when he first recorded Clark's "If You Gotta Make a Fool of Somebody" in 1961. The single became a Top 10 R&B hit in the United States in early 1962, and the Beatles soon added the song to their Liverpool nightclub repertoire. Sadly, within a year of enjoying his breakthrough hit and at the young age of twenty-two, James Ray died of a drug overdose—but not before recording an eponymous album.

In September 1963, George Harrison became the first member of the Beatles to set foot in the United States, when he visited his sister, Louise, in Benton, Illinois, for a few weeks. Louise introduced her brother to some local musicians, with whom he informally jammed. George also spent as much time as he could in listening to American radio and scouring the record bins at local shops for new American music. Among the albums he purchased on that fateful trip, including ones by Booker T. & the M.G.'s and Bobby Bland, was James Ray's debut album. Harrison was already familiar with Ray from "If You Gotta Make a Fool of Somebody." The album did not make much of an impression on the English guitarist, except for one number—also written by Rudy Clark—that had a swinging, Latinesque, horn-heavy arrangement, with banjo, orchestral strings, and a female choir that, despite Ray's gritty, soulful vocals, almost turned it into a big-band novelty track.

Fast-forward twenty-four years and move the scene to FPSHOT, Harrison's home studio, where, after a five-year hiatus, Harrison was recording an album of mostly new songs with coproducer Jeff Lynne, best known as cofounder and leader of Electric Light Orchestra, which shortened its name to ELO in the mid-1970s. During a recording session, Jim Keltner, sitting at his drum kit, began playing a jazzy, swinging beat. Harrison's longtime friend and keyboardist Gary Wright remarked that the beat reminded him of an old song called "Got My Mind Set on You." Harrison had no idea that anyone else was familiar with the James Ray song, which was on that album he bought back in 1963. The musicians began fooling around with the tune, and the next thing they knew, they had worked up a hard-rocking cover version that found its way onto the album they were recording, called *Cloud Nine*.

The song closed yet another circle for George Harrison. Having been the first member of the Beatles to have a number-one hit as a solo artist with "My Sweet Lord," Harrison became the last Beatle to hit number one when "Got My Mind Set on You" topped the charts in 1988. It marked the first time a Harrison song held the lead position since 1973's "Give Me Love (Give Me Peace on Earth)." "Got My Mind Set on You" snagged the top spot on January 16, 1988, just one week before the Beatles were to be inducted into the Rock and Roll Hall of Fame. To be "on cloud nine" is to be in a state of bliss, and Harrison must have felt something akin to bliss—or at the very least, some long-overdue satisfaction—to be riding high on the charts when he accepted the honor along with Ringo Starr and Yoko Ono, representing her deceased husband. (Paul McCartney boycotted the proceedings, as there were still Beatles lawsuits yet to be settled at the time and he felt it would be hypocritical to appear with the others and pretend that relations were amicable.) While the entire premise of the Rock Hall of Fame was based on history and nostalgia, here was Harrison who, at age forty-four, and for a brief, fleeting moment, was as current, relevant, and vital as any other artist making music at the time. (The other songs in the Top 10 the week that "Got My Mind Set on You" sat at number one included tracks by Whitesnake, Whitney Houston, Michael Jackson, INXS, Tiffany, George Michael, Elton John, and the Bangles.) Another person who undoubtedly felt a great deal of satisfaction that week was Rudy Clark, who must have gotten a huge kick out of hearing his old song become a global hit by a former member of the Beatles. Clark lived until 2020, when he passed away at the age of eighty-four.

When Harrison first made plans to record a new album, it had been five years since releasing his previous album, *Gone Troppo*. In the interim, Harrison spent his time largely on non-musical pursuits, including tending to HandMade Films, gardening, raising his son, flying around the world on the Formula One racing circuit, and vacationing for long stretches of time in far-flung places, including Hawaii and Australia. One thing he came to realize during this period is that if he was ever to make another album, he would need to collaborate with a hands-on producer, something that, with the exception of Russ Titleman's work on *George Harrison*, he had not really done since *All Things Must Pass*. Even in the latter case, most of the producing duties fell into his lap when the erratic Phil Spector was incapacitated or simply AWOL from the recording sessions. Harrison was the main producer of the rest of his solo albums, and he had grown to appreciate how much a producer or coproducer could ease the process and smooth out the stresses of making an album.

As anyone who ever listened to ELO could tell, Jeff Lynne was a huge Beatles fan. His group's entire aesthetic and approach was based upon psychedelic-era Beatles, especially in its aggressive use of orchestral instruments as part of the aural mix, along the lines of the Fab Four's "I Am the Walrus" and "Strawberry Fields Forever." Lynne also worshipped at the altar of Chuck Berry, and, tellingly, early in its career, Electric Light Orchestra recorded a version of "Roll Over Beethoven"—the same Chuck Berry tune the Beatles had performed and recorded, with George on lead vocals. Harrison was friendly with Welsh neo-rockabilly musician Dave Edmunds in the mid-1980s, contributing a number to the Edmunds-produced soundtrack to *Porky's Revenge!* and taking part in the Edmunds-directed TV tribute to Carl Perkins. Edmunds had been working with Lynne on several projects, including cowriting songs and having Lynne produce about half of Edmunds's 1984 album, *Riff Raff*. When Edmunds mentioned to Harrison that he was working with Lynne, Harrison asked Edmunds to tell Lynne that he wanted to get together with him to talk over the possibility of collaborating. One can only imagine how exciting this must have been for Lynne. The only thing that could possibly have been even more exciting than working with a former member of the Beatles would be to work with the Beatles themselves, which at the time must have seemed like an impossibility, given that John Lennon had been dead for half a decade. But at that moment, neither Lynne nor Harrison had any idea where their nascent collaboration would lead.

When *Cloud Nine* was released in November 1987, it was hailed as a "comeback" album for George Harrison. On at least one level, that term was absolutely correct. Having been mostly absent from the music scene for five years, Harrison had indeed come back. But had he not come back with the goods that demonstrated he was still a creative and commercial force, the term "comeback" would not have been bandied about so promiscuously. Powered mightily by the fluke success of "Got My Mind Set on You," *Cloud Nine* cracked the Top Ten of *Billboard*'s album chart, garnering itself "platinum" status by selling over one million copies. In contrast, his two previous albums, *Gone Troppo* and *Somewhere in England*, had not even earned "gold" status, awarded to albums that sell over a half million "units."

In addition to "Got My Mind Set on You," the album delivered another hit, "When We Was Fab," a gleefully nostalgic look back on the Beatle years, chock full of Beatles and other 1960s references (including nods to Bob Dylan and Smokey Robinson). The single bubbled under the Top 20 in both the United States and United Kingdom. The upbeat "When We Was Fab," however, illustrated a problem many had with George Harrison as produced by Jeff Lynne. Given the song's subject matter, it makes total sense that it would be presented as a latter-day musical update of "I Am the Walrus," complete with sawing cellos, phased vocals, backward loops, and even the brief return of sitar. What makes it sound less than authentic, however, is that in Lynne's hands, the Beatlesque touches come out sounding more like ELO than the Beatles. This does not make it a bad track per se, but it does serve as a reminder that when helmed by George Martin, the Beatles' sound was something magical, something that not even two Beatles—Ringo Starr played drums on the track—with a Beatles-worshipping producer could come close to recreating.

It was a sound and an aesthetic that George Harrison fans would grow accustomed to over the course of the next decade-plus. Lynne's production paws are all over the two albums by the Traveling Wilburys, the supergroup of Harrison's musician friends, including Bob Dylan, Tom Petty, Roy Orbison (on the first album only), and Lynne. In the mid-1990s, Lynne finally got his chance to put his stamp on the Beatles when, as part of the multimedia *Anthology* project—three albums, a documentary, and a book—Harrison, Paul McCartney, and Ringo Starr finally reunited in a studio to complete two raw, unfinished demo tracks left behind by John Lennon, overdubbing additional instruments, sounds, and vocals. Using state-of-the-art technology to bring the demos—poorly recorded at home by Lennon on a cassette recorder and turned over to them by Yoko Ono—up to par, the Fab Three and Lynne turned "Real Love" and "Free as a Bird" into new Beatles tracks, albeit ones that, again, sounded more like Electric Light Orchestra with guest vocalists than anything ever made by the Beatles. Lynne even had the audacity to include himself on the tracks, singing backing vocals and playing guitar. The group had Harrison to thank for that; one of his conditions for taking part in the endeavor was that Lynne would produce the tracks.

Lynne would once more work with Harrison on the latter's final album. Through the 1990s, Harrison sporadically wrote and recorded songs that would eventually become the posthumously released album *Brainwashed*. For much of the time, he worked closely with his son, Dhani, who had become an adept musician himself and someone Harrison could trust with his legacy. The 1990s and early aughts were marked by triumph and tragedy for George. A year after the release of the second Traveling Wilburys album, and after much badgering by Eric Clapton, Harrison embarked on a short tour of Japan in December 1991, with the assistance of Clapton and his touring group, which resulted in the release of a two-disk set, *Live in Japan*, featuring a mix of Harrison's Beatles hits, solo classics, and a handful of numbers from *Cloud Nine*. For a brief while, Harrison was able to put aside the disastrous fallout of the HandMade Films debacle. He also threw himself into the *Anthology* project, partly as a way to refill the personal coffers his erstwhile business partner, Denis O'Brien, had emptied. Harrison also had several bouts of throat cancer during the decade and survived an attempt on his life at Friar Park on December 30, 1999. Harrison never fully recovered from the brutal stabbings, and the cancer that had been at bay for several years returned with a vengeance, this time lodged in his lungs and his brain. Harrison had enough foresight to leave Dhani with detailed instructions for how to put the finishing touches on what would be his last album, which came out within days of the first anniversary of his death. Although Harrison had lost a lot of power and color in his vocals, the album marked a return to the sound and feel of Harrison's late-1970s solo albums. Coproducer Jeff Lynne treated the tracks with restraint and respect, and this time out he let Harrison be Harrison: a fitting way to conclude the latter's recording career.

The first thing a listener hears on *Brainwashed* is George Harrison saying, "Give me plenty of that guitar," presumably an instruction to a studio engineer to boost the guitar volume in the mix being fed to Harrison's headphones. The phrase resonates and echoes across the decades; have not we all been asking for plenty of George's guitar in the mix for as long as we can remember? The next thing we hear is an army of guitars and related stringed instruments: acoustic guitars, electric slide guitars, even banjolele—as the name indicates, a hybrid of banjo and ukulele, dating back to the early twentieth century and made famous by the British vaudevillian entertainer George Formby, a figure beloved by the Beatles and Harrison especially. The song is "Any Road," marking a return to spiritual themes about the life of the soul, originally written back in 1988, and with that knowledge sounding remarkably prescient, as if it were penned with George's knowledge that his days were numbered and that it would serve as a kind of valedictory. The song speaks of life's journey, over which the individual is relatively powerless and how ultimately it does not matter. The refrain, "If you don't know where you're going any road will take you there," is a paraphrase from Lewis Carroll's *Alice's Adventures in Wonderland*, demonstrating that even at his most serious, Harrison does not lose touch with his sense of humor or the absurd. But of course, absurdity can be quite serious, even when Harrison turns the mockery on himself with a mention of "watery grottoes," like the ones ribboning through the gardens of Friar Park.

Harrison returns to one of his favorite topics in "P2 Vatican Blues (Last Saturday Night)," jabbing at the perceived hypocrisies of the Roman Catholic Church practices of his youth. He continues in the same vein in the following song on the album, "Pisces Fish," which mocks the papacy with more glee than anything he has written going back at least as far as "Awaiting You All" on *All Things Must Pass*. "Pisces Fish," however, is about more than mere pope-bashing. Harrison finally puts into song a phrase he had been tossing around for years, decades even, when asked about what might be seen as personal contradictions. He would often explain that his dualities were an expression of his nature as a Pisces, whose symbol is a twisted fish, where "one half's going where the other half's just been." Here, the waters carrying the fish are like the journeys of our souls; indeed, the waters *are* the soul, and the river, as easy to take for granted as the air we breathe, flows through us until we arrive at the "unbounded ocean of bliss." Without intending to, Harrison finds common ground here between Freud and Hinduism, and probably a thousand other spiritual and psychological belief systems that pattern the human condition, in all its diversity and struggle, after natural world phenomena. Harrison reviewed similar territory in other songs on *Brainwashed*, including "Looking for My Life" and "Rising Sun," the latter of which mischievously invokes Paul McCartney's Beatles composition "Here, There and Everywhere."

The instrumental track "Marwa Blues," based upon a raga by Ravi Shankar and veritably sung here by Harrison's eloquent, precise slide guitar, has been widely praised as one of his greatest compositions, even winning a Grammy Award for Best Pop Instrumental Performance. *Brainwashed* also garnered Grammy nominations for Best Pop Vocal Album and Best Male Pop Vocal Performance, for "Any Road"; given Harrison's vocal limitations on the recording because of his treatment for throat cancer, these honors were obviously bestowed upon him in a posthumous sentimental gesture. The only Grammy Award that Harrison had previously won as a solo artist was Album of the Year for *The Concert for Bangladesh*—Carole King's *Tapestry* beat out *All Things Must Pass* for that honor. It was not until 2015 that the National Academy of Recording Arts and Sciences (NARAS) saw fit to bestow a Lifetime Achievement Award on Harrison, who as a member of the Traveling Wilburys and the Beatles (who won only five Grammy Awards in the 1960s and then another three in the 1990s) shared in other awards.

Brainwashed also included a ukulele-fueled, casual version of Harold Arlen's 1930 pop tune "Between the Devil and the Deep Blue Sea," and "Rocking Chair in Hawaii," both of which would have been thematically comfortable on *Gone Troppo*. The song "Brainwashed" served as more of a valedictory than anyone (at the time) could have expected, combining political protest, an attack on the world financial system, and warnings about the dangers of the media and advanced technology with invocations asking God to help humanity find its way—or at least to brainwash us, too. The song interpolates a spoken-word section drawn from *How to Know God: The Yoga Aphorisms of Patanjali*, even providing the page number from which the quotation was taken as a reference. And, at the very end of the last song on his final album, Harrison chants a Sanskrit devotional prayer, backed only by a drone and tabla, called "Namah Parvati," bringing the angry, hard-rocking title track—and George Harrison's life and career as a recording artist—to a serene, spiritual conclusion.

31
Everybody's Got Somebody to Lean On

The genesis of the Traveling Wilburys began with a song. The song led to the formation of a supergroup, featuring George Harrison, Bob Dylan, Roy Orbison, Tom Petty, and Jeff Lynne. While Harrison and Lynne supposedly fantasized at times during the making of *Cloud Nine* about forming a group of middle-aged (read: over-the-hill) rockers, the group came together through a series of accidents and coincidences, all surrounding Warner Bros. Records' insistence that Harrison record a new track for the B-side of the European release of *Cloud Nine*'s "This Is Love" as a single.

The basic version of the oft-told story is that Harrison was out to dinner with Jeff Lynne and Roy Orbison—Lynne was producing an album for Orbison at the time—and the subject of George's need for a new track came up. Time was of the essence, so Lynne took the helm as producer and, with Harrison's help, hastily assembled a recording session for the very next day. With no recording studios available on such short notice, Harrison called his pal Bob Dylan and asked if they could make use of his informal garage studio on his property in Malibu for the session. On his way to Dylan's the next day, Harrison swung by Tom Petty's house to pick up a guitar he had left there, and Petty, like Orbison before him, asked if he could tag along. So in short order, what was going to be an impromptu session whereby Lynne would record Harrison singing and playing guitar, with overdubs to be added later, became something of a party, with host Bob Dylan dishing up food from a grill. (Sadly, we don't know if that included grilled portobello mushrooms for vegetarian George.) But Harrison was not about to let the talents assembled go to waste, and soon enough, Petty, Orbison, and Dylan joined him and Lynne in the garage. Harrison and Lynne had sketched out the basic lines, chords, and melody to the song on their way to Dylan's, and Harrison, as only he could do, put Dylan on the spot and suggested he come up with some additional lyrics. When Dylan asked what the name of the song was, Harrison demurred, before his eyes landed on a crate with the words "Handle with Care" stenciled on it. That was the name of the song, he told Dylan.

As arranged, "Handle with Care" serves to casually introduce the Traveling Wilburys vocalists in succession, with lyrics that reflected their personas. It begins with Harrison on lead vocals, almost mocking himself with phrases that replicate the feeling he expressed in many of his songs throughout his career of having been held back and suppressed. By the time he gets to the part of the song where he complains about being stuck in airports and "terrorized," as well as being "overexposed" and "commercialized," he could well be singing straightforward autobiography—or at least an updated version of "Don't Bother Me."

After Harrison sings the first two verses, the heavenly voice of Roy Orbison floats in as if from on high, like some dream of rock 'n' roll heaven, singing about loneliness—his stock in trade. It is a beautiful moment, the subtext of which is to capture the bard of the forgotten and overlooked reminding listeners that he is still around, and, to some extent, mocking his own image as the guy who made ballads of vulnerability like "Only the Lonely," "Crying," "Running Scared," and "In Dreams" into Top 10 hits in the early 1960s. The Beatles and the British Invasion that followed in their wake wound up stopping the likes of Orbison and many other American pop-rock artists in the United States dead in their tracks. Decades later, while Orbison was beginning to enjoy the fruits of a career revival when Harrison and the Wilburys came calling, it was not to last; Orbison died about six weeks after the release of *Traveling Wilburys Vol. 1.*

After Orbison's vocal bridge, "Handle with Care" shifts to a second bridge, this one introducing listeners to another of the most distinctive and easily recognized voices of the rock era—the one belonging to Bob Dylan. Therefore, by the one-minute mark, the song has featured a veritable Mount Rushmore of rock royalty: a former member of the Beatles, a future Nobel Prize winner, and the beloved angel of "mercy," as Orbison famously sang on his number-one hit, "Oh, Pretty Woman," back in 1964. By the time Tom Petty, no bland vocalist himself, and Jeff Lynne added their voices to the mix, they sound merely like backing singers. Instrumentally, the song is powered by a five-handed acoustic-guitar army, peppered by jangly licks played by Harrison on his Rickenbacker twelve-string electric. Just as the song features an array of distinctive rock vocals, the outro showcases two of the most recognizable instrumental sounds in rock history: a duet between George Harrison's slide guitar and Bob Dylan's harmonica. The sweet smell of success, indeed.

When Harrison and Lynne presented the record company with the finished track, the wise men of Warner saw dollar signs in their eyes. "Handle with Care" was too good to bury on the B-side of an obscure European single. Instead, they asked if the quintet could come up with nine more tunes along these lines to make a complete album. Thus was born the Traveling Wilburys, a playfully, ostensibly anonymous—although everyone knew who they

were—new group that defied prevailing musical trends and offered a selection of diverse, timeless songs with touches of rockabilly, folk rock, roots rock,
and gleeful pop rock. The quintet reassembled for a few weeks in May 1988 to
write and record the basic tracks for a full album. Harrison and Lynne built
the final recordings around these mostly acoustic-guitar-based recordings
and *Traveling Wilburys Vol. 1* was released the following October.

Some of the songs bore the stamp of their chief singers and songwriters; several of them were tongue-in-cheek, loving tributes to their contemporaries.
"Dirty World," primarily the work of Bob Dylan, built an entire song around
nothing but double-entendres, many of them automotive in nature, lyrically
if not musically in the vein of Prince's "Little Red Corvette." Orbison's "Not
Alone Anymore" tweaked his lonely image, here celebrating the camaraderie
of his newfound bandmates. It also may have included a very Harrisonian
dig at Paul McCartney in the line "I never could see past yesterday," perhaps
echoing John Lennon's lyric, "The only thing you done was yesterday," in his
McCartney-bashing tune, "How Do You Sleep?" Dylan sends up his image
as the bard of divorce—think *Blood on the Tracks*—in "Congratulations,"
and attempts a Bruce Springsteen parody in "Tweeter and the Monkey Man."
Harrison plays it pretty straight on "Heading for the Light," on the surface
about spiritual salvation, but in hindsight an eerie foreshadowing of where
he would wind up in just a little over a decade. On "Margarita," Harrison
unleashes his inner Carl Perkins, sprinkling chunky guitar leads atop a bubbly
synth riff that recalls the one fueling Pete Townshend's "Let My Love Open
the Door." The album concludes with the aptly titled "End of the Line," with
Harrison, Petty, Orbison, and Lynne swapping lead vocals on a song gently
mocking survival and endurance, "even if you're old and gray."

The prevailing vibe was one of casual music-making among friends, albeit at
the highest possible level. Almost all the songs they wrote were funny on some
level, ranging from in-jokes to subtle parodies to out-and-out, laugh-out-loud
funny. While George Harrison was clearly the instigator and driving force behind the effort and the glue that kept everyone together, there was no sense of
the sort of ego trips or struggling for the spotlight that hindered or betrayed
previous such attempts. Tom Petty producer Rick Rubin often tells a story he
claims was related to him by Petty, a story that illustrates equally the lack of
ego and the sense of humor that ran through the quintet: Petty, Dylan, and
Harrison were together working on a song when George momentarily excused
himself. With Harrison out of earshot, Dylan leaned in close to Petty and said,
"You know, he was in the Beatles." It sounds too good to be true, and it may
be apocryphal, but it still perfectly captures the overall sensibility that comes
through on *Traveling Wilburys Vol. 1*, that of a mutual admiration society. The

death of Roy Orbison so soon after the album's release shrouded the effort in a mournful haze of wistfulness. It was probably unlikely that the Traveling Wilburys would have gotten their act together and taken it on the road even if Orbison had lived; each of the members had their own solo projects and concert tours to attend to. It was hard enough just getting each musician's record company to consent to allow their artist to appear on an album put out on another label; coordinating their tour schedules and other conflicts would have been a logistical nightmare. There was some talk of replacing Orbison with a historically or musically appropriate substitute. Names like Del Shannon, Johnny Cash, and Roger McGuinn were bandied about. But the remaining members wisely dispensed with the idea. They reunited in March 1990 to lay down tracks for a second album, which they mischievously titled *Traveling Wilburys Vol. 3*. Released almost two years to the day after their first album debuted in October 1990, the second album was very much in the same vein as the first one. But the loss of Orbison was felt deeply, and the element of awe that had greeted the previous album, the sheer excitement over the coming together of these all-time great rock legends—especially George Harrison and Bob Dylan—was no longer a factor. In the end, while the two albums and a few stray singles they released contained magical moments of musical inspiration and friendship, the Traveling Wilburys were more a legend than a band.

32

Brothers in Arms

"Write what you know" is a central commandment given to creative writers, passed down from writer to writer informally and taught in schools and writing workshops. Whether or not—and one assumes not—George Harrison ever heard that directive, his songs show that he intuitively understood it. Of all the Beatles songwriters, Harrison seems to have stuck closest to real life for writerly inspiration, whether it was a song about a feeling or an emotion ("Don't Bother Me," "Something"), a real-life incident ("Blue Jay Way," "This Song"), a belief ("Awaiting on You All," "Be Here Now"), or a friend ("Behind That Locked Door," presumably addressed to Bob Dylan during his reclusive phase; "Savoy Truffle," about Eric Clapton's fondness for sugary treats).

One of Harrison's favorite topics to write about, to which he returned repeatedly throughout his career, was the Beatles themselves and the experience of being a member of the Fab Four. Although perhaps calling it a "favorite topic" is imprecise; rather, George had a *penchant* for writing about his bandmates. He wrote about them as a group and as individuals, and he wrote about himself and his role or position in the group. But we cannot always say for sure if George was writing about the Beatles. For example, are we to interpret "I Me Mine" as a commentary on the egoism that ran rampant through the Fab Four, especially toward the end? Many pundits think so. I'm not one of them.

Harrison wrote "I Me Mine" during the difficult days in early January 1969, when the group was ensconced at Twickenham Film Studios, where the cameras were rolling while the Beatles wrote and rehearsed new songs, documenting the creative process that culminated in the famed rooftop concert at Apple headquarters. The footage was used in Michael Lindsay-Hogg's 1970 documentary *Let It Be*, and later in Peter Jackson's *Get Back*. Harrison did indeed get fed up with what was going on at Twickenham and stopped showing up to rehearsals for about five days, as his bandmates wondered if he would be returning or if he had quit the band for good. The confluence of Harrison writing "I Me Mine" at this very moment suggests that it was growing out of his frustration with one or more of his bandmates. But the lyrics themselves indicate a different impulse lying behind Harrison's song.

Harrison was writing about the Western concept of ego and how it traps one into a worldview based upon self-centeredness, very much an outgrowth of his studies in Eastern philosophy. In his memoir of the same title, Harrison credited the realizations that the song expresses to the result of taking LSD, the cosmic effects of which are said to break down the distinction between the individual and the universe. While one always must remain skeptical of what artists say about their own creations, Harrison did put the song in context quite succinctly when he wrote, "'I Me Mine' is the 'ego' problem."[1] Period.

In a final bit of irony, the recording of the song was left unfinished in January 1969 and was not picked up again until a year later, when, for the final time, the Beatles entered a recording studio to work together on a song. The Beatles, that is, minus John Lennon, who, unlike Harrison one year earlier, had in fact, and unbeknown to the outside world, quit the group the previous September. Harrison, Starr, and McCartney put the finishing touches on "I Me Mine," the song about the ego problem, without the participation of the man credited with founding the Beatles, the man whom many still count to this day as the most important member of the group.

Harrison had plenty of other opportunities to dish about the Beatles in song while he was still in the group and in his solo career. While Harrison himself said that "Savoy Truffle" was inspired by Eric Clapton's insatiable desire for chocolate treats and the deleterious effect his habit had on his teeth,[2] Harrison works in a reference to his group with an anomalous couplet, "We all know 'Ob-La-Di, Ob-La-Da' / But can you show me where you are?" The quasi-philosophical stance of the lyric stands out in a song that almost in its entirety merely lists the names of various chocolate treats—Creme Tangerine, Montelimar, Ginger Sling, Pineapple Heart—and cautions that they might cause tooth decay. But on closer examination, Harrison may also have been embedding some music criticism into the song. The line immediately preceding the one that refers to "Ob-La-Di, Ob-La-Da" warns that "what is sweet now, turns so sour." Was that a sly reference to the McCartney song that appears on the very same album? Harrison's and Lennon's distaste for the song itself is legendary—it is the one that prompted Lennon's characterization of Paul's compositions as "granny-music shit"—and the difficulties the band and studio personnel had while recording the song led the other musicians to stage a walkout, the normally even-tempered producer George Martin to blow his stack at McCartney, and longtime recording engineer Geoff Emerick to quit working with the group. (Emerick returned to the fold to engineer *Abbey Road* and wound up working with McCartney on the latter's solo albums and with his band Wings throughout the 1970s and beyond.) McCartney was left having to finish recording the track—generally considered one of the worst of the Beatles catalog and possibly one of the worst songs of all time—on his own.

With "Only a Northern Song," Harrison wrote a song with multiple layers of meaning and one wherein satire mixes with cynicism—all in the form of a musical critique (of the song itself). The self-referential aspect of the song announces itself right in the title, as Northern Songs was the name of the company that published Beatles songs. In a sense, almost every original Beatles song was a "Northern Song." Hailing from Liverpool, Lennon, McCartney, Harrison, and Starr were themselves considered to be from the north of England; thus, even if they or music publisher Dick James or manager Brian Epstein had not named the company Northern Songs, their output could still rightly be called Northern songs, along the same lines as American music from the south being called Southern songs, or Southern rock. And in England, being a Northerner had approximately the same stigma attached to it as being a Southerner in America: a Northerner in England was stereotypically less sophisticated, less educated, less modern, and less worldly than an English Southerner, meaning primarily one from London or its environs. The stereotype of Northerners as less worldly was especially fraught, especially in the case of Liverpudlians, who by virtue of living in England's largest port city were exposed to a panoply of foreign influences—not the least of which was early rock 'n' roll music from the United States.

The title phrase "only a Northern song" appears twice in the song, making it the closest thing to a refrain. The word "only" is used in the sense of devaluing the song in question (presumably the song we are hearing); it's *only* a Northern song. Why "only"? For one, as originally established, Northern Songs was owned almost entirely by four individuals, none of whom were George Harrison. Dick James and his business partner owned fifty percent; Lennon and McCartney owned twenty percent apiece; and Brian Epstein owned ten percent (the numbers are rounded off). Harrison and Starr wound up owning an amount measurable only in fractions. This meant that Lennon and McCartney earned many millions more than Harrison and Starr, which may have been justified, since they were the group's chief songwriters. But it also meant that Lennon and McCartney earned more money than Harrison did even on the songs that he wrote (including "Only a Northern Song"). So strictly from a financial perspective, the benefit that accrued to Harrison when the Beatles recorded one of his compositions was, to put it in musical terms, minor. A Harrison song, as it turned out, was not really a Harrison song, at least not in the sense of ownership or revenue. A Harrison song was therefore literally "only a Northern Song" until the expiration of his deal with the publishing company in 1968, after which his songs were published by his own company, Harrisongs.

But as noted, "Only a Northern Song"—which was recorded during the sessions for *Sgt. Pepper's Lonely Hearts Club Band* but not included on the album—is not solely a cynical take on Harrison's financial position within the group. It is also a satirical take on the Beatles themselves, a parody of a mockery of Beatles psychedelia, and a very meta one at that. The song opens, "If you're listening to this song, you may think the chords are going wrong / But they're not, we just wrote it like that." In two lines, Harrison punctures the aura of inscrutable complexity surrounding Beatles recordings going back at least as far as *Revolver* or even before then. He continues with reference to the harmonies being a little off and out of key, lampooning those who would criticize the Beatles along those lines, while also admitting that to a certain extent, those accusations are based in fact. But again, none of it really matters, because it's only a Northern song—however you understand the import of the phrase.

Another impetus behind "Only a Northern Song" may have been for George to write a nostalgic, northward-looking song in the vein of McCartney's "Penny Lane" and Lennon's "Strawberry Fields Forever," to make for a kind of triptych. Neither of those songs wound up on *Sgt. Pepper's*, either; "Only a Northern Song" was placed on the soundtrack album for the animated film *Yellow Submarine*, while the Lennon and McCartney tunes found their homes on the American LP version of *Magical Mystery Tour*.

Just as Paul McCartney did not set out to write an epitaph for the Beatles when he composed "Let It Be" in September 1968, George Harrison likely did not have the Fab Four in mind when he wrote "All Things Must Pass." In hindsight, however, both songs—each of which gave its title to the album on which it appeared—have come to be viewed as resigned farewells to the Beatles. Perhaps McCartney and Harrison were channeling unconscious feelings and thoughts when they wrote these songs, subtexts that are almost impossible to hear or even think of without attaching them to the breakup of the Beatles.

When it came time for Harrison to create his debut solo album, he had a backlog of songs he had written in recent years to draw upon, and "All Things Must Pass" was at the top of the list. The context had changed, and therefore the song's meaning had changed or evolved. To debut his post-Beatles solo career with an album and song called "All Things Must Pass" was a simple statement in and of itself, one of resignation and acceptance, very much in keeping with the Eastern-influenced spiritual philosophies that Harrison had come to embrace. Everyone knew, or thought they knew, to what the things that passed referred. And to contextualize the passing of the Beatles as part of the natural life cycle—that he "must be leaving" and that "none of life's strings can last"—must have been alluring, even though Harrison probably did not have this meaning in mind when he originally penned the lyrics. Other songs on *All Things Must Pass* variously comment on the Beatles experience, including "Run of the Mill," "Wah-Wah," "Isn't It a Pity," and "Apple Scruffs."

"Run of the Mill," written shortly after the troubled *Get Back* sessions, is a heartbreaking letter to an erstwhile friend, examining their relationship, what went wrong, and what it means now. It can easily be read as a message to Paul McCartney or John Lennon—or perhaps both. "You've got me wondering how I lost your friendship," sings Harrison, as he questions why he was repeatedly put down by his friend, who, he points out, could clearly have chosen to do otherwise.

George Harrison wrote "Wah-Wah" the same day he walked out of the *Get Back* sessions in January 1969. Harrison was obviously in a bad mood that day, and "Wah-Wah" has always been understood as an expression of Harrison venting his anger and frustration with his bandmates. The emotions of the day inspired Harrison to greatness, and when he finally recorded the song—the first track recorded for *All Things Must Pass*, on May 28, 1970—it featured an ineffable guitar hook, a fierce vocal, and a delirious arrangement and production courtesy of Phil Spector. But the song is not a naked primal scream along the lines of some of John Lennon's Beatles commentary, even with its "Wah-Wah" title and refrain, alluding to the cries of babies. The song also functions as a simple tribute to the recently introduced wah-wah effects pedal, making it one of a number of Harrison songs that reference musical instruments, along with "While My Guitar Gently Weeps" and "This Guitar (Can't Keep from Crying)." Only marketed for the first time in early 1967, the wah-wah pedal soon became standard equipment in an electric guitarist's toolbox. It's just too bad that Harrison did not think to rhyme "wah-wah" with "sitar."

Like other songs on *All Things Must Pass,* "Isn't It a Pity" was written several years before it was recorded, and therefore it took on new meaning, given the context of its release. Its origins are vague but are said to date back to 1966, and various insiders claim it was submitted—and rejected—for inclusion on *Revolver, Sgt. Pepper, The Beatles,* and *Let It Be.* The quartet finally gave it a half-hearted run-through in January 1969, which can be heard briefly in the *Get Back* documentary. The lyrics do not address the Beatles or their breakup in any pointed matter. The song is rather a universal lament for a perceived human weakness: an easy trap we fall into whereby we fail to express gratitude and appreciation for the very people we love. If Harrison did not originally see the song as a commentary on the Beatles breakup—and how could he have back in 1966 when he wrote it?—he certainly was aware that, given what had gone down in the ensuing years, it had taken on new meaning, especially in the context of *All Things Must Pass*. And in case there was any doubt, without changing any chords, Harrison had the song's long fade-out morph into a reprise of the long fade-out section of the Beatles' "Hey Jude." Point made; point taken.

Harrison also included "Apple Scruffs," his loving tribute to a small group of hardcore, mostly female fans who continuously kept watch on the Beatles coming and going from Apple headquarters. The "Apple scruffs"—Harrison came up with the coinage—were not groupies in the commonly used sense of the term. Rather, they saw their role as something more maternal or sisterly and protective; they specifically saw themselves as a first line of defense against maniacal fanatics. They did not scream at the sight of a Beatle; they issued membership cards after vetting potential new "scruffs"; and they even published their own newsletter. The Beatles came to know most of them by name; the scruffs sometimes gave them flowers; and their interactions were brief and cordial. There were a little over a dozen authorized scruffs, and though they were predominantly young working women (who would leave their day jobs and go directly to 3 Savile Row to keep vigil overnight), there were at least a few gay men among them.[3] A couple of the scruffs even graduated to official positions at Apple. "There was a code of behavior for the Scruffs and that separated us from the normal fans," said one.[4] "We sometimes surrounded the unruly ones, so they knew they were out of line. We were quite severe, a little militia of girls protecting their idols."

The scruffs continued their vigils even after the Beatles broke up. Band members were still in and out of Apple headquarters frequently, having meetings, conducting business, and using the recording studio. Harrison recorded *All Things Must Pass* there, and that further cemented his connection with the scruffs. One of the scruffs admitted that, while still there out of loyalty and a sense of mission, many of the scruffs had "a George fixation." She recalled, "We used to call him 'The Body' because we imagined what he was like underneath. Very skinny, all muscle, you know?"[5] Not only did Harrison express his mutual fondness for the scruffs by immortalizing them in song—he even surprised them one night by having Mal Evans open the front door and invite them inside, an unprecedented event, so they could be the first to hear the new song he recorded for them.

Harrison was not always so philosophical in song about the breakup of the Beatles. Once the split devolved into a series of meetings with lawyers and the subsequent filing of lawsuits, Harrison wrote "Sue Me, Sue You Blues" in disgust over how the legal situation had deteriorated. The song mentions lawyers, attorney fees, affidavits, joint escrow, court receivers, and being served with papers—not the ordinary stuff of a rock song. But this is the kind of thing that Harrison was great at: turning the inane details of daily life into compelling songs. In case anyone did not draw the circle completely, Harrison nails it with the line "Now all that's left is to find yourself a new band." He similarly transformed the pain of paying taxes in "Taxman" and being accused of plagiarism in "This Song."

Harrison was not done wrestling with his Beatles demons on *All Things Must Pass*. The title track to the follow-up album, *Living in the Material World*, was something of a transitional number. He was still trying to sort out what happened with his former bandmates and come to some kind of understanding, at least for himself, of what it all meant. And for the most part, he succeeds. The song is largely another of his statements of philosophical belief—that a human lifetime is merely one physical incarnation of an eternal spirit, and how the challenge life presents is for one to realize that material existence has little to no value. Harrison is not critical of the Beatles here, neither the experience nor the individuals, even as he refers to them each by name: John, Paul, and "Richie." Never one to waste a good pun, Harrison employs Ringo Starr's real first name in its secondary meaning as wealthy. He offers a bit of biography by noting that the four Beatles grew up in dire straits—at least three of them did, John Lennon having enjoyed more of a middle-class existence, albeit one marked by terrible family dysfunction and tragedy—before they became rich and famous. While he laments that the Fab Four "got caught up in the material world," there is more acceptance rather than blame in his tone; he seems more concerned with addressing the inevitability of the situation while offering a way out of the spiritual wasteland of consumer capitalism.

"Who Can See It," also on *Living in the Material World*, is a heartbreaking ballad, a plea for understanding, recognition, and reconciliation. Featuring one of Harrison's most memorable vocal performances, nakedly emotional, the kind of song his voice was made to perform, the singer talks about having toed the line the past few years and asks for his life back. He talks about living in fear—a reference to the constant, low-level anxiety Harrison especially felt being in the public spotlight (and, as the future would prove, for good reason). Having been "held up" and "run down," and having been "denied" what he had "earned," the singer now realizes "my life belongs to me." There is no blame implied or imputed, no resentment or regret, just sadness and hope for clarity of purpose (and perhaps a bump up of his royalty rate). "Who Can See It" is an overlooked gem worthy of reconsideration. It also marks a transition point for how Harrison will address the Beatles in song in the future, bringing down the curtain on past hurts and inequities, putting them to bed under a blanket of equanimity. Future references to the Fab Four would wax much more nostalgic, and eventually Harrison would even break the ice that had frozen his relationship with Paul McCartney, at least enough so that the two of them, along with Ringo, could join together again in the studio, albeit on just a few, rare occasions.

A few Beatles allusions pop up on songs that otherwise have little or nothing to do with the Beatles themselves. "Simply Shady" on *Dark Horse* is one of Harrison's more autobiographical songs. It's about losing self-control, falling off the wagon, winding up imprisoned in a vortex of dissolute chaos, and about the hangover—both literal and figurative—that inevitably follows. Damaged relationships and the karma are the price he must pay. Harrison says there is nothing special about this dynamic in particular—"it's all been done before"—but that still does not make it any easier to deal with the fallout. In the end, he borrows an image from John Lennon when he sings, "You may think of Sexy Sadie," and warns the listener not to let her in, lest one is willing to jeopardize peace on the home front.

It took the tragedy of John Lennon's murder in New York City in December 1980 to reunite Harrison, Starr, and McCartney on record for the very first time since the Beatles split. The previous month, Harrison had been working with Ringo Starr on a few songs for his next album, *Stop and Smell the Roses*, which would eventually be released in late October 1981. Harrison produced a version of the 1952 pre-rock pop confection, "You Belong to Me," made popular by Jo Stafford, the sort of number that always suited Ringo, bearing a strong musical resemblance to "You're Sixteen." Starr also recorded "Wrack My Brain," a Harrison original that was one of a pair of songs George wrote concurrently in response to his record company's demand to churn out more radio-friendly material, the other being "Blood from a Clone," which appeared on his June 1981 album, *Somewhere in England*. "Wrack My Brain" did well for Starr, riding its galloping rhythm into the Top 40.

In another case of Harrison offering a song to another artist only to have it be rejected and later become a huge hit in his own version, Starr had recorded an early version of "All Those Years Ago." The song was never finalized because Ringo felt it was beyond his reach vocally and out of his wheelhouse lyrically. (We will never know if he was right, because the track has never surfaced.) When Harrison returned to work on *Somewhere in England*, he constructed a new version of the song atop the basic tracks he had laid down with Starr, including Ringo's drumming, adding his own vocals and new lyrics that addressed Lennon's legacy, both in personal and universal terms. While Lennon is never named, it is obvious about whom Harrison is singing, not the least reason being allusions to John in lines including "you point the way to the truth when you say all you need is love" and "You were the one who imagined it all." Putting a capstone on the effort, Harrison had Paul McCartney lend backup vocals to the effort, which he did along with his wife Linda and his Wings bandmate Denny Laine. Thus did three-quarters of the Fab Four wind up on a new recording paying tribute to their fallen bandmate in 1981. (McCartney recorded his own sweet tribute to Lennon, "Here Today," a "Yesterday"-style track featuring string quartet, on his 1982 *Tug of War* album.)

Harrison went whole hog for nostalgia in his 1987 song "When We Was Fab," whose title alone speaks volumes about the song, which appeared on Harrison's "comeback" album, *Cloud Nine*. Besides bringing in Ringo Starr to play drums on the number, Harrison and producer Jeff Lynne stuffed the tune with sonic references to the Beatles: vocals panning right to left, tones oscillating in dizzying patterns, tympani thumping, sitars crackling, vocals reversing. They availed themselves of all the elements in the psychedelia toolbox.

This time around, Harrison steers clear of any overt lyrical quotations beyond repetition of the term "fab" and that other Liverpudlian synonym for "cool" that the Beatles hipped the world to: "gear." Another direct Beatles reference was Harrison once again complaining about Inland Revenue, an obsession of his dating at least as far back as *Revolver*'s "Taxman," here described as "back when income tax was all we had." George did not expressly write the song with only the Beatles in mind—indeed, the group is never named. Rather than invoking the Beatles exclusively, Harrison included two of the Beatles' greatest influences and his personal favorites—Bob Dylan and Smokey Robinson—namechecking their songs "It's All Over Now Baby Blue" and "You've Really Got a Hold on Me," respectively. Thus, "When We Was Fab" was a tribute as much to the greater musical context of the 1960s as to the Beatles themselves. (The Beatles had recorded a version of the Smokey Robinson tune, with George and John sharing lead vocal duties.) "When We Was Fab" performed well on the charts, reaching number twenty-three in the United States and number twenty-five in the United Kingdom.

33

The Great Depression

Was George Harrison depressed?

That is a question that can never be answered definitively and one that raises a whole host of other questions: What does it mean to be depressed? Are we talking about clinical depression (whatever that is) or a depressive emotional state or a generally depressed outlook on life? Without recourse to a determination by a psychologist who engaged George in talk therapy or who treated Harrison for mood disorders, we can never truly know the answer. And if we cannot know the answer, then why are we even asking the question?

We ask the question simply as another way to explore Harrison, to get within him in order to understand what made him tick—or what did not make him tick. And we ask it because there is enough evidence in his songs and behavior to suggest that an understanding of a George Harrison who was depressed, or prone to depression, or one who partially or wholly, occasionally or permanently, had a depressed outlook, might help enhance our appreciation for his art and for the obstacles he struggled with throughout his life.

If George Harrison was afflicted with mood disorders that led him to be prone to depression, it would be bound to show up in his creative life, in his work, and in his personal relationships. Perhaps only those who were closest to him—his two wives, his brothers, a few close friends, and possibly his former bandmates—could shed light on the question. All of them, however, are ultimately unqualified to render such a judgment, entwined as they were in their own narratives they built around their lives with George, narratives that are bound to be self-serving or self-justifying or protective of their friend or loved one—or not, as the case may be.

Beatles author Candy Leonard first proposed to me the notion that George Harrison may have been depressed. Leonard points out that a good number of George's songs have the word "blue" in the song title, or other nouns and adjectives that we often associate with depression. There are the most obvious: "For You Blue" on *Let It Be*, "Deep Blue" on *Living in the Material World*, "So Sad" on *Dark Horse*, "Tired of Midnight Blue" on *Extra Texture*, "Grey Cloudy Lies," also on *Extra Texture*, "Teardrops," on *Somewhere in England*, and "Stuck Inside a Cloud" on *Brainwashed*. Even when George Harrison used a term denoting bliss, he opted for one with the word "cloud" in it, as in the title track to the album, *Cloud Nine.*

The lyrics to songs like "Deep Blue" and "Stuck Inside a Cloud" are virtual lists of symptoms of clinical depression: suffering in darkness, crying out loud, talking to oneself. "Grey Cloudy Lies" describes a feeling of loneliness so hopeless it could drive someone "insane" to the point of wanting to take a gun to one's head. In "Teardrops," the singer recalls crying buckets of them, so many that they are indistinguishable from rain. And while he undoubtedly meant their titles and key lines to be taken metaphorically, Harrison opted for sadness as the governing emotion of "While My Guitar Gently Weeps" and "This Guitar (Can't Keep from Crying)." It is no great stretch to conclude that Harrison viewed the world through eyes full of tears hidden behind blue-tinted glasses.

Harrison established the baseline of depression in his very first song for the Beatles, 1962's "Don't Bother Me," in which the song's narrator refuses company, preferring the comfort he finds in being alone, a common symptom of depression. Almost a decade later, the title track to Harrison's first solo album, "All Things Must Pass," is replete with poetic references to depression: darkness, grayness, and clouds.

Harrison has often been described as "moody," a promiscuously loose, casual term, and one probably overused, misused, and abused. Everyone has moods, after all. But the distance between having a moody personality and having a mood disorder is not such a great one, especially when combined with the frustrations Harrison experienced as a creative artist somewhat stifled and stuck inside the greatest show on earth. Anyone who has ever been depressed knows that hanging around someone with a perpetual smile on his face, with a sunny disposition no matter what day or time it is, and who approaches the world as if nothing can disarm or debilitate him, can be a recipe for annoyance at best or loathing at worst. As much as Harrison may have struggled with Paul McCartney over creative differences and just getting a chance to be heard, it's easy to see without looking too far that it may have been the latter's eternally youthful, puppy-dog grin that eventually wore down Harrison to the point that he could not stand being in the same room with him. And so he walked out.

Even a song like "Give Me Love (Give Me Peace on Earth)," hopeful as it may sound, comes from a place of underlying sadness, viewing life as a heavy burden to transcend. "Here Comes the Sun," ostensibly about dawn and rebirth, dwells to a certain extent on the darkness that precedes it and a long cold lonely winter that has seemingly gone on forever. Winter lasts only a few months—well, maybe half a year in England—and for those prone to seasonal affective disorder, it could well feel as if it had not been sunny and warm for years. But it is also possible that Harrison is writing metaphorically about the lifting of the long, dark winter of depression in favor of the promise of the sun bringing warmth and contentment. Harrison recycled much of the imagery of "Here Comes the Sun" in his 1974 song "So Sad," which dispenses with the former song's optimism and chooses merely to wallow in the gloom of a broken relationship.

In "It's All Too Much," Harrison compares the world to a birthday cake, an image that evokes a nostalgic waft of happiness in most people. But Harrison does not just leave it that; he admonishes the listener to "take a piece but not too much." Can you say Debbie Downer? In "For You Blue," from *Let It Be*, one line sticks out from what otherwise is a song full of simple pledges and promises of love: "I want you at the moment I feel blue." How did that image wind up in what otherwise sounds like a casual, tossed-off love song? But the number is a rare example of the Beatles doing a classic, twelve-bar blues, and it has the word "blue" in its title, so something in the otherwise upbeat, happy ditty had to earn the song its "blues" status.

Even in his iconic love song, "Something," Harrison feels impelled to protest, "I don't want to leave her now," and when pressed to the wall, being asked if his love will grow, the best he can come up with is an impassioned "I don't know, I don't know." On one level, that response is remarkable for its emotional honesty, acknowledging the complexities of the heart and not papering them over them with teenage-level romantic vows (see Dolly Parton's "I Will Always Love You"). Perhaps that is partly why the song now reigns as one of the most often streamed Beatles tracks. Will love keep us together or will it tear us apart? Credit Harrison with handling the topic with psychological complexity and adult sophistication. But then again, are his inner doubts about the duration and perpetuation of this love about which he sings yet another sign or symptom of a troubled mind (if not a fickle heart)?

In discussing the nature of the songs on *Extra Texture*, Harrison displayed some self-awareness of his depressive nature when he said, "I was in a real down place. . . . 'Grey Cloudy Lies' described clouds of gloom that used to come down on me. A difficulty I had. I've found over the years that I'm more able to keep them away, and am quite a happy person now."[1] And Harrison's wife Olivia once told an interviewer, "He had a bit of a cloud over his head. He had a furrowed brow we used to call 'the mark of the beast.'"[2]

One hesitates to medicalize Harrison's lifelong yearning for equanimity. But experimentation with mind-altering substances, immersion in somewhat alien holistic belief systems, addictive behavior, and other forms of escapism are various tools—some more effective, some less—that, at least momentarily, help an individual cope with a brain whose default setting is sadness.

One of Harrison's most explicit statements of his depressive state is contained in his song "That Which I Have Lost," an overlooked gem from 1981's *Somewhere in England* album, in which he describes turning inward as a "refuge inside himself" and begs for someone to "remove the dark from in me."

In the end, it does not much matter if George Harrison was clinically depressed to the point of its determining his emotions, his life choices, and his creative life. The question itself, however, illuminates his work in a unique way, and is thus worth asking.

Then again, it was John Lennon who penned the words, "Help me if you can, I'm feeling down. . . ."

34
The Art of Dying

In 1966, when George Harrison was twenty-three years old, he began writing a song about death, dying, and reincarnation. There was always something precocious about Harrison, and given what we know today about his world outlook at the time, both within and without the Beatles, it may not seem as surprising as it might on face value that someone so young was developing an ideology around death.

Harrison had begun his studies of Hinduism and spirituality in 1966 as an outgrowth of his interest in Hindustani classical music, urged on by his mentor, Ravi Shankar, who made clear to Harrison that the music did not exist in a vacuum, but that it was part and parcel with Hindu practices and beliefs. Harrison had been reading Western authors like Baba Ram Dass and Eastern classics like *The Tibetan Book of the Dead*, and, along with his experience of tripping on acid, he was beginning to form his own views about what it all meant and how it all applied to George Harrison, and, eventually, to his listeners.

From what we can tell, many of these concepts about transcending earthly experience through meditation and chanting, as well as beliefs in the existence of a spiritual plane where our souls reside untethered to our bodies, brought great comfort and solace to Harrison. From an even earlier age, Harrison seemed more sensitive than his bandmates to the darker side of their fame— the indignity of being pelted onstage with hard candies by so-called fans, the acts of violence against the Fab Four perpetrated by audience members in their club days, before they were able to insulate themselves behind barriers and bodyguards, the phoned-in bomb threats and death threats before concerts, and too many near-misses in puddle-jumper airplanes experiencing momentary engine failures, turbulence, and other weather-related hazards.

Michael Lindsay-Hogg remembers a conversation he had with Harrison about their mutual distrust of flying. "George said, 'Once there was a plane we were on and the door opened. I didn't like that one so much.'" Once at the Cavern Club, when a "fan," furious that the Ringo Starr had replaced the popular Pete Best, came gunning for the newer drummer, George stepped in to protect his bandmate and took a punch to his eye, winding up with a shiner that seemingly lasted for weeks. Harrison saw that being a Beatle could be hazardous to one's health. Harrison knew that lurking underneath the adoration of Beatlemania was a dangerous undercurrent of mania and hysteria that could turn on a dime into actual violence. And he saw much of this playing out in real time, with organized US protest rallies featuring bonfires into which erstwhile fans were urged to toss their Beatles records in the wake of John Lennon's misunderstood comparison of the Beatles to Jesus, and with the frightening run-ins with "angry Marcos partisans"[1] at the airport in Manila, urged on by that nation's first lady, Imelda Marcos, who felt snubbed when the Fab Four failed to show up to a party she had planned for them at her palace. All the madness and the real and threatened violence combined to make Harrison, foremost among his bandmates, decide to eschew touring after completing their US summer tour in 1966.

This is when Harrison first began putting words to paper for a song that would become "Art of Dying," finally surfacing four years later on his first solo album, *All Things Must Pass*. In "Art of Dying," Harrison sung about a time in life when hopelessness would reign, when the simplest verities would "become an awful pain." His point in the song is to purport his belief in reincarnation, in the near-endless recycling of souls into human bodies as they strive for perfection, a perfection that would bring about an end to the cycle and grant a soul a permanent existence on a spiritual plane. As discussed in Chapter 19 about *All Things Must Pass*, the song "Art of Dying" was just one of many songs about death on the album, an album that can be heard as Harrison's distinctive musical statement in response to his burgeoning Hindu beliefs. To put it simply, a concept album about death.

As it turned out, Harrison's obsession with death and violence would prove to be morbidly prescient: two of the four Beatles eventually succumbed to extreme violence at the hands of crazed attackers. John Lennon would be struck down within weeks of turning forty years old, shot to death in front of his Upper West Side New York City apartment right in front of his wife Yoko Ono. And despite the barrier fences and other security measures taken to turn his beloved Friar Park estate into a safe zone, Harrison would find himself face to face with a mad intruder in his own home on December 30, 1999, fighting off a knife attack that led to several dozen puncture wounds, deflating one of his lungs and nearly killing him. Olivia may have saved George's life when she picked up a lamp and smashed it over the attacker's head.

"I was lying there. I can't believe it," he said to Olivia. "After all I've been through—I'm being murdered in my own house. And because of that I'd better start letting go of this life so that I can do what I've been practicing to do my whole life."[2]

Harrison had successfully fought off several bouts of throat cancer in the years preceding the attack, but by May 2001, a recurrence led to an operation to remove a tumor from his lungs. Within half a year, the cancer had metastasized to his brain. George sought medical treatment around the world, including in Switzerland and in a specialty hospital in Staten Island, but doctors concluded that the cancer was incurable and recommended that Harrison should spend his final few weeks in the comfort of friends and loved ones.

Michael Lindsay-Hogg recounts,

> When George was dying, and Paul went to see him, Paul said to someone that it was George who comforted him more than he was able to comfort George. Because of his beliefs, George was able to understand that there was going to be this transition from life to death. But Paul had been his schoolfriend, and his own wife had died . . . maybe three years before, Linda had died. So, George was holding Paul's hand more than Paul was holding George's hand.

George Harrison died at the age of fifty-eight on November 29, 2001—just a few months after the world-shattering events of 9/11. In the Martin Scorsese–directed documentary film, *Living in the Material World*, Olivia Harrison said, "There was a profound experience when he left his body. Let's just say you wouldn't need to light the room if you were trying to film. He just lit the room."

Acknowledgments

Special thanks to interlocutors who went above and beyond the call of duty: Lauren Passarelli, professor of guitar at Berklee College of Music and a specialist in playing the music of George Harrison and the Beatles, and author Wesley Stace, aka singer-songwriter John Wesley Harding. Their insights and fellowship proved invaluable.

Thanks to those who gave so freely and generously of their time, observations, and expertise, including Michael Lindsay-Hogg, Robyn Hitchcock, Allan Kozinn, Candy Leonard, Sarah Beth Driver, Gary Lucas, Joel Harrison, and Dr. Hankus Netsky, co-chair, Contemporary Musical Arts at New England Conservatory in Boston, Massachusetts.

Thanks especially to my hometown pal and fellow Bob Dylan author Harold Lepidus, who waited patiently over the decades for me to succumb to the allure of the Beatles.

Thanks, as always, to my mentor and friend, Richard Ford.

Thanks to Jessie Lee Montague for friendship, humor, and Sanskrit consultation.

Thanks to my college pals Annik La Farge, for her enthusiastic support and Scrivener tutorials, and to filmmaker Stacy Cochran, for sharing her love of George.

Thanks also to Holly George-Warren, Alan Light, Howard Fishman, Michael Chabon, Morgan Narkiewicz, Jen Chapin, Wim de Lang, Aleba Gartner, Kathryn King, Peggy Marcus, Carol Bosco Baumann, and the good folks at the Hudson (New York) Area Library.

Thanks to my dear friends Frank London, Tine Kindermann, Dan Jacobs, Merlin Shepherd, Eleanor Reissa, Karen Karp, Ken Opengart, and Cassio Saverino.

Thanks to Adam Langer, my longtime editor at the Forward.

Thanks to Alex Cowen and Lucas Cowen.

Thanks especially to Paul Bresnick, for believing in me and for being my strongest advocate.

Thanks to my editor, Norm Hirschy, and to everyone else at Oxford University Press, especially Zara Cannon-Mohammed, Nirenjena Joseph, Emily Tobin, Jo Wojtkowski, Amy Stewart, Scott Greenway, and Leslie Safford.

To my children, Anna Peretz Rogovoy and Willie Watkins: Without you there's no point to this book.

This book would not have been possible without the love, encouragement, and support of my wife, Linda Friedner.

Notes

Why George Harrison?

1. Mikal Gilmore, in *Harrison,* by the Editors of Rolling Stone (New York: Simon & Schuster, 2002), 18.
2. Walter Everett, *The Beatles as Musicians: The Quarry Men Through "Rubber Soul"* (New York: Oxford University Press, 2001), 193.
3. Joshua M. Greene, *Here Comes the Sun: The Spiritual and Musical Journey of George Harrison* (Hoboken, NJ: Wiley, 2006), 65.
4. Graeme Thomson, *George Harrison: Behind the Locked Door* (London: Overlook Omnibus, 2013), 389.

Chapter 3

1. Brian Epstein, *A Cellarful of Noise* (London: Souvenir Press, 2021), 53.

Chapter 4

1. Stark, *Meet the Beatles*, 59.
2. Gilmore, in *Harrison*, 18.
3. Rob Sheffield, *Dreaming the Beatles: The Love Story of One Band and the Whole World* (New York: Dey Street Books, 2017), 52.
4. Kenneth Womack and Jason Kruppa, *All Things Must Pass Away: Harrison, Clapton, and Other Assorted Love Songs* (Chicago: Chicago Review Press, 2021), 21.

Chapter 5

1. David Sheff, *All We Are Saying* (New York: St. Martin's Griffin, 2000), 165.
2. Alan W. Pollack, *Soundscapes.info website*, https://www.icce.rug.nl/~soundscapes/DATABA SES/AWP/dywtkas.shtml.
3. Walter Everett, *The Beatles as Musicians: The Quarry Men Through "Rubber Soul"* (New York: Oxford University Press, 2001), 207.

Chapter 6

1. Everett, *The Beatles as Musicians*, 236.
2. Jonathan Gould, *Can't Buy Me Love: The Beatles, Britain, and America* (New York: Three Rivers Press, 2007), 417.
3. *The Beatles Bible*, https://www.beatlesbible.com/features/hard-days-night-chord.

Chapter 7

1. Sheff, *All We Are Saying*, 176.
2. Allan Kozinn, *The Beatles: From the Cavern to the Rooftop* (New York: Phaidon Press, 1995), 117–118.
3. Ian MacDonald, *Revolution in the Head: The Beatles' Records and the Sixties* (Chicago: Chicago Review Press, 2007), 144.

Chapter 8

1. John Kruth, *This Bird Has Flown:* The Enduring Beauty of Rubber Soul, Fifty Years On (Milwaukee, WI: Backbeat Books, 2015), 106–107.
2. Matthew Bannister, "The Beatle Who Became a Man," in Russell Reising, *"Every Sound There Is":* The Beatles' "Revolver" and the Transformation of Rock and Roll (Burlington, VT: Ashgate, 2002), 186.
3. Dave Rybaczewski, Beatles Music History website, http://www.beatlesebooks.com/day-tripper.
4. Alan W. Pollack, Soundscapes.info website, http://www.icce.rug.nl/~soundscapes/DATABA SES/AWP/dt.shtml.
5. Sheffield, *Dreaming the Beatles*, 48.
6. Simon Leng, *While My Guitar Gently Weeps:* The Music of George Harrison (New York: Hal Leonard, 2006), 18.
7. Philip Glass, "George Harrison, World-Music Catalyst and Great-Souled Man; Open to the Influence of Unfamiliar Cultures," *New York Times*, December 9, 2001.

Chapter 9

1. David R. Reck, "Beatles Orientalis: Influences from Asia in a Popular Song Tradition," *Asian Music*, 83–149.
2. Timothy White, *George Harrison: Reconsidered*, Kindle edition (London: Larchwood & Weir, 2013), 6.

Chapter 11

1. MacDonald, *Revolution in the Head*, 16.
2. MacDonald, *Revolution in the Head*, 243.

Chapter 12

1. "The Beatles Have Taken Refuge," Ellen Willis, *The New Yorker*, February 1, 1969, as cited in Gould, *Can't Buy Me Love*, 494.
2. George Harrison, *I Me Mine* (San Francisco: Chronicle Books, 2007), 126.

Chapter 15

1. Rob Sheffield quoted in Nathan Brackett and Christian Hoard, eds., *The New Rolling Stone Album Guide, Fourth Edition* (New York: Fireside/Simon & Schuster, 2004), 53.
2. Sheffield, *Dreaming the Beatles*, 171.
3. Kenneth Womack, *Long and Winding Roads:* The Evolving Artistry of the Beatles (New York: Continuum, 2007), 195.
4. Elvis Costello quoted in *The New York Times,* May 15, 1991, C13.

Chapter 18

1. Alan Light, "Ringo Starr Can't Bring Himself to Practice Alone," *Esquire*, March 16, 2021, https://www.esquire.com/entertainment/music/a35842463/ringo-starr-interview-zoom-in-ep-taylor-swift-here-comes-the-sun.

Chapter 20

1. Alan Clayson, *George Harrison* (London: Sanctuary, 2001), 355.

Chapter 23

1. Harrison, *I Me Mine*, 258.
2. Interview conducted by Elliot Mintz, originally broadcast on August 29, 1977, on the program *Innerview*. In addition to his long-standing career in radio, Mintz served as publicist for Bob Dylan and John and Yoko. http://www.beatlesinterviews.org/db1976.00rs.beatles.html
3. Harrison, *I Me Mine*, 268.
4. Harrison, *I Me Mine*, 254.
5. Harrison, *I Me Mine*, 226.
6. Philip Norman, *Paul McCartney: The Life* (New York: Little Brown, 2016), 449.
7. Harrison, *I Me Mine*, 232.

Chapter 25

1. Ronnie Spector, with Vince Waldron, *Be My Baby* (New York: Henry Holt, 2022), 77.
2. Spector, *Be My Baby*, 79.
3. Spector, *Be My Baby*, 78.
4. Spector, *Be My Baby*, 80.
5. Spector, *Be My Baby*, 82.
6. Spector, *Be My Baby*, 200.
7. Spector, *Be My Baby*, 200.
8. Spector, *Be My Baby*, 201.
9. Spector, *Be My Baby*, 203.

Chapter 27

1. Glass, "George Harrison, World-Music Catalyst and Great-Souled Man; Open to the Influence Of Unfamiliar Cultures."
2. *The Guardian*, October 22, 1999, https://www.theguardian.com/friday_review/story/0,3605,258749,00.html.
3. Robert Sellers, *Always Look on the Bright Side of Life:* The Inside Story of HandMade Films (London: John Blake, 2003), 54.
4. Sellers, *Always Look on the Bright Side of Life,* 263.

Chapter 28

1. George Harrison quoted in *Rolling Stone*, April 19, 1979.
2. Everett, *The Beatles as Musicians*, 203.

Chapter 32

1. Harrison, *I Me Mine*, 158.
2. Harrison, *I Me Mine*, 128.
3. Cliff Jones, "The Apple Scruffs: 'We're waiting for The Beatles,'" *MOJO*, 1996, http://www.rocksbackpages.com/Library/Article/the-apple-scruffs-were-waiting-for-the-beatles.
4. Jones, "The Apple Scruffs."
5. Jones, "The Apple Scruffs."

Chapter 33

1. White, *George Harrison*, 21.
2. Olivia Harrison quoted in *AARP Magazine,* June 2022, https://www.aarp.org/entertainment/books/info-2022/olivia-george-harrison-book-of-poetry.html.

Chapter 34

1. Gould, *Can't Buy Me Love*, 339.
2. Olivia Harrison, *George Harrison: Living in the Material World* (New York: Abrams, 2011), 12.

Bibliography

Allison, Dale C., Jr. *The Love There That's Sleeping: The Art and Spirituality of George Harrison*. New York: Continuum, 2006.

Asher, Peter. *The Beatles from A to Zed*. New York: Picador/Henry Holt, 2019.

Beatles. *The Beatles: Get Back*. New York: Callaway, 2021

Blauner, Andrew, ed. *In Their Lives: Great Writers on Great Beatles Songs*. New York: Blue Rider Press, 2017.

Boyd, Jenny. *Jennifer Juniper: A Journey Beyond the Muse*. Urbane Publications: Great Britain, 2020.

Boyd, Jenny. *It's Not Only Rock 'n' Roll*. With Holly George-Warren. London: John Blake, 2013.

Boyd, Joe. *White Bicycles: Making Music in the 1960s*. London: Serpent's Tail, 2006.

Boyd, Pattie. *Wonderful Tonight*. With Penny Junior. New York: Three Rivers Press, 2007.

Bragg, Billy. *Roots, Radicals and Rockers: How Skiffle Changed the World*. London: Faber & Faber, 2017.

Braun, Michael. *Love Me Do! The Beatles' Progress*. Graymalkin, 2019.

Brothers, Thomas. *Help! The Beatles, Duke Ellington, and the Magic of Collaboration*. New York: W.W. Norton, 2018.

Brown, Craig. *150 Glimpses of the Beatles*. New York: Farrar, Straus & Giroux, 2020a.

Brown, Craig. *One Two Three Four: The Beatles in Time*. London: 4th Estate, 2020b.

Brown, Peter, and Steven Gaines. *The Love You Make: An Insider's Story of the Beatles*. New York: New American Library. 2002.

Editors of *Rolling Stone*. *Harrison*. New York: Simon & Schuster, 2002.

Clapton, Eric. *Clapton: The Autobiography*. New York: Crown Archetype, 2007.

Clayson, Alan. *George Harrison*. London: Sanctuary, 2001.

Connolly, Ray. *Being John Lennon: A Restless Life*. New York: Pegasus Books, 2018.

Craske, Oliver. *Indian Sun: The Life and Music of Ravi Shankar*. New York: Hachette, 2020.

Davies, Hunter. *The Beatles*. New York: W.W. Norton, 2009.

de Herrera, Nancy Cooke. *All You Need Is Love*. San Diego: Jodere, 2003.

Doggett, Peter. *You Never Give Me Your Money: The Beatles After the Breakup*. New York: Harper, 2010.

Emerick, Geoff, and Howard Massey. *Here, There and Everywhere: My Life Recording the Music of the Beatles*. New York: Gotham Books, 2006.

Engelhardt, Kristofer. *Beatles Deeper Undercover*. Ontario: Collector's Guide Publishing, 2010.

Epstein, Brian. *A Cellarful of Noise*. London: Souvenir Press, 2021.

Everett, Walter. *The Beatles as Musicians: The Quarrymen Through "Rubber Soul."* New York: Oxford University Press, 2001.

Everett, Walter. *The Beatles as Musicians: "Revolver" through the Anthology*. New York: Oxford University Press, 1999.

Everett, Walter, and Tim Riley. *What Goes On: The Beatles, Their Music, and Their Time*. New York: Oxford University Press, 2012.

Forsthoefel, Thomas A., and Cynthia Ann Humes, eds. *Gurus in America*. Albany: State University of New York Press, 2005.

Giuliano, Geoffrey. *Dark Horse: The Life and Art of George Harrison*. New York: Da Capo Press, 1997.

Goldberg, Philip. *American Veda*. New York: Three Rivers Press, 2010.

Gould, Jonathan. *Can't Buy Me Love: The Beatles, Britain, and America*. New York: Three Rivers Press, 2007.

Greene, Joshua M. *Here Comes the Sun: The Spiritual and Musical Journey of George Harrison*. Hoboken, NJ: Wiley, 2006.

Guesdon, Jean-Michel, and Philippe Margotin. *All The Songs: The Story Behind Every Beatles Release*. New York: Black Dog & Leventhal, 2013.

Harrison, George. *I Me Mine*. San Francisco: Chronicle Books, 2007.

Harrison, Olivia. *Came the Lightening: Twenty Poems for George*. Guildford, UK: Genesis Publications, 2022.

Harrison, Olivia. *George Harrison: Living in the Material World*. New York: Abrams, 2011.

Harvey, Bill. *The George Harrison Encyclopedia*. London: Virgin Books, 2003.

Herbert, Trevor. *Music in Words*. New York: Oxford University Press, 2009.

Holoman, D. Kern. *Writing About Music: A Style Sheet*. Oakland: University of California Press, 2014.

Humphries, Patrick. *Lonnie Donegan and the Birth of British Rock and Roll*. London: The Robson Press, 2012.

Idle, Eric. *Always Look on the Bright Side of Life: A Sortabiography*. New York: Crown Archetype, 2018.

Inglis, Ian. *The Beatles in Hamburg*. London: Reaktion Books, 2012.

Kahn, Ashley, ed. *George Harrison on George Harrison: Interviews and Encounters*. Chicago: Chicago Review Press, 2020.

Kane, Larry. *When They Were Boys: The True Story of the Beatles' Rise to the Top*. Philadelphia: Running Press, 2013.

Kozinn, Allan. *The Beatles: From the Cavern to the Rooftop*. New York: Phaidon Press, 1995.

Kruth, John. *This Bird Has Flown: The Enduring Beauty of Rubber Soul, Fifty Years On*. Milwaukee, WI: Backbeat Books, 2015.

Lapham, Lewis. *With the Beatles*. Hoboken, NJ: Melville House, 2005.

Lavezzoli, Peter. *The Dawn of Indian Music in the West*. New York: Bloomsbury, 2006.

Leng, Simon. *While My Guitar Gently Weeps: The Music of George Harrison*. New York: Hal Leonard, 2006.

Leonard, Candy. *Beatleness: How the Beatles and Their Fans Remade the World*. New York: Arcade, 2014.

Lewisohn, Mark. *All These Years: Tune In Extended Special Edition*. London: Little, Brown, 2013.

Lewisohn, Mark. *The Beatles Day By Day*. New York: Harmony Books, 1990.

Lewisohn, Mark. *The Complete Beatles Recording Sessions*. London: Hamlyn, 1988.

Lindsay-Hogg, Michael. *Luck and Circumstance*. New York: Knopf, 2011.

Martin, George, and Jeremy Hornsby. *All You Need Is Ears*. New York: St. Martin's Press, 1979.

MacDonald, Ian. *Revolution in the Head: The Beatles' Records and the Sixties*. Chicago: Chicago Review Press, 2007.

McCartney, Paul, edited by Paul Muldoon. *The Lyrics*. New York: Liveright, 2021.

McKinney, Devin. *Magic Circles: The Beatles in Dream and History*. Cambridge, MA: Harvard University Press, 2003.

Mellers, Wilfrid. *Twilight of the Gods: The Music of the Beatles*. New York: Viking Press, 1973.

Melly, George. *Revolt into Style: The Pop Arts*. Garden City, NY: Anchor Books/Doubleday, 1971.

Moore, Allan F. *The Beatles: "Sgt. Pepper's Lonely Hearts Club Band."* New York: Cambridge University Press, 1997.

Norman, Philip. *John Lennon: The Life*. New York: Ecco, 2008.

Norman, Philip. *Paul McCartney: The Life*. New York: Little Brown, 2016.

Norman, Philip. *Shout! The Beatles in Their Generation*. New York: Fireside, 2005.

O'Dell, Chris, and Katherine Ketcham. *Miss O'Dell: Hard Days and Late Nights with the Beatles, the Stones, Bob Dylan, and Eric Clapton.* New York: Touchstone, 2009.

Pawlowski, Gareth L. *How They Became the Beatles: A Definitive History of the Early Years: 1960–1964.* New York: E.P. Dutton, 1989.

Reck, David R. "Beatles Orientalis: Influences from Asia in a Popular Song Tradition." *Asian Music* 16, no. 1 (1985), 83–149.

Reising, Russell, ed. *"Every Sound There Is": The Beatles' "Revolver" and the Transformation of Rock and Roll.* Burlington, VT: Ashgate, 2002.

Riley, Tim. *Tell Me Why: The Beatles Album by Album.* New York: Knopf, 1988.

Robertson, Robbie. *Testimony.* New York: Crown Archetype, 2016.

Rodriguez, Robert. *"Revolver": How the Beatles Reimagined Rock 'n' Roll.* Milwaukee, WI: Backbeat Books, 2012.

Ross, Alex. *The Rest Is Noise: Listening to the Twentieth Century.* New York: Farrar, Straus & Giroux, 2007.

Sawyers, June Skinner. *Read the Beatles.* London: Penguin Books, 2006.

Scott, Ken, and Bobby Owsinski. *"Abbey Road" to Ziggy Stardust: Off the Record with the Beatles, Bowie, Elton and So Much More.* Los Angeles: Alfred, 2012.

Sellers, Robert. *Always Look on the Bright Side of Life: The Inside Story of HandMade Films.* London: John Blake, 2003.

Shankar, Ravi. *Raga Mala: The Autobiography of Ravi Shankar.* New York: Welcome Rain Publishers, 1997.

Shapiro, Marc. *All Things Must Pass: The Life of George Harrison.* London: Virgin Books, 2002.

Sheff, David. *All We Are Saying.* New York: St. Martin's Griffin, 2000.

Sheffield, Rob. *Dreaming the Beatles: The Love Story of One Band and the Whole World.* New York: Dey St., 2017.

Spector, Ronnie. *Be My Baby.* With Vince Waldron. New York: Henry Holt, 2022.

Spitz, Bob. *The Beatles: The Biography.* New York: Little, Brown, 2005,

Stark, Steven D. *Meet the Beatles: A Cultural History of the Band That Shook Youth, Gender, and the World.* New York: Harper Collins, 2005.

Taylor, Derek. *As Time Goes By.* London: Faber and Faber, 2018.

Taylor, James. *Break Shot: My First 21 Years.* New York: Audible Originals, 2020.

Thomas, Nick. *The Traveling Wilburys: The Biography.* Green, OH: Guardian Express Media, 2017.

Thomson, Graeme. *George Harrison: Behind the Locked Door.* London: Overlook Omnibus, 2013.

Tillery, Gary. *Working Class Mystic: A Spiritual Biography of George Harrison.* Wheaton, IL: Quest Books, 2011.

Turner, Steve. *The Complete Beatles Songs.* New York: Dey Street Books, 2015.

Wald, Elijah. *How the Beatles Destroyed Rock 'n' Roll.* New York: Oxford University Press, 2009.

White, Timothy. *George Harrison: Reconsidered.* Kindle edition. London: Larchwood & Weir, 2013.

Winn, John C. *That Magic Feeling: The Beatles' Recorded Legacy, Volume Two, 1966–1970.* New York: Three Rivers Press, 2009.

Winn, John C. *Way Beyond Compare: The Beatles' Recorded Legacy, Volume One, 1957–1965.* New York: Three Rivers Press, 2003.

Womack, Kenneth, ed. *The Cambridge Companion to the Beatles.* Cambridge: Cambridge University Press, 2009.

Womack, Kenneth, *Long and Winding Roads: The Evolving Artistry of the Beatles.* New York: Continuum, 2007.

Womack, Kenneth. *Solid State: The Story of Abbey Road and the End of the Beatles.* Ithaca, NY: Cornell University Press, 2019.

Womack, Kenneth, and Jason Kruppa. *All Things Must Pass Away: Harrison, Clapton, and Other Assorted Love Songs*. Chicago: Chicago Review Press, 2021.

Womack, Kenneth, and Kit O'Toole, eds. *Fandom and the Beatles: The Act You've Known for All These Years*. New York: Oxford University Press, 2021.

Wright, Gary. *Dream Weaver: Music, Meditation, and My Friendship with George Harrison*. New York: Jeremy P. Tarcher/Penguin, 2014.

Zanes, Warren. *Petty: The Biography*. New York: Henry Holt, 2015.

Index

For the benefit of digital users, indexed terms that span two pages (e.g., 52–53) may, on occasion, appear on only one of those pages.